NISEI DAUGHTER

Nisei Daughter

by
MONICA SONE

Introduction by S. Frank Miyamoto

UNIVERSITY OF WASHINGTON PRESS

Seattle and London

To Father and Mother

University of Washington Press
PO Box 50096
Seattle, WA 98145-5096, U.S.A.
www.washington.edu/uwpress

Library of Congress Cataloging-in-Publication Data
Sone, Monica Itoi, 1919–
Nisei daughter.
1. Sone, Monica Itoi, 1919–   2. Japanese Americans—
Washington (State)—Seattle—Biography.   3. Seattle—Biography.
4. Japanese Americans—Evacuation and relocation, 1942–1945.
I. Title.
F899.S49J376   1979   79-4921
979.7'77'004956[B]   CIP
ISBN 978-0-295-95688-6 (pbk.)

The paper used in this publication is acid-free and recycled from 20
percent post-consumer and at least 50 percent pre-consumer waste.
It meets the minimum requirements of American National Standard
for Information Sciences—Permanence of Paper for Printed Library
Materials, ANSI Z39.48-1984. ♾ ♲

Contents

THE title of this book, *Nisei Daughter*, is well chosen—better chosen than most readers will realize. This is an autobiographical account by a Japanese-American woman that describes her childhood, adolescence, and young womanhood while growing up in a Japanese immigrant family in Seattle. The title of course is appropriate to such a narrative. But the title also carries less obvious meanings which deserve comment.

I believe it is illuminating to regard *Nisei Daughter* as a statement of self-identity, and in the second half of the book, as a search for identity. The identity question asks, "Who am I?"; or more specifically, "What is my place in this world?" In the period before World War II, an answer to this question for a Nisei was not simple. He or she faced two worlds which gave conflicting answers: the world of the Japanese community, and the world of the larger American society. As a further complication, the first world was divided into two sub-worlds, that of the Issei and that of the Nisei. I need to describe these two sub-worlds in some detail before attempting to show how they formed a part of Ms. Sone's identity statement.

The Japanese character *sei* means "generation." By adding a numerical counter as a prefix, as in Issei, Nisei, and Sansei, the concepts of first, second, and third generation respectively are produced, referring of course to the generation of the immigrant group in the United States. In the Japanese communities of the Pacific Coast, these generational distinctions acquired an inordinate degree of significance. The generation gap is present in some measure in every parent-child relationship, and is generally a notable feature of immigrant communities. In the Japanese communities, circumstances conspired to give special prominence to generational distinctions.

The Issei immigration to the United States occurred mainly in the first quarter of the present century. Almost from the beginning, powerful anti-Japanese groups in California campaigned to halt this immigration, and ultimately succeeded in gaining passage of the Immigration Act of 1924, the principal effect of which was to arrest the flow of Japanese immigrants. This sudden interruption of the migration produced a singular effect on the age structure of the Japanese communities of the West Coast. The Issei immigrants, who were almost entirely men and women twenty or thirty years of age at their arrival, consituted an age cluster that was no longer replenished. Their Nisei children consituted a second age cluster a full generation younger. Because the Japanese communities unlike normal ones lacked persons in the intermediate ages, the generation gap was in them a palpable, visible reality.

Furthermore, the wide difference between the language and culture of the parents and of the children, which generally was greater than between European immigrants and their children, accentuated the gap. The most critical factor, however, was the condition that the Issei were by law ineligible for citizenship, in contrast to their Nisei children who were citizens by birth in this country. Because of their permanent alien status, the Issei were generally oriented nationally and culturally in a direction opposite to that of the Nisei.

The Seattle Japanese community of the 1920s and 30s, which is the principal setting of Ms. Sone's narrative, thus was a community organized at two related but separate levels—organized into two distinct subcultures—and organized intensely as we shall note. I want to describe this community setting, beginning with a sketch of the physical layout.

The city of Seattle spreads north and south between two bodies of water—Elliott Bay to the west on the saltwater side, and Lake Washington to the east—and is somewhat constricted in the middle in an hourglass form. Main Street, a west-to-east street that bisects the city at the waist of the hourglass, could in 1930 be described as the main axis of the Japanese community. Skid Road, the "area of homeless men" where Ms. Sone's father managed a hotel and where she grew up, lay at the western end of Main Street between the waterfront and Fourth Avenue. The center of the Japanese business district was located at Sixth and Main. From that point Main Street rose steadily to the east up First Hill, and up a second hill called Cherry Hill, until it descended steeply at the eastern end to the lake shore. In 1930 when the Japanese minority population of Seattle numbered about 8,500, the majority of that population resided in a belt approximately half a mile wide on either side of Main Street, concentrated on the western slope of the two hills.

The community was, as I noted, highly organized. The hub was located in the business center surrounding Sixth and Main Street where a dense cluster of shops and offices served the needs of an ethnic population. Two Japanese-language newspapers vied for subscribers and advertisers. The Japanese Association, the most wide-reaching organization in the community, which served a quasi-governmental role and also functioned as a loose confederation of clubs and associations, had its headquarters here. The most important of these associations were the *kenjinkai*, prefectural associations, which served both mutual aid and social purposes. The Japanese Chamber of Commerce, constituted mostly of business associations (hotel, restaurant, grocers, etc.), also shared offices with the Japanese Association. Nippon-kan Hall, an old auditorium located near the business center, was heavily used for ceremonial gatherings, political meetings, *shibai* (Japanese plays), Japanese musical events, and *judo* and *sumo* (wrestling) matches. Eastward, uphill from the business center, apartment houses and rooming houses were displaced by rowhouses and multiplexes, and finally by single-family dwellings. Intermingled among the homes were at least two Buddhist temples and six or seven Japanese Christian churches representing all the major denominations. The Japanese Language School, a substantial building, was also located here.

This was the world of the Issei. On the streets when two Issei met, one would see much bowing and hear the soft modulations of the Japanese language. Ritual acknowledgments of obligations incurred and to be incurred were an almost invariant part of such conversations. Also, references often were made to families, relatives, friends, and the *kenjin* (prefectural countrymen)—in short, to the network of relations which bound community members together. These relational networks were the bases of much of the organizational activity in the community whether in the home and family, shops and businesses, clubs and association, or churches. And in all the networks one tended to observe the play of what Chie Nakane has called the vertical structure of Japanese society, the tendency to grant special rights, privileges, and authority to those in higher status: elders over youths, males over females, employers over employees, and teachers over students.

By comparison, the Nisei subculture was rudimentary. Basically, the Nisei were Americans. They spoke English, knew its idioms and slang; they knew the popular songs and danced the latest dance steps; and their idols were the favorites of all Americans: Babe Ruth, Joe DiMaggio, Clark Gable, and Katharine Hepburn. They attended American schools, and except for racial characteristics seemed scarcely distinguishable from the majority-group students. But socially they generally were isolated from white American society, and participated only marginally in it. As for the Japanese culture of the Issei, because of the Nisei's poor command of the Japanese language and scant knowledge of Japanese traditions, the Nisei had limited means for participating in it. Yet because of their necessarily intimate relations with their Issei parents and their participation in some Japanese functions in the community, most Nisei absorbed more of Japanese culture than they realized.

The Nisei community, like that of the Issei, was highly organized. The Japanese Language School, which the majority of Seattle Nisei attended at one time or another, was minimally successful in teaching the language but highly effective in establishing lasting associations. The most typically Nisei organizational activity occurred in sports and churches. In the Nisei community, teen-age sports leagues involving dozens of teams were organized long before the Little Leagues and Babe Ruth Leagues ever appeared in the white communities. And the sports clubs sometimes became social clubs. In the churches, Nisei activities, which were almost totally separated from those of the Issei, were not only organized into the usual clubs, choirs, and socials, but also into active regional interdenominational conferences and associations.

Thus a Nisei was American, but not truly a part of American society. A Nisei was certainly not Japanese, but Japanese influences seeped into aspects of his character and behavior. The intermingling of backgrounds was especially evident in the Nisei's attitudes and personality. Compared to white Americans the Nisei were generally more aware of self and of others, less direct and spontaneous, and less assertive; but compared to the Issei, the Nisei were clearly more like Americans. These characteristics affected their interpersonal style; and the Nisei, within their own society, developed a way of relating to one other that was distinctive to their group.

Having described the world typical of the Issei and Nisei, I must now point out that Mr. and Mrs. Itoi, Ms. Sone's parents, were not typical Issei, and that Kazuko (Ms. Sone's name in childhood) was not a typical Nisei. Mr. Itoi came to this country with some training in law and the aim of entering a major law school, a rare aspiration among Issei immigrants. Mrs. Itoi was the daughter of a Japanese Christian minister, which is unusual, and she was a poet who wrote Japanese poetry all her adult life. Both of the Itoi parents, in short, appear to have had intellectual and cultural backgrounds well above those of the average Issei. Perhaps because their backgrounds were unusual, but also because both parents came from *ken* (prefectures) with relatively few *kenjin* (prefectural members) in the Seattle area, they appear not to have been drawn as heavily into the organized life of the community as were some Issei.

Similarly, Kazuko seems to have been less closely tied to Nisei society than many of her peers, and more closely related to her mother, as a companion, than was typical of mother-daughter relations in most immigrant families. And perhaps because of this relationship, Kazuko's grasp of the Japanese language and of Japanese conventions appears to have been stronger than for most Nisei girls. There is another fact of interest. Because Kazuko grew up in a Skid Road hotel operated by her father, she appears to have had more direct contacts with a cross-section of white society than was true for most Nisei, and therefore a greater sense of ease in that society.

Nevertheless, Kazuko was clearly a Nisei and identified herself as such. It was particularly her relationship as a Nisei daughter to Issei parents that defined the role for her. As one reads the first several pages of her book and adapts oneself to seeing the world through Kazuko's eyes, it is obviously an American perception of the world that emerges, or at least a world as it might have been seen by any lively, imaginative, and resourceful child. In the pages that follow, however, Kazuko tells of the curious, sometimes comical, and sometimes wonderful ways of the Issei which are revealed to her and, without expressing it in so many words, shows how these experiences influenced her. One thing missing in her account is any reference to certain basic value principles which generally underlay all Issei-Nisei family relations—the principles of *ôn* and *oya-kōkō* which defined obligations and responsibilities between parents and children—but it seems evident that these are implicit in Kazuko's relations with her parents. In sum, these appear to have been the conditions which defined for Kazuko her status as a Nisei daughter.

In the last half of the book, however, which describes the years leading up to World War II, and the war years themselves, the identity question for Kazuko takes on a new form. By the late 1930s she, like hundreds of her contemporaries, reached an employable age but found that job opportunities in white American communities, except in menial services, were virtually closed to them. Similarly, the search for better homes outside the central Japanese community was likely to yield bitter experiences of prejudice and discrimination. The irony was that in the prewar years the American emphasis with respect to immigrant communities was what Milton Gordon has called "Anglo conformity," assimilation into the ways of the Anglos, but as the Nisei gradually realized, the majority group had no intention of permitting the Nisei access to those means needed for attaining Anglo conformity. This was the paradox of Nisei identity in the years just before the war.

The outbreak of war between Japan and the United States, and the evacuation of the Japanese minority, drastically changed the status of the Nisei. The Nisei were basically American and they were American citizens, but a serious question now arose as to whether they had any standing at all in American society. So much has already been written about the Nisei's identity dilemma during World War II that it is pointless to attempt a review of the matter here. Suffice it to say that in the latter part of the book, Kazuko seeks an answer to the question "What is my place in this world?" and in the concluding chapter hints at the answer that was forming for her.

Some writers seem to assume that the identity problem for Japanese Americans emerged primarily with the Sansei, but the fact is that the problem was no less serious for the Nisei in the years preceding the outbreak of World War II. The main difference was that the problem then was less well articulated. Indeed, one may question the need for imposing a theoretical conception upon Ms. Sone's lively, ingenuous, and charming book. She certainly makes no pretense of theorizing or philosophizing. Nevertheless, the identity problem was a very genuine issue for most Nisei in the prewar era, and I believe consideration of Ms. Sone's book within that context may add to its understanding.

S. FRANK MIYAMOTO

TWENTY-six years have passed since *Nisei Daughter* first came out in 1953. My narrative ended at a point where my brother, sister, and I left camp to go to our respective destinations, St. Louis, New Jersey, and Indiana. Our parents still remained in camp. They could not return to Seattle since the West Coast was still off limits to the Japanese.

The ten concentration camps, which received 120,000 of us in 1942, were finally closed in 1946.

From Hanover College in southern Indiana, I went on to Western Reserve University to study clinical psychology. I married Geary Sone, a Nisei veteran from California. We moved from Detroit, to Lansing, to Des Moines, to Iowa City, and are now in Canton, Ohio. Nisei daughter became Nisei mother to Philip Geary, Susan Mari, Peter Seiji, and John Kenzo. And very recently, we became grandparents to an infant named Andrew Harold Geary, first child of Susan and Gary Davison.

Today my mother, brother, Henry, and his wife, Minnie, live in Seattle. My sister, Sumiko, and her husband, Shirley Brinsfield, reside in Illinois. Mother is now an American citizen, thanks to the efforts of the Japanese American Citizens League with Congress. It was too late for father, who died in 1949.

As a result of years of reflection by the Nikkeis about their unique experience as Americans of Japanese ancestry, certain ideas and feelings have become distilled and crystallized into a strong determination. The Nikkeis are moving out into the public eye, to attend to unfinished business with the government. Their primary goal is to have the government address the constitutional issue of the evacuation. There will also be a petition for redress from Congress.

In our bicentennial year of 1976, upon recommendation of the Japanese American Citizens League, President Gerald R. Ford rescinded Executive Order 9066. He acknowledged that the mass incarceration was a national mistake. This was a small, but significant step toward righting a wrong.

During Thanksgiving of 1978, the Japanese American Citizens League began its redress campaign by observing its first "Day of Remembrance" ceremony in Seattle. Similar public ceremonies followed in Portland, San Francisco, and Los Angeles.

So that their story will not be forgotten and lost to future generations, the Nikkeis are telling the nation about 1942, a time when they became prisoners of their own government, without charges, without trials. This happened because the President and Congress yielded to the pressures of agricultural and other economic interest groups on the West Coast, which for fifty years had tried to be rid of the Nikkeis. Mass media assisted in molding public opinion to this end. Most astounding of all, the Supreme Court chose not to touch the issue of the Niseis' civil liberties as American citizens. In the Hirabayashi, Yasui, and Korematsu cases, the Court carefully avoided ruling on the basic constitutional issue of curfew and mass incarceration of a particular group of citizens, selected solely on the basis of ancestry. The Court overlooked the vital American principle that consideration of guilt and punishment is to be carried out on an individual basis, and is not to be related to the wrongdoing of others. Justice Robert Jackson, in dissent, wrote, "The Supreme Court for all time has validated the principle of racial discrimination in criminal procedure."

The Nikkeis hope that this redress movement may discourage similar injustices to others. They aim to work together with white America, to carry out our mutual task which Professor V. Rostow of Yale delineated in his writing: "Until the wrong is acknowledged and made right, we shall have failed to meet the responsibility of a democratic society . . . the obligation of equal justice."

MONICA SONE

NISEI DAUGHTER

CHAPTER I

A Shocking Fact of Life

THE first five years of my life I lived in amoebic bliss, not knowing whether I was plant or animal, at the old Carrollton Hotel on the waterfront of Seattle. One day when I was a happy six-year-old, I made the shocking discovery that I had Japanese blood. I was a Japanese.

Mother announced this fact of life to us in a quiet, deliberate manner one Sunday afternoon as we gathered around for dinner in the small kitchen, converted from one of our hotel rooms. Our kitchen was cozily comfortable for all six of us as long as everyone remained in his place around the oblong table covered with an indestructible shiny black oilcloth; but if more than Mother stood up and fussed around, there was a serious traffic jam — soy sauce splattered on the floor and elbows jabbed into the pot of rice. So Father sat at the head of the table, Kenji, Henry, and I lined up on one side along the wall, while Mother and baby Sumiko occupied the other side, near the kitchen stove.

Now we watched as Mother lifted from a kettle of boiling water a straw basket of steaming slippery noodles. She directed her information at Henry and me, and I felt uneasy. Father paid strict attention to his noodles, dipping them into a bowl of fragrant pork broth and then sprinkling finely chopped raw green onion over them.

"Japanese blood — how is it I have that, Mama?" I asked, surreptitiously pouring hot tea over my bowl of rice. Mother said it was bad manners to wash rice down with tea, but rice was delicious with *obancha*.

"Your father and I have Japanese blood and so do you, too. And the same with Henry, Ken-chan, and Sumi-chan."

"Oh." I felt nothing unusual stirring inside me. I took a long cool sip of milk and then with my short red chopsticks I stabbed at a piece of pickled crisp white radish.

"So, Mama?" Henry looked up at her, trying to bring under control with his chopsticks the noodles swinging from his mouth like a pendulum.

"So, Papa and I have decided that you and Ka-chan will attend Japanese school after grammar school every day." She beamed at us.

I choked on my rice.

Terrible, terrible, terrible! So that's what it meant to be a Japanese — to lose my afternoon play hours! I fiercely resented this sudden intrusion of my blood into my affairs.

"But, Mama!" I shrieked. "I go to Bailey Gatzert School already. I don't want to go to another!"

Henry kicked the table leg and grumbled, "Aw gee, Mama, Dunks and Jiro don't have to — why do I!"

"They'll be going, too. Their mothers told me so."

My face grew hot with anger. I shouted, "I won't, I won't!"

Father and Mother painted glowing pictures for me. Just think you'll grow up to be a well-educated young lady, knowing two languages. One of these days you'll thank us for giving you this opportunity.

But they could not convince me. Until this shattering moment, I had thought life was sweet and reasonable. But not any more.

Why did Father and Mother make such a fuss just because we had Japanese blood? Why did we have to go to Japanese school? I refused to eat and sat sobbing, letting great big tears splash down into my bowl of rice and tea.

Henry, who was smarter and adjusted more quickly to fate, continued his meal, looking gloomy, but with his appetite unimpaired.

Up to that moment, I had never thought of Father and Mother as Japanese. True, they had almond eyes and they spoke Japanese to us, but I never felt that it was strange. It was like one person's being red-haired and another black.

Father had often told us stories about his early life. He had come from a small village in the prefecture of Tochigi-ken. A third son among five brothers and one sister, Father had gone to Tokyo to study law, and he practiced law for a few years before he succumbed to the fever which sent many young men streaming across the Pacific to a fabulous new country rich with promise and opportunities.

In 1904 Father sailed for the United States, an ambitious young man of twenty-five, determined to continue his law studies at Ann Arbor, Michigan. Landing in Seattle, he plunged into sundry odd jobs with the hope of saving enough money to finance his studies. Father worked with the railroad gang, laying ties on virgin soil, he toiled stubbornly in the heat of the potato fields of Yakima, he cooked his way back and forth between Alaska and Seattle on ships of all sizes and shapes, but fortune eluded him. Then one day he bought a small cleaning and pressing shop on Tenth and Jackson Street, a wagon and a gentle white dobbin, "Charlie." The years flew by fast, but his savings did not reflect his frenzied labor. With each passing year, his dream of Ann Arbor grew dimmer.

At last Father's thoughts turned toward marriage. About this time the Reverend Yohachi Nagashima — our grandfather — brought his family to America. Grandfather Nagashima was a minister of a Congregational church in Sanomachi, about twenty miles north of Tokyo in Tochigi-ken prefecture. He had visited the United States twice before on preaching missions among the Japanese. Grandfather had been impressed with the freedom and educational opportunities in America. He arrived in Seattle with his wife, Yuki, three daughters, Yasuko, my mother Benko, and Kikue, twenty-two, seventeen and sixteen years of age respectively, and two little round-eyed sons, Shinichi and Yoshio, six and four years.

Mother and her sisters sailed into the port looking like exotic tropical butterflies. Mother told us she wore her best blue silk crepe kimono, Yasuko chose a deep royal purple robe, and Kikue, a soft rose one. Their kimonos had extravagantly long, graceful sleeves, with bright red silk linings. Over their kimonos, the girls donned long, plum-colored, pleated skirts, called the *hakama*, to cover the kimono skirts that flipped open as they walked. Shod in spanking white *tabis* — Japanese stockings — and scarlet cork-soled slippers, the young women stood in tense excitement at the rails of the ship. Yasuko, the eldest, held a picture of a young man in her hand, and she could hardly bring herself to look down at the sea of faces below on the dock where her prospective husband, whom she had never met, stood waiting. Mother told us she and Kikue scanned the crowd boldly and saw hundreds of young, curious masculine faces turned upward, searching for their picture brides.

Father heard of the Nagashimas' arrival. He immediately called to pay his respects. Seeing three marriageable daughters, Father kept going back. Eventually he sent a mutual friend to act as go-between to ask for the hand of the first daughter, Yasuko, but the friend reported that Mr. Nagashima had already arranged for Yasuko's marriage to a Mr. Tani. Undaunted, Father sent his friend back to ask for the second daughter, Benko. Mother said that when her father called her into his study and told her that a Mr. Itoi wanted to marry her, she was so shocked she fled to her room, dived under her bed and cried in protest, "I can't, Otoh-san, I can't. I don't even know him!"

Her father had got down on his hands and knees and peered at her under the bed, reprimanding her sternly. "Stop acting like a child, Benko. I advise you to start getting acquainted with Mr. Itoi at once."

And that was that. Finally Mother gave her consent to the marriage, and the wedding ceremony was performed at the Japanese mission branch of the Methodist Episcopal Church on Fourteenth and Washington Street. Years later, when Henry and I came upon their wedding picture in our family album, we went into hysterics over Mother's face which had been plastered white and immobile with rice powder, according to Japanese fashion. Only her piercing black eyes looked alive. In deference to Occidental tradition, she wore a white gown and bridal veil in which she looked tiny and doll-like beside Father, who stood stiff and agonized in formal white tie and tails.

For about a year Mother helped Father haphazardly at his dry-cleaning shop, intent on satisfying the customer's every whim. She scribbled down the strangely garbled phone messages. More than once Mother handed Father an address at which he was supposed to pick up clothes, and he found himself parking his wagon in front of an empty, weed-choked lot or cantering briskly out of the city limits as he pursued phantom house numbers.

In January, 1918, their first child was born, Henry Seiichi — son of truth. Shortly after, Father sold his little shop and bought the Carrollton Hotel on Main Street and Occidental Avenue, just a stone's throw from the bustling waterfront and the noisy railroad tracks. It was, in fact, on the very birth site of Seattle when the town began its boisterous growth with the arrival of pioneer Henry Yesler and his sawmill on the waterfront. In its early days, the area south of Yesler Hill, where we lived, was called Skid Road because loggers used to grease the roads at intervals to help the ox teams pull the logs down to the mills. Nearly a hundred years later, the district bore the name Skidrow, a corrupted version of Skid Road, with its shoddy stores, decayed buildings, and shriveled men.

The Carrollton had seen its heyday during the Alaskan gold rush. It was an old-fashioned hotel on the second floor of an old red brick building. It had twenty outside rooms and forty inside ones, arranged in three block formations and separated by long corridors. The hallways and inside rooms were lighted and ventilated by the ceiling skylight windows. During the cold of winter, these inside rooms were theoretically warmed by a pot-bellied stove in the lobby, which was located just at the left of the top stair landing. There was only one bathroom, with a cavernous bathtub, to keep sixty-odd people clean. A separate restroom, For Gents Only, eased the bathroom congestion somewhat. For extra service all the rooms were equipped with a gigantic pitcher of water, a mammoth-sized washbowl, and an ornate chamber pot.

When Father took over the hotel in 1918, the building fairly burst with war workers and servicemen. They came at all hours of the day, begging to sleep even in the chairs in the hotel lobby. Extra cots had to be set up in the hallways.

Father and Mother loved to tell us how they had practically rejuvenated the battered, flea-ridden Carrollton by themselves. Father had said firmly, "If I have to manage a flophouse, it'll be the cleanest and quietest place around here." With patience and care, they began to patch the aches and pains of the old hotel. The tobacco-stained stairways were scrubbed, painted and lighted up. Father varnished the floors while Mother painted the wood-work. New green runners were laid out in the corridors. They re-papered the sixty rooms, one by one. Every day after the routine room-servicing had been finished, Mother cooked up a bucket of flour and water and brushed the paste on fresh new wallpaper laid out on a long makeshift work table in the hall.

All the while Father tried to build up a choice selection of cus-tomers, for even one drunkard on a binge always meant fist fights and broken furniture. Father quickly found that among the flot-sam of seedy, rough-looking characters milling around in Skid-row were men who still retained their dignity and self-respect. There were lonely old men whose families had been broken up by the death of wives and departing children, who lived a sober existence on their meager savings or their monthly pension allot-ment. Father also took in sea-hardened mariners, shipyard work-ers, airplane workers, fruit pickers and factory workers. He tried to weed out petty thieves, bootleggers, drug peddlers, perverts, alcoholics and fugitives from the law. At first glance it was hard to tell whether a stubble-bearded, wrinkled, and red-eyed man had just returned from a hard day's work or a hard day at the tavern. Father had a simple technique. If the man smelled of plain, honest-to-goodness perspiration, he was in. But if he reeked of wood alcohol or bay rum, the office window came crashing down in front of his nose.

Shortly after the Armistice of World War I was signed, I was born and appropriately named Kazuko Monica, the Japanese name meaning "peace." (Mother chose Monica from her reading about Saint Augustine and his mother, Saint Monica.) Two years later Kenji William arrived, his name meaning "Healthy in body and spirit." Mother added "William" because she thought it sounded poetic. And two years after that, Sumiko, "the clear one," was born.

For our family quarters, Mother chose three outside rooms looking south on Main Street, across an old and graying five-story warehouse, and as the family increased, a fourth room was added. Father and Mother's small bedroom was crowded with a yellow brass bed that took up one wall. Mother's dainty white-painted dresser and a small square writing table piled with her books and papers occupied another wall. Father's brown dresser stood off in another corner, its only ornament a round, maroon-lacquered collar box. A treadle sewing machine squatted efficiently in front of the window where Mother sat in the evenings, mending torn sheets and pillowcases. Their closet was a pole slung against the fourth wall, covered with a green, floral-print curtain.

The living room was large, light, and cheerful-looking, with a shiny mahogany-finished upright piano in one corner. Right above it hung a somber picture of Christ's face which looked down upon me each time I sat in front of the piano. Depending on my previous behavior, I felt restless and guilty under those brooding eyes or smugly content with myself. Against another wall, next to the piano, stood an elegant-looking, glass-cased secretary filled with Father's Japanese books, thick hotel account books, a set of untouched, glossy-paged encyclopedias, and the back numbers of the *National Geographic*. In the corner, near the window, was a small square table, displaying a monstrous, iridescent half of an abalone shell and a glass ball paperweight filled with water, depicting an underwater scene with tiny corals and sea shells lying on the ocean bottom. In front of the other two windows was a long, brown leather davenport with a small gas heater nearby. A round dining table in the center of the room was surrounded by three plain chairs.

The children's bedrooms were simply furnished with brown iron cots and old-fashioned dressers. Although rugs were laid out in the living room and our parents' bedroom, our rooms had toe-chilling, easy-to-keep-clean linoleum. Sumiko and I occupied the room next to the living room while Henry and Kenji had the last room.

At first glance, there was little about these simple, sparse furnishings to indicate that a Japanese family occupied the rooms. But there were telltale signs like the *zori* or straw slippers placed neatly on the floor underneath the beds. On Mother's bed lay a beautiful red silk comforter patterned with turquoise, apple-green, yellow and purple Japanese parasols. And on the table beside the local daily paper were copies of the *North American Times,* Seattle's Japanese-community paper, its printing resembling rows of black multiple-legged insects. Then there was the Oriental abacus board which Father used once a month to keep his books.

Our kitchen was a separate room far down the hall. The kitchen window opened into an alley, right above the Ace Café. An outdoor icebox, born of an old apple crate, was nailed firmly to our kitchen window sill.

Father had put in a gas stove next to the small sink. The huge stove took up nearly all the floor space. He had nailed five layers of shelves against the opposite wall almost up to the ceiling, and next to this, he installed a towering china cabinet with delicate, frosted glass windows. A large, oblong table was wedged into the only space left, in a corner near the door. Here in the kitchen were unmistakable Oriental traces and odors. A glass tumbler holding six pairs of red and yellow lacquered chopsticks, and a bottle of soy sauce stood companionably among the imitation cut-glass sugar bowl and the green glass salt and pepper shakers at the end of the table. The tall china cabinet bulged with bright hand-painted rice bowls, red lacquered soup bowls, and Mother's precious *somayaki* tea set.

The tea set was stunningly beautiful with the uneven surface of the gray clay dusted with black and gold flecks. There was a wisp of soft green around the rim of the tiny cups, as if someone had plucked off grass from the clay and the green stain had remained there. At the bottom of each teacup was the figure of a galloping, golden horse. When the cup was filled with tea, the golden horse seemed to rise to the surface and become animated. But the tea set was only for special occasions and holidays, and most of the time we used a set of dinnerware Americana purchased at the local hardware store and a drawerful of silver-plated tableware.

In the pantry, the sack of rice and gallon jug of *shoyu* stood lined up next to the ivory-painted canisters of flour, sugar, tea and coffee. From a corner near the kitchen window, a peculiar, pungent odor emanated from a five-gallon crock which Mother kept filled with cucumbers, *nappa* (Chinese cabbage), *daikon* (large Japanese radishes), immersed in a pickling mixture of *nuka*, consisting of rice polishings, salt, rice and raisins. The fermented products were sublimely refreshing, delicious, raw vegetables, a perfect side dish to a rice and tea mixture at the end of a meal.

Among the usual pots and pans stood a dark red stone mixing bowl inside of which were cut rows and rows of minute grooves as on a record disc. The bowl was used to grind poppy seeds and *miso* (soybeans) into soft paste for soups and for flavoring Japanese dishes. I spent many hours bent over this bowl, grinding the beans into a smooth, fine paste with a heavy wooden club. For all the work that went into making *miso shiru,* soybean soup, I thought it tasted like sawdust boiled in sea brine. Mother told me nothing could be more nutritious, but I could never take more than a few shuddering sips of it.

In our family we ate both Western and Oriental dishes. Mother had come to America just fresh out of high school and had had little training in Japanese culinary art. In the beginning, Father taught Mother to cook all the dishes he knew. Father had a robust, mass-cooking style which he had learned in the galleys of Alaska-bound ships and he leaned heavily toward ham and eggs, steaks and potatoes, apple and pumpkin pies. Later Mother picked up the technique of authentic Japanese cooking herself and she even learned to cook superb Chinese dishes. Although we acquired tastes for different types of food, we adhered mostly to a simple American menu.

So we lived in the old Carrollton. Every day, amidst the bedlam created by four black-eyed, jet-propelled children, Father and Mother took care of the hotel. Every morning they went from room to room, making the beds and cleaning up. To help speed up the chores, we ran up and down the corridors, pounding on doors. We brutally woke the late sleepers, hammering with our fists and yelling, "Wake up, you sleepyhead! Wake up, make bed!" Then someone would think of pushing the linen cart for Father and the rest of us would rush to do the same. We usually ended up in a violent tussle. One of our favorite games, when neither Father nor Mother was looking, was "climbing the laundry." We vied with each other to see who could climb highest on an ill-smelling mountain of soiled sheets, pillowcases and damp towels, piled high to the ceiling. Henry always reached the top by giving himself a running start halfway down the hall. He flew light-footed up the mound like a young gazelle. He hooted scornfully when I scrambled up, red faced and frantic, grabbing at the sheets and tumbling down when I snatched a loose pillowcase. Kenji and Sumiko squealed happily at the foot of the linen pile and slapped each other with the sopping wet towels. Whenever Mother discovered us, she shrieked in dismay, *"Kita-nai, mah, kita-nai koto!* It's dirty and full of germs. Get right out of there!"

Yes, life to us children was a wonderful treat — especially during hot summer nights when Father slipped out to a market stand down the block and surprised us with an enormous, ice-cold watermelon. It was pure joy when we first bit into its crisp pink succulence and let the juice trickle and seeds fall on old newspapers spread on the round table in the parlor. Or sometimes on a wintry evening, we crowded around the kitchen table to watch Father, bath towel-apron draped around his waist, whip up a batch of raisin cookies for us. It wasn't everybody's father who could turn out thick, melting, golden cookies. We were especially proud that our father had once worked as a cook on romantic Alaska-bound freighters.

Life was hilarious whenever Mother played *Jan-ken-pon! Ai-kono-hoi!* with us. This was the game played by throwing out paper, scissors, and rock symbols with our hands, accompanied by the chant. The winner with the stronger symbol had the privilege of slapping the loser's wrist with two fingers. Mother pretended to cry whenever our small fingers came down on her wrist. With her oval face, lively almond-shaped eyes, and slender aquiline nose, Mother was a pretty, slender five feet of youth and fun.

I thought the whole world consisted of two or three old hotels on every block. And that its population consisted of families like mine who lived in a corner of the hotels. And its other inhabitants were customers — fading, balding, watery-eyed men, rough-tough bearded men, and good men like Sam, Joe, Peter and Montana who worked for Father, all of whom lived in these hotels.

It was a very exciting world in which I lived.

I played games with a little girl I liked, Matsuko, who lived in Adams Hotel, two blocks away. Sometimes Henry and his friends Dunks and Jiro joined us to explore dingy alleys behind produce warehouses, looking for discarded jars of candies. Sometimes we fished from Pier Two, dipping a long string with bread tied to its end in the briny, moldy-green water. It was pleasant to sit on the sun-warmed old timber which creaked with the waves, and bask in the mellow sun, waiting for the shiners to nibble.

Our street itself was a compact little world, teeming with the bustle of every kind of business in existence in Skidrow. Right below our living quarters was a large second-hand clothing store. It was guarded by a thin, hunchbacked, gray woolly-bearded-man who sat napping on a little stool at the entrance. Its dust-misted windows were crammed with army and navy surplus clothes, blanket bathrobes, glistening black raincoats, stiff lumber jackets which practically stood up by themselves and a tangled heap of bootery from romeo house slippers to hip-length fishing boots. Oddly, the shop was very susceptible to fire, and every now and then smoke would seep up through our bedroom floor boards and we would hear fire engines thundering down our street. After each such uproar, the old man would put up huge, red-lettered signs: *Mammoth Fire Sale . . . practically a giveaway!*

Next to the clothing store was the tavern, the forbidden hall of iniquity, around which we were not supposed to loiter. The swinging door was sawed off at the bottom, but with our heads hanging down we managed to get an upside down view of it. All we could see were feet stuck to brass rails. A nickelodeon played only one song, day in and day out, a melancholy, hillbilly tune of which we could make out just one phrase. "When they cut down that old pine tree. . . ." It was drowned out by the heaven-splitting songs from the mission hall next door, which was filled with hollow-eyed, graying old men, sitting impassively with battered hats balanced on their knees.

Next to our hotel entrance, Mr. Wakamatsu operated the Ace Café. We liked him, because he was such a tall, pleasant-mannered, handsome man. He had a beautiful clear tenor voice which floated out into the alley up to our kitchen as he called out, "Veal, French fries on the side . . . !" Mr. Wakamatsu's window display was always a splendid sight to see. There would be a neat row of purple strawberry shortcakes, or a row of apple pies shining with the luster of shellac, or a row of rigid, blood-red gelatin puddings planted squarely in the center of thick white saucers.

Next to the Ace Café was Dunks's father's small barbershop. Then there was the little white-painted hot-dog stand where we bought luscious hot dogs and hamburgers smothered with onions and the hottest of chili sauce which brought tears brimming to our eyes. The hot-dog man was constantly swatting flies on the meat board, and I hate to think how many mashed flies were in the red ground meat.

Then came another forbidden place, the burlesque house. A brunet-haired woman with carefully powdered wrinkles sat in the ticket booth, chewing gum. She always winked a shiny purple eyelid at us whenever we passed, and we never knew for sure whether we should smile back at her or not. The theater marquee was studded with dingy yellow light bulbs, spelling out the "Rialto," and the doors were covered with the life-size paintings of half-naked girls, about to step out from behind feathers, balloons and chiffon scarves.

On the corner of Occidental and Washington Street stood a small cigar shop. We were sure that the storekeeper, who constantly rattled dice in a dirty leather cylinder box, had been a big-time gambler in the past. He was just the type, with his baggy eyes, cigar stuffed in his mouth, and his fingers covered with massive jeweled rings.

Just around the corner was a teamsters' union office. Hairy-armed, open-shirted, tattooed men clomped continually in and out of the smoke-filled room. Twice a day, a man hustled out of there carrying a wooden cratebox. He beckoned to the men loafing on the corner to gather near and listen to what he had to say. We stood watching on tiptoes at the fringe of the crowd until the orating man had worked himself into a passion, alternatingly purring at and berating his apathetic audience.

". . . tell me, my friends, what the hell are you anyway . . . men or beasts? To the goddamned capitalist, you're nothin' but beasts! Are you going to grovel under their feet the rest of your life? CRUMBS! That's all they give you . . . CRUMBS! Are you going to be satisfied with that? I say 'NO!' None of that for us anymore. We have to break them now . . . now!"

"Hallelujah," someone would respond dryly.

Across on the opposite corner there was another small crowd, gawking at a man with flowing, silver-white hair and full beard. Tears would be rolling down his uplifted face and disappear into his beard as he pleaded with his audience to "repent before it is too late." Listening to him, I always felt the urgency to repent before it was too late, but I was never sure which of my sins was worth confessing.

The Salvation Army was always there, marching along the

street, keeping in time with the brass drum. Wheeling expertly into semicircle formation near the curb, the uniformed men and women would lift their bugles and trumpets and blare out a vigorous hymn. When the tambourine was passed around for our offering, we would move on guiltily, having already spent our nickles for hot dogs.

This was the playground where I roamed freely and happily. And when I finally started grammar school, I found still another enchanting world. Every morning I hurried to Adams Hotel, climbed its dark flight of stairs, and called for Matsuko. Together we made the long and fascinating journey — from First Avenue to Twelfth Avenue — to Bailey Gatzert School. We always walked over the bridge on Fourth Avenue where we hung over the iron rails, waiting until a train roared past under us, enveloping us completely in its hissing, billowing cloud of white, warm steam. We meandered through the international section of town, past the small Japanese shops and stores, already bustling in the early morning hour, past the cafés and barber shops filled with Filipino men, and through Chinatown. Then finally we went up a gentle sloping hill to the handsome low-slung, red-brick building with its velvet green lawn and huge play yard. I felt like a princess walking through its bright, sunny corridors on smooth, shiny floors. I was mystified by a few of the little boys and girls. There were some pale-looking children who spoke a strange dialect of English, rapidly like gunfire. Matsuko told me they were *"hagu-jins,"* white people. Then there were children who looked very much like me with their black hair and black eyes, but they spoke in high, musical singing voices. Matsuko whispered to me that they were Chinese.

And now Mother was telling us we were Japanese. I had always thought I was a Yankee, because after all I had been born on

Occidental and Main Street. Montana, a wall-shaking mountain of a man who lived at our hotel, called me a Yankee. I didn't see how I could be a Yankee and Japanese at the same time. It was like being born with two heads. It sounded freakish and a lot of trouble. Above everything, I didn't want to go to Japanese school.

CHAPTER II

The Stubborn Twig

THE inevitable, dreaded first day at Nihon Gakko arrived. Henry and I were dumped into a taxicab, screaming and kicking against the injustice of it all. When the cab stopped in front of a large, square gray-frame building, Mother pried us loose, though we clung to the cab door like barnacles. She half carried us up the hill. We kept up our horrendous shrieking and wailing, right to the school entrance. Then a man burst out of the door. His face seemed to have been carved out of granite and with turned-down mouth and nostrils flaring with disapproval, his black marble eyes crushed us into a quivering silence. This was Mr. Ohashi, the school principal, who had come out to investigate the abominable, un-Japanesey noise on the school premises.

Mother bowed deeply and murmured, "I place them in your hands."

He bowed stiffly to Mother, then fastened his eyes on Henry and me and again bowed slowly and deliberately. In our haste to return the bow, we nodded our heads. With icy disdain, he snapped, "That is not an *ojigi*." He bent forward with well-oiled precision. "Bow from the waist, like this."

I wondered, if Mr. Ohashi had the nerve to criticize us in front of Mother, what more he would do in her absence.

School was already in session and the hallway was empty and cold. Mr. Ohashi walked briskly ahead, opened a door, and Henry was whisked inside with Mother. I caught a glimpse of little boys and girls sitting erect, their books held upright on the desks.

As I waited alone out in the hall, I felt a tingling sensation. This was the moment for escape. I would run and run and run. I would be lost for days so that when Father and Mother finally found me, they would be too happy ever to force me back to Nihon Gakko. But Mr. Ohashi was too cunning for me. He must have read my thoughts, for the door suddenly opened, and he and Mother came out. He bowed formally again, "*Sah*, this way," and stalked off.

My will completely dissolved, I followed as in a terrible nightmare. Mother took my hand and smiled warmly, "Don't look so sad, Ka-chan. You'll find it a lot of fun when you get used to it."

I was ushered into a brightly lighted room which seemed ten times as brilliant with the dazzling battery of shining black eyes turned in my direction. I was introduced to Yasuda-sensei, a full-faced woman with a large, ballooning figure. She wore a long, shapeless cotton print smock with streaks of chalk powder down the front. She spoke kindly to me, but with a kindness that one usually reserves for a dull-witted child. She enunciated slowly and loudly, "What is your name?"

I whispered, "Kazuko," hoping she would lower her voice. I felt that our conversation should not be carried on in such a blatant manner.

"*Kazuko-san desuka?*" she repeated loudly. "You may sit over there." She pointed to an empty seat in the rear and I walked down an endless aisle between rows of piercing black eyes.

"Kazuko-san, why don't you remove your hat and coat and hang them up behind you?"

A wave of tittering broke out. With burning face, I rose from my seat and struggled out of my coat.

When Mother followed Mr. Ohashi out of the room, my throat began to tighten and tears flooded up again. I did not notice that Yasuda-sensei was standing beside me. Ignoring my snuffling, she handed me a book, opened to the first page. I saw a blurred drawing of one huge, staring eye. Right above it was a black squiggly mark, resembling the arabic figure one with a bar across the middle. Yasuda-sensei was up in front again, reading aloud, "*Meh!*" That was "eye." As we turned the pages, there were pictures of a long, austere nose, its print reading "*hana,*" an ear was called "*mi-mi,*" and a wide anemic-looking mouth, "*ku-chi.*" Soon I was chanting at the top of my voice with the rest of the class, "*Meh! Hana! Mi-mi! Ku-chi!*"

Gradually I yielded to my double dose of schooling. Nihon Gakko was so different from grammar school I found myself switching my personality back and forth daily like a chameleon. At Bailey Gatzert School I was a jumping, screaming, roustabout Yankee, but at the stroke of three when the school bell rang and doors burst open everywhere, spewing out pupils like jelly beans from a broken bag, I suddenly became a modest, faltering, earnest little Japanese girl with a small, timid voice. I trudged down a steep hill and climbed up another steep hill to Nihon Gakko with other black-haired boys and girls. On the playground, we behaved cautiously. Whenever we spied a teacher within bowing distance, we hissed at each other to stop the game, put our feet neatly together, slid our hands down to our knees and bowed slowly and sanctimoniously. In just the proper, moderate tone, putting in every ounce of respect, we chanted, "*Konichi-wa, sensei.* Good day."

For an hour and a half each day, we were put through our paces. At the beginning of each class hour, Yasuda-sensei punched a little bell on her desk. We stood up by our seats, at strict attention. Another "ping!" We all bowed to her in unison while she returned the bow solemnly. With the third "ping!" we sat down together.

There was *yomi-kata* time when individual students were called upon to read the day's lesson, clear and loud. The first time I recited I stood and read with swelling pride the lesson which I had prepared the night before. I mouthed each word carefully and paused for the proper length of time at the end of each sentence. Suddenly Yasuda-sensei stopped me.

"Kazuko-san!"

I looked up at her confused, wondering what mistakes I had made.

"You are holding your book in one hand," she accused me. Indeed, I was. I did not see the need of using two hands to support a thin book which I could balance with two fingers.

"Use both hands!" she commanded me.

Then she peered at me. "And are you leaning against your desk?" Yes, I was, slightly. "Stand up straight!"

"*Hai!* Yes, ma'am!"

I learned that I could stumble all around in my lessons without ruffling sensei's nerves, but it was a personal insult to her if I displayed sloppy posture. I must stand up like a soldier, hold the book high in the air with both hands, and keep my feet still.

We recited the Japanese alphabet aloud, fifty-one letters, over and over again. "Ah, ee, oo, eh, *OH!* Kah, kee, koo, keh, *KOH!* Sah, shi, soo, seh, *SOH!*" We developed a catchy little rhythm, coming down hard on the last syllable of each line. We wound up the drill with an ear-shattering, triumphant, "Lah, lee, loo, leh, *Loh!* WAH, EE, OO, EH, OH! UN!"

Yasuda-sensei would look suspiciously at us. Our recital

sounded a shade too hearty, a shade too rhythmic. It lacked something . . . possibly restraint and respect.

During *kaki-kata* hour, I doubled up over my desk and painfully drew out the *kata-kanas*, simplified Japanese ideographs, similar to English block printing. With clenched teeth and perspiring hands, I accentuated and emphasized, delicately nuanced and tapered off lines and curves.

At five-thirty, Yasuda-sensei rang the bell on her desk again. "Ping!" We stood up. "Ping!" We bowed. "Ping!" We vanished from the room like magic, except for one row of students whose turn it was to do *otohban*, washing blackboards, sweeping the floor, and dusting the desks. Under sensei's vigilant eyes, the chore felt like a convict's hard labor.

As time went on, I began to suspect that there was much more to Nihon Gakko than learning the Japanese language. There was a driving spirit of strict discipline behind it all which reached out and weighed heavily upon each pupil's consciousness. That force emanated from the principal's office.

Before Mr. Ohashi came to America, he had been a zealous student of the Ogasawara Shiko Saho, a form of social conduct dreamed up by a Mr. Ogasawara. Mr. Ohashi himself had written a book on etiquette in Japan. He was the Oriental male counterpart of Emily Post. Thus Mr. Ohashi arrived in America with the perfect bow tucked under his waist and a facial expression cemented into perfect samurai control. He came with a smoldering ambition to pass on this knowledge to the tender Japanese saplings born on foreign soil. The school-teachers caught fire, too, and dedicated themselves to us with a vengeance. It was not enough to learn the language. We must talk and walk and sit and bow in the best Japanese tradition.

As far as I was concerned, Mr. Ohashi's superior standard

boiled down to one thing. The model child is one with deep *rigor mortis* . . . no noise, no trouble, no back talk.

We understood too well what Mr. Ohashi wanted of us. He yearned and wished more than anything else that somehow he could mold all of us into Genji Yamadas. Genji was a classmate whom we detested thoroughly. He was born in Seattle, but his parents had sent him to Japan at an early age for a period of good, old-fashioned education. He returned home a stranger among us with stiff mannerisms and an arrogant attitude. Genji boasted that he could lick anyone, one husky fellow or ten little ones, and he did, time and time again. He was an expert at judo.

Genji was a handsome boy with huge, lustrous dark eyes, a noble patrician nose, jet crew-cut setting off a flawless, fair complexion, looking every bit the son of a samurai. He sat aloof at his desk and paid strict attention to sensei. He was the top student scholastically. He read fluently and perfectly. His handwriting was a beautiful picture of bold, masculine strokes and curves. What gnawed at us more than anything else was that he stood up as straight as a bamboo tree and never lost rigid control of his arms or legs. His bow was snappy and brisk and he always answered "*Hai!*" to everything that sensei said to him, ringing crisp and clear with respect. Every time Mr. Ohashi came into our room for a surprise visit to see if we were under control, he would stop at Genji's desk for a brief chat. Mr. Ohashi's eyes betrayed a glow of pride as he spoke to Genji, who sat up erect, eyes staring respectfully ahead. All we could make out of the conversation was Genji's sharp staccato barks, "*Hai!* . . . *Hai!* . . . *Hai!*"

This was the response sublime to Mr. Ohashi. It was real man to man talk. Whenever Mr. Ohashi approached us, we froze in our seats. Instead of snapping into attention like Genji, we wilted and sagged. Mr. Ohashi said we were more like *"konyaku,"* a colorless, gelatinous Japanese food. If a boy fidgeted too nervously under Mr. Ohashi's stare, a vivid red stain rose from the back of Mr. Ohashi's neck until it reached his temple and then there was a sharp explosion like the crack of a whip. *"Keo-tsuke! Attention!"* It made us all leap in our seats, each one of us feeling terribly guilty for being such an inadequate Japanese.

I asked Mother, "Why is Mr. Ohashi so angry all the time? He always looks as if he had just bitten into a green persimmon. I've never seen him smile."

Mother said, "I guess Mr. Ohashi is the old-fashioned schoolmaster. I know he's strict, but he means well. Your father and I received harsher discipline than that in Japan . . . not only from schoolteachers, but from our own parents."

"Yes, I know, Mama." I leaned against her knees as she sat on the old leather davenport, mending our clothes. I thought Father and Mother were still wonderful, even if they had packed me off to Nihon Gakko. "Mrs. Matsui is so strict with her children, too. She thinks you spoil us." I giggled, and reassured her quickly, "But I don't think you spoil us at all."

Mrs. Matsui was ten years older than Mother, and had known Mother's father in Japan. Therefore she felt it was her duty to look after Mother's progress in this foreign country. Like a sharp-eyed hawk, she picked out Mother's weaknesses. Why did Mother find it necessary to stay up late every night to read and write poetry? She should be resting her body for the next day's work. Each time Mrs. Matsui called, Mother was on tenterhooks, wishing desperately for some sort of remote control over our behavior. It was impossible for us to remember the endless little things we must not do in front of Mrs. Matsui. We must not laugh out loud and show our teeth, or chatter in front of guests, or interrupt adult conversation, or cross our knees while seated, or ask for a piece of candy, or squirm in our seats.

I knew I could never come up to Yaeko, Mrs. Matsui's only daughter. She was a few years older than I, and plump and vicious like her mother. Yaeko would sit quietly beside her mother, knees together, dress pulled down modestly over the ankles, hands folded demurely in her lap, and eyes fixed dully on the floor. Whenever Mother gave her a magazine to look at, Yaeko would bow graciously. "*Arigato gozai masu.*" And she would stare politely at one picture for a long, long time, turn a page so slowly and quietly that I felt like tearing into her and rattling the paper for her. But whenever we were given permission to play outside, Yaeko became a different person. She would look at me scornfully, "Let's not play jacks again! It's baby stuff. Don't you have some good magazines to read . . . like *True Love?*"

I did not have *True Love* magazines. So we played an ill-tempered game of jacks at which time she would cheat, pinch and jar my elbows whenever she felt I was taking too long.

Mrs. Matsui thought Mother's relationship with her children was chaotic. She clucked sympathetically at Mother, "Do they still call you 'Mama' and 'Papa'?"

"Oh, yes," Mother smiled to hide her annoyance. "You know how it is. That's all they've ever heard around here. In fact, my husband and I have been corrupted, too. We call each other 'Mama' and 'Papa.' It just seems natural in our environment."

Mrs. Matsui drew herself up stiffly. "I taught my young ones to say '*Otoh-san*' and '*Okah-san*' from the very beginning."

"That's wonderful, Mrs. Matsui, but I'm afraid it's too late for us."

"Such a pity! You really ought to be more firm with them, too,

Itoi-san. When I say 'no,' my children know I mean it. Whenever I feel they're getting out of hand, my husband and I take steps."

Mother looked interested.

"We give '*okyu*' quite often." Mrs. Matsui folded her hands neatly together. *Okyu* was an old-country method of discipline, a painful and lasting punishment of applying a burning punk on a child's bare back. "Believe me, after *okyu*, we don't have trouble for a long, long time."

Henry, Kenji, Sumiko and I eyed each other nervously. We wished Mrs. Matsui would stop talking about such things to Mother.

Mr. Ohashi and Mrs. Matsui thought they could work on me and gradually mold me into an ideal Japanese *ojoh-san*, a refined young maiden who is quiet, pure in thought, polite, serene, and self-controlled. They made little headway, for I was too much the child of Skidrow. As far as I was concerned, Nihon Gakko was a total loss. I could not use my Japanese on the people at the hotel. Bowing was practical only at Nihon Gakko. If I were to bow to the hotel patrons, they would have laughed in my face. Therefore promptly at five-thirty every day, I shed Nihon Gakko and returned with relief to an environment which was the only real one to me. Life was too urgent, too exciting, too colorful for me to be sitting quietly in the parlor and contemplating a spray of chrysanthemums in a bowl as a cousin of mine might be doing in Osaka.

One of my driving ambitions was to win the $3000 reward offered in the true detective magazines to anyone who helped capture a fugitive murderer. I studied the rogues' gallery and tried to memorize the faces of criminals . . . especially those bringing the highest rewards. I was sure that our hotel was a gold mine since so many of our customers looked like fugitives from the law, haggard, tough and unkempt. From time to time, real detectives appeared at our office window, flashing their badges. They studied the hotel register silently and departed with a mysterious air. I was sure that behind one of our doors was a frightened fugitive, lying low in his room.

I became suspicious of one gaunt, furtive-looking man who stayed in his room day after day, never showing himself in broad daylight. Only at night, he slunk out, cap pulled down over his gray, bleak eyes. I looked for his name in the register — Jack Montane. I inquired casually about Jack's background. No one seemed to know much about him, but Sam, the old-timer, told me that Jack worked nights as watchman. He was a hard-working man who sent money regularly to his old mother in Nebraska. This was a terrible blow to my plans, but one disappointment did not deter me. Day after day, as I kept an eager watch out for criminals, Mother worried about my dark mind and predatory soul.

I would have liked to turn over Kirby Dare to the police, but his picture had never appeared in the crime magazine. Kirby was a slender, pint-sized young man in his middle twenties. He had electric blue eyes, a Pinocchio nose, and a ruddy, odd face which wrinkled up like an old man's when he laughed. When he was in high spirits, he cackled and pranced up and down the corridor like a rooster. He flapped his arms and crowed with such a piercing shriek that his face reddened and his neck veins stood out. We always knew he was around by his loud abandoned singing, "K-K-K-Katy! You're the only girl that I adore . . . tum te tum ta, tum te ta ta, da da daaaaa!" Father thought Kirby must be a little *kichi-gai*, mad. So the name "Kichi-gai" stuck to Kirby.

Kirby took baths a half a dozen times a day. Looking like a boiled lobster, he declared, "I believe in keeping clean, because to be clean is to be like God!" He also carried a giant-sized Bible under his arm. When anyone was around, he would open the Bible and read aloud.

If Kirby was not sitting on top of the world, then he was at his rudest and meanest. Passing by one of us children in the hallway, he would reach out and pinch our arms or cheeks hard. It hurt. I sometimes managed to kick him on his shin bones and dart away, taunting him, "You, Kichi-gai!"

Father warned Kirby many times to keep away from us. Kirby was all graciousness, assuring Father that he loved children and he would never think of harming us. Then he began trying to lure us into his room with candy and toys. We were afraid of him, but we wanted the candy so badly that one day, we stepped across the threshold, grabbed it out of his hand and ran pell-mell down the hall. We told Father about it, we were so pleased with ourselves. Father turned pale, and his voice shook with anger. He made us promise we would never, never, go into anyone's room or accept gifts without his permission. And Kirby was firmly told to leave.

People in Skidrow were not all queer like Kirby Dare. There were nice, quiet men like Sam, Joe, Peter and Montana. We thought of them as part of the family.

Sam Orland was a tall, rugged, blue-eyed retired mariner with a photographic mind. He knew every man's character and habit in Skidrow. When Father first took over the hotel management, Sam used to sit near the office window and screen the hotel clients for Father. He would shake his head darkly whenever he knew the man to be a bad actor or a "wino."

When the large mission hall next door was vacated in 1928,

Father rented it and converted it into a mammoth dormitory with row upon row of neat-looking beds. He turned it over to Sam who managed it with great pride. Sam saw to it that it was shipshape and clean, patrolling the aisles like a sea captain up on deck. He kept a sharp eye out for stray characters who might sneak in for a cat nap. Because Sam was muscular as well as iron-willed, drunks and brawlers found themselves being swiftly escorted down the stairs.

Joe Subotich was a portly, cheerful man with a tiny black mustache and a deep dimple on his chin. He reminded us of a swarthy version of Santa Claus, for his pockets were always bulging with chocolate bars, apples and nuts. Joe had left Oregon years ago after a family breakup, and he had wandered into Father's hotel, broken in spirit and finance. Sometimes when Joe lost his job, it might be weeks before he found another. Father trusted him, and Joe's gratitude knew no bounds. Eventually Joe became our night watchman and Father's loyal friend.

Peter was a soft-spoken, gentle old Bohemian who delighted us by performing impromptu folk dances and singing gay little Bohemian songs. No matter how often we asked him, with each passing year, he solemnly told us he was seventy years old. He had a translucent, pale, bald head which he kept covered day and night with a cap. He was thin and delicately put together, but he had the most durable health and energy I have ever seen in a man. When Father placed Peter in charge of the second new dormitory, Peter came into his own. He fussed all day in the dormitory like a high-strung housekeeper, patting pillows into shape, smoothing wrinkles out of bedspreads, and sweeping the spotless, bare floor a dozen times a day.

Montana was our self-appointed bouncer. A bouncer was a necessity, not only in the taverns, but every place in Skidrow.

Well over six feet tall with a tightly curled, black beard growing rampant down over his faded flannel shirt, Montana was an awesome figure. He weighed two hundred and fifty pounds and required two sturdy chairs to hold his massive bulk as he sat dozing in the lobby. His ears were especially sensitive to loud, quarreling voices. Knowing that Father was never one for violence, by temperament or size, Montana hovered around him like a huge St. Bernard. "Now, Boss, anyone give you trouble, and you want 'em out, just give me the sign and I'll show 'em the way out, pronto!"

Father, barely reaching Montana's bulging shoulders, felt that it would not be diplomatic to refuse his services, so he merely smiled noncommittally. Father usually managed to extricate himself from trouble with hardly a hubbub.

I remember one evening Father was called to the front office by the bell. We heard a loud voice echoing down the hall to our kitchen.

"Goddammit! I demand my money back! I'm not staying here tonight, so gimme my dollar back."

Henry and I rushed out to see what was the matter. A grizzly bear of a man was stalking Father. "No, suh! I don't owe you a penny!" Father said as he turned and went inside the office, intending to close the subject.

The man narrowed his eyes, hitched his trousers up and followed Father belligerently. He bellowed, "You damn Jap! You know who I am? I graduated from a big university and I'm a lawyer. I can turn you in to the law for cheating me."

"That so? I'm lawyer, too, and I know American law. You come in five o'clock this morning. You sleep all morning until afternoon. No law say I owe you money just because you don't sleep all day and night."

"Why, you stinking little rat! I'll bash your head in, you runty son of a . . . !"

Henry and I stood paralyzed, as the man picked up a chair and lifted it above his head to bring it crashing down over Father, just like in the movies.

"Wait!" Father held up his hand. "You want to fight? You know judo?"

"What? Nah, I don't know nothing about judo."

"Well, I do. But you don't know? I'm sorry, I can't fight you. Get out o' here . . . don't make any more trouble."

Father knew nothing about judo and he could have been twisted like a pretzel if the man had called his bluff. Instead the man dropped the chair and crashed heavily out of the office. On the stair landing, he turned around and discharged a last round of profanity.

Just then massive Montana appeared. Montana stared at the man quietly, from head to feet, from feet to head and waited patiently for the man to finish his speech. The man's voice died to a mere whisper and his eyes bulged at Montana's size. Montana asked him with deceptive courtesy, "Are you through talking to the Boss?"

The poor man let out a tiny squeak. Father said, "Montana! It's all right. Everything's all right."

Montana heard nothing. He simply gripped the man's coat collar, lifted him off the floor as if he were picking up a stray pup, and dropped him casually over the stairs. The man clattered and bounced down the long flight of stairs, heels over head, without uttering a sound. Montana watched as impassively as if he were looking at a sack of potatoes rolling down. The frightened man picked himself up and hurtled out into the street.

At first glance, Sam, Joe, Peter and Montana presented a rough and shabby front, but we were willing to swear by them against a stack of policemen. Like true natives of Skidrow, we instinctively disliked the beet-cheeked, paunchy policemen who patrolled our streets in twos. We were accustomed to the sight of policemen dragging a drink-befuddled man into the privacy of a store entrance. There, one would hold the sagging figure upright while the other shook him down, expertly frisking the drunkard's pockets. We would stop our games, walk up to them, curious to see how much they would find. The policemen, feeling boring, black eyes upon them, would shake their billys at us, "Get going, you kids! Watch out for the big stick."

With an impudent laugh, we would skip away, knowing that we could outrun them any time.

During those impressionable years, the police became our sworn enemies, especially after two of them shoved their way into our household one night and arrested Father as a bootlegger. It happened so suddenly and it was so unexpected that we magnified the incident as catastrophic and the most harrowing experience of our lives.

It was suppertime and the family was seated as usual around the kitchen table. Henry said grace for us in his high, piping voice. ". . . and we ask Thy blessing upon us as we partake of the food. Amen." A chorus of small voices rang out with a clear, "Amen!" Father and Mother responded fervently with a Japanese-accentuated, "Ahamen!"

Four round black heads bobbed up quickly. Henry played drums on his rice bowl with the wooden chopsticks and soon everyone was copying him, singing and shrieking.

"Where are your manners?" Father scolded gently.

We watched Mother fill six porcelain bowls with steaming,

fluffy rice. We screeched with delight when we saw her ladling our favorite homemade egg noodles cooked in hot pork broth into the red lacquer bowls — a perfect meal for a frosty fall evening. When I lifted my bowl of noodles up to my mouth I paused to feel the warm mist of the hot, clear brown soup rise to my cold face and to breathe in its rich fragrance.

Little Sumiko snatched Mother's long chopsticks in her chubby fists and wrestled violently with the slippery noodles which slithered away on the table like live eels. Unable to bring the noodles up to her drooling lips, she burst into frustrated screams. Just as Mother seated herself to feed Sumiko, someone rapped on the door, rattling the transom window overhead. Mother sighed, "Somebody wants to borrow money again." She reached around Father's shoulders and opened the door a crack.

A bass voice boomed through the opening, "Hello, Mama!"

A heavy-jowled, oyster-eyed head popped into the kitchen and then a huge policeman squeezed himself through, forcing Father to get up from his chair to make room. The officer glanced quickly around the tiny kitchen.

Father said impatiently, "Yes?"

The officer watched Father closely as he drew from his hip pocket a flask filled with a light yellow liquid. "You know what this is, Shorty? In case you don't remember, this happens to be yours."

Father's eyes flashed indignantly. "Mine? It's not. I don't drink. I see you new man here on block. You don't know me, but I'm not drinking man."

"Well, maybe you don't drink, but you sell 'em. I just picked up a fellow down the street who said he bought this bottle from you."

"I don't sell nobody no bottle. You make big mistake. I just starting dinner. I was here, not outside!" Just then a sharp clang of the office bell vibrated down the hall. "You wait. I go see who it is at the office."

Father hurried away, annoyed and worried. We smiled at the policeman. It was all very funny that he thought Father would do such a thing. Father would prove to him that he was not a bootlegger. The officer would realize his mistake, apologize to Father, and we would go back to our dinner.

To our dismay, the officer whipped the curtain on the pantry aside and started rummaging through the shelves, tossing bags and cans of food to the floor. Mother tapped him on the back and asked coldly, "What's matter? What you looking for?"

"All right, Mama, all right. Just don't get excited. I wanted to see if you have any more of this stuff that your husband makes. Ah! What's in this jug here . . . more sake, rice wine?" The policeman picked up a gallon jug and lifted it up against the light bulb.

Mother exploded, "What's matter you? That's *shoyu*, Japanese sauce. Taste it, taste it."

Mother wrested the jug away from the officer and angrily poured the soy sauce into a cup. She shoved it into his face. The officer sniffed at it cautiously, saying, "Now, don't get so excited, Mama. Everything's going to be all right. Don't worry. Yeah, I guess this stuff's bug juice."

Mother shook her finger at him. "See! We don't have sake. We don't make it. We don't drink it. You make mistake. Somebody else. Not Mr. Itoi."

"All right, all right. Just calm down now. Don't worry about a thing." He dropped his voice and whispered soothingly, "Just fifty dollars, Mama, just fifty dollars. No trouble then, see?"

Mother stood speechless for a second. Then she blurted out in Japanese, "Don't think we're such fools!" Mother laughed into the officer's face. Kenji and Sumiko giggled, hearing Mother laugh. Henry and I glared hotly at the policeman.

When Father reached the front office, he found that the customer at the window was another officer.

"Say, Charlie, I'd like to speak to you in private. Let me inside the office."

Father let him in. The policeman said to him in a confidential tone of voice, "Say we found a man who says he bought the whisky from you. You know what the charges are for peddling liquor like that. It's going to be hard on you . . . the law, you know."

Father felt as if he were talking to a stone wall. "But you have the wrong man. I never drink, never make it, never sell it. What you thinking about?"

"But we have proof, definite proof, man. You can't get away with anything like this."

"No, suh! I don't do nothing wrong."

"Oh, so you're going to be stubborn about it. Maybe you want to explain everything to the judge, Charlie. Come on, get your hat. We're going places." Father fumed as he flew down the hall to the kitchen, the policeman following close at his heels.

Mother clutched Father by the arm and spoke rapidly in Japanese. "It's awful! The policeman just asked me to give him fifty dollars to hush everything up for you!"

"*Nanda!* I'll never give an *ichi-mon* to these beggars. We'll see who's breaking the law!"

Father clapped his hat on and looked up defiantly at the officers. "*Sah,* let's go. I ready. I want to talk to the judge."

One of the officers suddenly laughed good-naturedly and patted Father's back. "Wait a minute, Shorty. Why don't you settle this thing like a smart guy? We want to give you another chance. Fifty dollars will make it even."

Father shouted in wrath. "But I tell you, I don't sell sake. I don't do it."

"Oh, what the hell! Let's quit stalling and take him in."

"*Iku tomo!* I certainly will go!"

Paralyzed with fright, we watched the men grab Father's arms roughly and whisk him out. Father trotted along, so impatient was he to get to court and clear the matter up.

Suddenly Kenji let out a shriek, "Mama! Don't let them take Papa away! Not Papa!"

Henry tried to calm him. "Don't worry, Ken-chan. Papa can take care of himself. He'll be back in no time, won't he, Mama?" His voice petered out toward the end.

"Yes, of course," Mother replied emphatically. Then without another word, Mother ran out into the hall to the telephone. With nervous fumbling fingers, she dialed a number and waited tensely for an answer.

"Halloh, Kato-san! Will you please come over quickly? My husband has just been taken to jail. They accuse him of selling sake."

Within ten minutes, Mr. Kato, who operated the hotel across our back alley, was bounding up the long flight of stairs. He was a prominent and respected figure in the community who always seemed to know what to do in a crisis. He pushed his way through a small group of men gathered around our tearful family scene. Many of the hotel clients had heard and seen the Boss being rushed out of the hotel, flanked by two red-faced policemen. Mother was walking up and down the hall with Sumiko in her arms. Kenji was sobbing into Henry's shirt.

Mother briefly described to Mr. Kato all that had happened. He listened intently, his head cocked to one side.

"It sounds odd to me. They didn't even have a warrant for search or arrest. Mr. Itoi didn't have to go at all under such circumstances. He was a bit rash. It may not be such a simple task to get him out right away, but I'll go up to the police station and see what can be done. Hmmmm, I have an idea!" His face lit up as he drew out a card from his vest pocket. "Maybe this will do it." He dashed out with Mother's cries of gratitude following him down the stairs.

In the meantime, Father told us later, the two policemen had pulled him along, handcuffed between them, through the dark, littered streets. They headed for the telephone box on a corner a few blocks away. Loitering men stared impassively. A few bold characters hooted, "What's up, copper? Did l'il Tokyo get into trouble?" "Keep your eyes open, Tokyo, don't let 'em put anything over on ya."

The officers pulled Father up to the blue iron box. "Well, Charlie, I'm calling the wagon . . . that is, unless you want to settle this thing the easy way."

Father dryly ordered him to telephone. The officer hesitated, then slowly unlocked the door, barked a curt order into the phone, and slammed the box shut.

The police station was only five blocks away, at the foot of Yesler Hill, and in a short while the Black Maria careened down Washington Street and screeched to a halt on the corner. The policemen lifted Father through the back door and slammed the door in the faces of the staring, open-mouthed men.

At the police station, Father was booked at the desk and told by the sergeant that unless he posted a $500 bail, he could not be released. Father refused to pay it, protesting his innocence, and without further ado, he was hustled into the bull pen. There he found two cellmates. One confided that he had been picked up on a vagrancy charge and the other lay prone on the floor, reeking with liquor. Father remained aloof. It seemed like hours later that the cell door clanged open. "Hey . . . you there! Come on, you're getting out."

Bewildered, Father hurried after the guard. In the hallway was Mr. Kato.

"Oh, Kato-kun! This is most embarrassing. You didn't pay that exorbitant bail fee, did you?"

Mr. Kato laughed, "No, it wasn't necessary. I showed them my name card which I had printed when I president of the Japanese Chamber of Commerce. They were willing to release you under my custody. But you'll have to go on trial later on."

"Yes, I know that. By the way, Kato-kun, you had that office last year. Yoshida-kun is president now."

"Of course, but the sergeant didn't ask me when I was president."

A week passed before Father received the summons to appear in court. He appeared there accompanied by Mr. Kato, Mr. Naka, a young Nisei lawyer, and Mr. Lubeck, the minister of our church. The trial was postponed because one of the officers was ill. The next week, the officers pleaded for another postponement because their star witness was ill.

Father became suspicious. "Those rascals are up to something. I think they're trying to escape from the trial."

But the day of the trial finally arrived. Mother went with Father, while we children remained at home, frightened to death. The policemen would lie and Father might be put in jail. Mother told us all about it later. One of the officers stated the charges against Father. Mr. Naka questioned the officer.

"On what day and time did you pick up the person who bought this bottle?"

"It was on the twenty-fourth of October, Tuesday evening, about 6:15 P.M."

"Where did this take place?"

"On Washington and Occidental Avenue."

"Please tell us what happened at the time."

"We found a man drunk, sitting on the curb. We questioned him and found out that he bought the liquor from a Japanese man who operated a hotel on Occidental."

Mr. Naka questioned the officer about his conversation with the defendant's wife.

The officer's eyes flickered. "All I asked was where she kept the other bottles of sake."

"Are you sure that that is all you asked?"

"Yes . . . yes, of course."

"Did you not ask the woman for fifty dollars to keep the matter quiet?"

"I did not." The officer looked straight into Mr. Naka's eyes.

Later on the prosecution's star witness was called. An officer led a decrepit, ragged old man to the chair. He sat down nervously, his gnarled hands fumbling at a crumpled, greasy old cap.

"From whom did you buy this flask?"

A pair of pale, watery blue eyes squinted up at Mr. Naka. "I . . . I bought it from a Jap fer two bits."

"Where did this take place?"

"Uh, in front of the hotel?"

"What's the name of the hotel?"

"Uh, Carl . . . Carlson Hotel."

"Where is it located?"

"It's, uh . . . down there . . . I don't exactly remember the name of the street, but I kin show you the place."

"Now, will you point out for the court the man from whom you bought the liquor?"

Mr. Naka assisted the witness down from the stand, led him to the bench where Father and Mr. Kato sat, side by side. The old man bent down and peered into their faces near-sightedly, then pointed a knobby, shaky finger at austere-looking Mr. Kato.

"That's him. That's the guy!"

A roar of laughter broke out in the court. Someone shouted, "Frame-up! Ahhhh, it's just a frame-up."

The judge pounded his gavel to restore order. The case was dismissed.

Exonerated and jubilant, Father and his friends stepped out of the courtroom. A handful of reporters who had heard the uproar in the court swept up to Father to find out what had happened. Just then the two officers who had arrested Father elbowed their way into the group. They whispered something to the reporters and led them away. Father became apoplectic. "Did you see that? They're trying to cover themselves up. I'm going to expose those rascals and see to it that they stop their little racket!"

Mr. Kato calmed him, "I know just how you feel, but try to forget the whole thing. The police have the upper hand. If you try to settle scores, there's no telling what other miseries they might think up for you."

Father sadly agreed. "Yes . . . I have a family to think of."

At least it had been a tie. The police had put him into trouble, but they had failed to extract money from him. Yet it was a long time before I outgrew my hostility toward policemen. Every time I saw an officer, my lips curled and I felt an undignified impulse to kick his shin bones and run for dear life.

An Unpredictable Japanese Lady

FATHER was a great admirer of Gandhi. Sometimes I thought he even looked like him, especially after a bath, when Father would sit tailor fashion on the davenport, warming himself in front of the small gas heater, clad only in his B.V.D.'s. As he peered through black-rimmed reading spectacles to manicure his toenails, he wore the same patient expression on his face that I had seen in newspaper pictures of the Indian leader.

Father talked a great deal about the merits of Gandhi's ideas on nonviolence and moral resistance. Father did not approve of violence, and would never fly into a wild rage like Dunks's father, Mr. Oshima. Mr. Oshima loved his rice wine so much that he often closed his barbershop when he felt the need to commune with his porcelain wine bottle. When Henry and I went to call on Dunks, we often saw him scrambling out the door, urged on by flying hair-tonic bottles and Mr. Oshima's roars, "You nuisance, get out of here!"

Yes, it was nice to have Father sober and self-controlled like Mr. Gandhi, but I thought it unfair when he practiced moral resistance on us. For his part, Father found it the only way to deal with a daughter who was growing to be alarmingly head-strong — like the time I decided to be a dancer.

One day I attended a children's talent show at the Pantages Theater. I was enchanted by the fairylike grace of the dancers in their cloud pink tutus and satin slippers. Right then and there I knew I had to be a ballet dancer or die.

I ran all the way home and pounced on Mother, "Mama, Mama . . . may I take ballet lessons? I want to be a dancer!"

Mother laughed as I babbled and whirled excitedly around the table in the parlor. She was relieved that I had given up being a detective. She confessed to me that she had been waiting nervously for the day when I would announce that I wanted to be an international spy.

That evening I asked Father about taking dancing lessons. He looked at me intently through his bifocals. He quietly said, "No."

I was baffled. It was such a wonderful idea. Mother had thought so too. "Why no?"

Father said he didn't wish to discuss the subject with me any more and he turned back to his newspaper. I wheedled, "But, Papa, why? Why?"

I rattled the newspaper, I tickled his foot. Father kept on reading stoically. I finally asked Mother to talk it over with Father alone and find out why he disapproved. I found out the next day.

By Father's standard, I had hit an all-time low. In Japan, dancing was associated with geisha girls and he would never consent to his daughter's entering *that* profession!

Besides, Father had never recovered from his first introduction to Western dancing. He had gone to a burlesque show at the Palace Theater on First Avenue soon after he had arrived from Japan, expecting to see an American version of the classic *kabuki* drama. Father's eyes spun in their sockets at the sight of half-naked girls who came prancing on to the stage like a frenzied team of horses. Not only had those girls flung themselves all over the place like crazy, but they had kicked their legs way up in the air in the most scandalous manner.

Father said to Mother in a quaking, outraged voice, "I'd die of disgrace if my daughter were to appear like that in public."

If Father had to make a choice between the two evils, Oriental or Western dancing, he would choose the former. At least the Japanese women were decently clothed. But that was why I would have nothing to do with Japanese classic dancing. I would have to be completely entombed like a cocoon, under layers of garments and miles of sash. True, the kimonos were exotically beautiful with long, flowing sleeves, and butterfly sashes, but that was all the good I could see in the Japanese dance.

"How can Papa call that dancing? Those Japanese girls don't even move a muscle in the *odori*."

My views about *odori* were as distorted as Father's opinion about the Western dance. The first time Father and Mother took me to Nippon Kan Hall to see a Japanese classic dance recital I was all eyes and breathless with anticipation. The curtain rose on the first performance. Someone behind the stage dramatically clapped wooden blocks, slowly and deliberately, increasing the tempo faster and faster. I saw a small girl standing as motionless as a statue in the center of the stage, her back turned to the audience. Her wide sash of glittering old brocade was tied into an elaborate butterfly bow. Suddenly a chorus of women's voices, which sounded as if it were being strained through a sieve, drifted out from offstage, accompanied by the plucking of samisens, banjolike instruments. The singing sounded alarmingly like growling, moans and strangulation. Then the girl turned slowly around.

Her face was masked in deathly white rice powder, with jet black eyes and eyebrows, and a tiny red dot of a mouth. On her head, she wore a huge, black pompadour wig, decorated with bright, glittering hair ornaments. Her rich purple kimono was patterned with gorgeous golden chrysanthemums. I waited for her to start dancing . . . that is, to leap and whirl and get going, but all I saw were undulating, butter-soft hands, a slight tremor of the head, and a delicate foot stamp which could hardly have hurt an ant. During the entire performance, the dancer did not cover more than a few square inches. And she never smiled.

Well, I should not have expected her to do more than that. I knew how it felt to be wound up inside a kimono. I had worn such a costume once for a festival at Bailey Gatzert School. A Japanese woman had come to school to dress us. First I wore a short, white silk kimono called *hada-jiban,* and on top of it a floor-length, brilliant orange kimono, *naga-jiban,* which shimmered like a saffron jewel. Then the woman adjusted the third kimono, a light apple-green, which looked pale and vapid compared to the second. After that she carefully unfolded a wide sash which she wrapped around my chest, wound and tightened, wound and tightened until I felt my ribs caving inward. I was sure that only decorum kept her from bracing both her feet against my back to bind me tighter. When she had finished with me, I was breathing just on the surface of life. I lumbered out to the main auditorium to help serve tea, reeling like a grounded butterfly. I could never have turned cartwheels or done the splits in the boa grip of a Japanese *obi.*

Again and again I attacked Father on the subject of ballet lessons. I explained to him that there was a great difference between burlesque and ballet dancing. Father passively resisted all my pleadings and arguments. He said politely, "No. Do you mind if I read the evening paper?"

"No, not at all . . . but . . ."

"Thank you." Father retired gratefully behind the paper and I lost contact with him for the evening. He was gentle. He did not go into a rage. He always remained courteous and polite. And he always said "No."

At length I capitulated to Father's resistance, but my passion for dancing suffered a hard death. At grammar school and high school, I always chose dance courses, any and all kinds . . . square dances, folk dances, tap dances, modern interpretation, acrobatics, instead of baseball and basketball. Whenever the school put on an entertainment program, I always volunteered to take part in the dancing. Once at Central Grammar School, I offered to create and perform a duet acrobatic dance for a gala Christmas program. I called it, "The Clown and the Lady." I headed off Father's objections by assuring him that I would be the clown and fully clothed. The lady was one of my classmates, Grace Doi. She would wear the pink sleeveless bodice, a limp cheesecloth version of a tutu skirt, and she was the one who was barelegged and barefooted. Gracie begged me not to talk about it in front of her parents since they were even more strict than mine.

The day of the Christmas program arrived and Gracie and I made our debut. When we were on stage, performing with gusto, landing on our feet so that we rattled the windows and shook the curtains, it suddenly occurred to me that we sounded like two rollicking baby elephants. We perspired and panted audibly as we tried to keep up with a nervous pianist's runaway accompaniment. The faster we twisted and rolled to catch up with the music, the faster the girl played. She finished first and left us in a horrible silent vacuum which we filled with a crashing cartwheel exit, but the school audience was gratifyingly appreciative. For many days I recalled its wild applause, but always with a writhing in my breast. I could never admit it to Father, but I decided that he had been right as usual.

Mother was different from Father in that she was not always right, but she was a lot of fun. Unlike Father, who took life with the unwavering calm of a philosopher, Mother vibrated on a higher frequency. In fact, she rattled the sensibilities of some of the more correct women in the neighborhood. It was because Mother had come to America at the wrong age, when she was an energetic and curious seventeen-year-old on whom the cement of Japanese culture had not yet been set. Mother tried hard. She cultivated a gentle and soft-spoken manner and even managed a poker face when the occasion demanded, but underneath, Mother was a quivering mass of emotions.

We were satisfied with her just as she was. I was glad that she wasn't like slow-as-molasses Mrs. Kato, chubby Jiro's mother. Once Mother and I went downtown with Mrs. Kato. Just as we were about to board the Second Avenue streetcar, the three of us became separated in the swarming crowd. The car door opened and people surged inside, but all of a sudden the movement stopped. The bottleneck was slow-motion Mrs. Kato smiling and bowing graciously to Mother who was submerged in the crowd.

"*Sah*, Itoi-sama, *dozo osaki ni*. Please, after you."

I screamed at Mother to tell Mrs. Kato to please get in and dispense with the ceremony. Mrs. Kato was standing hesitantly, waiting for Mother to emerge from the tight crowd. Mother's voice floated out to her in Japanese. "Please go ahead, we're right behind you."

Reluctantly, Mrs. Kato climbed up into the car and bowed to the conductor as she dropped a token into the box. All this time people were turning around and staring at us, attracted to the Japanese dialogue.

When we neared our destination and should have been moving toward the rear door, Mrs. Kato again started bowing and urging

Mother to go ahead. Mother, firmly wedged between a mountain of a woman clutching two shopping bags of groceries, and a crotchety old man, declined the invitation. "*Iiye . . . dozo*, after you."

I suppressed a scream, fought my way through the packed bodies and leaped off the streetcar first, not caring whether Mrs. Kato made it or not. Mother emerged successfully, but we lost Mrs. Kato then and there.

One of Mother's many consuming desires was to learn to speak the English language. Mother's younger sister, Kikue, had the opportunity to attend high school and in a short time, Kikue was able to speak fluently. Mother had been married too soon and missed out on this chance, but she was determined to master the language with whatever facilities she had. If her four children could learn to speak it, there was no reason why she couldn't. Still, we felt something was amiss whenever we were welcomed home by Mother with a beaming smile, "Well, did you guys have a good time?"

Mother was really too busy and we were too impatient to sit down and teach her in a systematic way. It was mostly a trial and error method . . . a great trial to us while she made the errors. She drove us frantic by asking us the meaning of odd phrases to which she was invariably attracted. She liked the lilt of a phrase in a song which she had heard over the radio, "nothing but a nothing." She repeated it over and over to master the difficult "th" sound. We told her it meant nothing at all and that no one ever talked that way, really, so there was no sense in memorizing it.

Father had no practical need to learn a polite version of the English language because his contacts were with Skidrow men and it was better for him to speak to his rambunctious guests on equal earthy terms. But Mother simply could not get away with a similar dialect. She had to attend teas, P.T.A. meetings, and festivals at school and carry on conversation with our teachers. Many Japanese mothers never appeared at these functions because it was such an excruciating experience. Some who did attend stayed close to their children, smiled tirelessly, and said, "yes," "no," "thank you," and laughed at the wrong time. But Mother was not satisfied with just a spiritual evening of good will. Although I was secretly proud that Mother showed spunk in wading into a full-sized conversation, I often wished that she was not quite so spirited with her words. As she chatted with my teacher, I listened in agony, for it was always a mangled dialogue in which the two parties never seemed to be talking about the same thing at the same time. Miss Powers would smile at Mother, "So you are KaZOOko's mother." Miss Powers could never remember that there is no accent on any syllable in pronouncing my Japanese name. "You seem so young, Mrs. Itoi, you look more like her big sister."

"Yes, I am, thank you." Mother smiled back, more intent on being gracious at the moment than on the subject matter. Miss Powers remained unruffled.

"Did KaZOOko tell you we're having a special program for the May Festival soon?"

"Oh yes, it was very nice. I enjoyed program so much." Mother nodded her head enthusiastically. I curled inside. I had not yet told Mother about May Festival and I knew she had become lost after the words, "special program." Mother was speaking about the Christmas program. Miss Powers's blue eyes fluttered, but she quickly figured that Mother was thinking about last year's May Festival.

"Oh yes, we had a nice time all right, but KaZOOko wasn't in my class then. This year she's going to be one of the crocuses and we want her to dress in a real pretty costume . . . a lavender skirt and purple petal hat made from crepe paper. Do you think you could help us make the dress if I sent the instructions home with KaZOOko?"

"Oh yes, I make them all the time," Mother smiled with great assurance. It was a bare-faced lie. Mother had never made a single crocus costume for me nor had she ever seen one; but Mother did make lots of pretty dresses for me for which she thought Miss Powers was complimenting her. I had to bolster this crippled dialogue.

"Mother can help with the costume, Miss Powers. She made this for me," I said, holding out the skirt of my new dress. It was a flaming, candy-red taffeta dress, crawling with dainty ruffles, according to my tyrannical specifications. Miss Powers was back on the track and she gushed politely, "Did she really? My what a wonderful seamstress you are, Mrs. Itoi. And I love that color! It's as lovely as can be."

"Oh, no, it's not so good," Mother said modestly. She could have said "thank you" at this moment, but I was content that Mother was talking about the same thing as Miss Powers. All of a sudden Mother burst out, "It's too red, but my daughter, she likes red. I think it's *lousy!*"

A tense silence followed. Miss Powers was struggling to keep a straight face. I felt as if I were standing inside a furnace. I managed to tug at Mother's elbow and whisper, "*Kairo*, Mama, let's go home."

I thought, miserably, as I walked home with Mother, how much the other teachers would laugh when Miss Powers told them about Mother's *faux pas*. I pointed out to Mother in a tearful, disgraced-for-life voice that she had made a terrible mistake.

"Mama, you should have said, loud, loud! not lousy! Lousy is a vulgar word, a bad word like goddamn and hell."

"Soh? I didn't know. I heard you children using it all the time so I thought it was perfectly all right." Mother didn't sound at all sorry. I fell into a morose silence the rest of the way home, wondering how I was ever going back to school and face my teacher. But when I saw her next she seemed to have forgotten all about the episode.

Mother's haphazard way with the language did not always work against her. I remember once she became involved in a switch of identity and lived for a day like royalty, suddenly swept into high society. It happened when Sumiko and I were rabid fans of Mickey Mouse and members of the Mickey Mouse Club at the Coliseum Theater which met every Saturday morning. We sang Mickey Mouse songs, we saw Mickey Mouse pictures, we wore Mickey Mouse sweaters, we owned Mickey Mouse wrist watches. Because the club had the endorsement of the Parent-Teacher Association, Father and Mother raised no objections to our latest craze.

One Saturday there was to be a very special party to which we could invite our mothers. There would be a Mickey Mouse drawing contest for the members and refreshments for everyone. Mother said although she would like to be there, she was too busy Saturday morning. Sumiko and I wept.

"But, Mama, everybody else's mother will be there. We'll be the *only* ones without a mother. People will think we're orphans."

Fortunately, a few days before the event, Mother went to a P.T.A. meeting at Bailey Gatzert School at which time Miss Mahon, our school principal, pleaded with the Japanese mothers to go to this particular party with their children. Women of different nationalities would be there and Miss Mahon wanted to see the Japanese represented. Miss Mahon stirred Mother's conscience. Mother decided to go. Sumiko and I knew it was going to be one of the biggest, happiest parties we would ever attend.

That bright Saturday morning Sumiko and I put on our best red coats and matching red berets. We bounded down the long flight of stairs, clutching our Mickey Mouse sketches and ran all the way downtown. Mother had promised that she would follow later, as soon as she had finished the hotel chores. We had drilled Mother on the location of the theater building. With a thick red crayon, we printed the name of the theater, its address and the name "Pike Street," the block where she was supposed to get off the streetcar, on a big sheet of paper so Mother could not lose it or herself.

Having taken these precautions, Sumiko and I relaxed. At the Coliseum Theater, we pushed our dimes through the box-office window, deposited our drawings in a large chest in the foyer and slid into our seats, breathless with hope that one of us would win a prize. The meeting started off as usual. The same, double-chinned master of ceremonies greeted us, shook with laughter at his jokes and raved a great deal about what a wonderful time we were going to have. He introduced a bouncy, Dutch-bobbed five-year-old girl named Patsy who tap danced and sang for us. Later the lights were dimmed, the words of songs were flashed on the screen and Patsy led us in singing our Mickey Mouse songs. Soon it was time for the judging of the picture contest. Sumiko and I also thought it was time for Mother's appearance. We went to the lounge where we had agreed to meet her. No one was there. Little Sumiko's lips started to tremble. I said, hastily, "She'll be here soon. Let's wait."

We sank deep into the luxurious low sofa and waited silently.

Hours seemed to pass and still there was no Mother. We hurried back to our seats to see what was going on, but it was hard to keep our attention focused on the stage. We learned that the pictures were still being judged upstairs. Everyone was getting restless, and two boys started wrestling in the aisle. Soon a team of usherettes swooped down the aisles, distributing ice cream in Dixie cups, and cookies. While we thoughtfully ate our refreshment, the master of ceremonies suddenly appeared and announced the names of three contest winners. Our spirits sagged when neither of our names was mentioned; and worse than that Mother was lost.

The party over, the auditorium, hallway, and lounge soon filled with chattering boys and girls and their smiling, bright-eyed mothers. We made one last inspection of the theater without success. Maybe Mother was wandering downtown, lost and bewildered. Or maybe she had just decided not to attend.

We headed back home with an ache lodged deep in our throats. How could Mother have failed us, after she had promised us a dozen times. We climbed heavily up the hotel stairs, made our way to our living quarters with a solemn expression on our faces, all set to reprove Mother. The rooms were empty. We scurried through the dim labyrinth of halls until we found Father in the last room at the other end of the hotel. He was busily making the bed. Indignantly I asked, "Papa, where is Mama? Why didn't she come to the party?"

"*Nani?* Why, Mama left about half an hour after you both had gone. I was afraid she would be late so I told her to take a taxi. Where could she have gone?"

We were thoroughly alarmed. Sumiko burst out crying. Father, looking harried, put the finishing touches on the bed, picked Sumiko up and led me out of the room.

"Now, now, don't start that. Mama's all right, wherever she is. She's been downtown before by herself. Maybe she just walked into the wrong place. If Mama isn't home in an hour, I'll call the police."

At the word "police," I started to cry, too. Father sighed and took us into the kitchen where he tried to stifle our sobs with cookies. "Now, why don't you two go back to the parlor and play a while. I have a little more work to do."

No, we didn't feel like it. We wanted to be with him. We trailed after him with wet faces and damp cookies, really feeling like orphans now. As Father pushed the carpet sweeper carefully over the frayed edges of the rug, he asked questions about the party. Between sniffles and bites, we managed to give Father all the boring details. Then all of a sudden behind us, we heard the sweetest voice in the world. It was Mother.

"Ka-chan, Sumi-chan," she said happily, "wasn't that a lovely party?"

Father stopped sweeping. Sumiko and I stared at her, wondering what party she had attended. Mother was still glowing with excitement. She looked exquisite and beautiful, in her best gown of pale lavender silk velvet. Delicate floral patterns were traced in velvet, woven over a background of sheer voile. A huge butterfly rhinestone pin held the drape on the side of the skirt. Mother also wore a close-fitting, beige helmet over her freshly marcelled black hair. The long length of hair was coiled into a low, thick bun at the nape of her neck. She looked pretty and out of place, standing in the doorway near the mop and the laundry pile. She turned brightly to Father, "By the way, what does 'consul's wife' mean?"

"Consul's wife? What in the world . . . why, that's the wife of a *ryoji*. Why do you ask?"

"Arrra!" Mother shrieked in horror. "A *ryoji's* wife! *Doshima sho!*"

Mother clapped her hand to her mouth, then to her head as if she didn't know what to do next. Sumiko and I jumped all over her, trying to get her attention.

"Mama, Mama, what happened? Where were you anyway? We waited for you all morning."

Mother then burst into hysterical laughter and the only words we could get out of her were, "*Mah, iyayo!* What shall I do? *Tondemo nai kotoyo.*"

We went back to the parlor and waited impatiently for Mother to subside. Father scolded her, "Where were you all this time? The children have been crying all morning."

With tears of laughter in her eyes, Mother told us the whole story. She had gone to our Mickey Mouse party. The taxi driver had delivered her to the front of the Coliseum Theater. Just as soon as she had stepped out of the cab, a suave, beautifully groomed woman pounced on Mother and escorted her into the theater. "We're so glad you could come, Mrs. Saito. We're having quite a party this morning."

Mother felt slightly overpowered with this warm reception, but she smiled politely back at the nice lady as if she were quite used to such cordiality.

"Thank you. I'm late little bit. I'm so sorry."

"It doesn't matter in the least, Mrs. Saito. You're in time for the important part of the program."

Mother didn't completely understand what the woman was saying, but she realized she was being addressed as Mrs. Saito. She corrected her new friend, "I'm Mrs. Itoi."

"Oh? Er . . . you're the Japanese consul's wife, aren't you?"

Mother didn't know what she meant, but she knew very well

she should be agreeable at all times. She said, "Yes, thank you."

Obviously, the hostess had been assigned the special task of taking charge of the Japanese consul's wife, Mrs. Saito. The eager hostess had stepped out of the theater door several times and when at last a beautifully gowned Oriental woman had stepped out of a cab she thought the quarry was safe in her hands. The woman trilled to Mother, "Oh, Mrs. Saito, I wonder if you would do us the honor of acting as one of the judges for our Mickey Mouse drawing contest?"

"Yes, yes," Mother answered absent-mindedly, wondering why the woman kept calling her Mrs. Saito. "I'm Mrs. Itoi."

"I beg your pardon, Mrs. Itoi." The hostess paused for a moment and then began again, "You *are* the consul's wife?" This time she asked the question slowly and loudly. "Yes!" Mother replied, almost snapping. The woman was certainly asking a lot of questions. The hostess finally seemed satisfied with Mother's positive reply.

Just then, a woman walking in front of her stumbled. Her high heel had caught the edge of the carpet and both heel and shoe came off. Mother dove for the torn heel and shoe. She had fixed many a broken heel. The woman with the broken heel said, "Dear me, it would happen now."

"I fix for you," Mother assured her.

The hostess's eyes widened, "Please, Mrs. Saito, er, Mrs. Itoi, the maid will do that." She turned in desperation to the woman, "I'd like you to meet Mrs. Saito, the Japanese consul's wife."

The introductions were made, but Mother ignored them both, adjusted the heel into the nail holes, kneeled down and pounded it back into place on the marble floor.

"Fixed now, I think." Mother returned the shoe to the pink-faced woman while the hostess made high-pitched sounds.

Mother was led upstairs to a luxuriously furnished room which glittered with mirrors and elegant crystal chandeliers, the like of which Mother had never seen. The room was filled with the subdued murmurs of distinguished-looking guests. The hostess introduced Mother to many gay, enchanting people. Mother caught words like "Swedish . . . English . . . German . . ." and heard the same mysterious expression, "consul's wife" over and over again. Soon everyone was addressing Mother as Mrs. Saito and Mother let it pass good-naturedly. Far be it from her to keep correcting these lovely people. Nobody seemed to mind that Mother hardly said anything except, "I'm glad to meet you," and "Yes, thank you" whenever refreshments were offered to her, and "I think so" when she couldn't understand the topic of conversation.

Mother sipped delicious coffee from a tiny, doll-sized cup and nibbled at dainty sandwiches of all shapes and colors. On the tables were gleaming silver platters of bonbons, cookies and assorted nuts. Mother felt as if she were part of a movie set.

Soon the hostess came up to Mother again and closeted her in a small, adjoining room with three other smartly dressed women who spoke English with heavy foreign accents. No one understood what the other was saying, but somehow they picked the prize pictures of Mickey Mouse. They went back to the reception room again for some more polite chatter and laughter. Half an hour later the party drew to a close. Mother bade farewell to her new acquaintances, the French consul's wife, the English consul's wife, the German consul's wife and a few more. They all shook her hand cordially, "Goot-by, Mrs. Saito. It was just loavely meeting you. . . ."

What charming manners! What delightful ladies! The same attentive hostess escorted Mother out of the theater, hailed a taxi for her and waved farewell. Mother sank back in the rear seat, feeling positively giddy with the personal attention and hospitality that had surrounded her from the beginning to the end. The cab driver had to ask her, "Where to lady?"

"Yes, please. Oh! . . . 217 Occidental Avenue."

The driver glanced back at her twice. Mother, looking like an Oriental princess of the court, sat fanning herself with her perfumed silk handkerchief and sighing . . . my, my what a grand party it had been and such cultured, gentle people. Miss Mahon will be certainly glad to know I took part and helped with the picture contest. The taxicab sped through the downtown shopping district and plunged into the fish and barnacle atmosphere of the waterfront where our hotel was located.

We have often wondered if the reception committee of the gala Mickey Mouse Club party ever discovered this error. We thanked God that Mrs. Saito, the Japanese consul's wife, had not appeared. Mother might have been hustled out of the theater as an impostor and criminal. Then we thought of something worse . . . maybe Mrs. Saito did attend, but nobody had met her at the door. She would have had to pay an admission fee at the box office to get in and been forced to find a seat for herself in the audience of screaming, squirming youngsters. I wondered if an usherette had handed her a Dixie cup of ice cream and a cookie, too. She probably would have resented such shabby treatment and reported it to her husband, the Japanese consul. We saw international complications arise and diplomatic relationships slip a notch between America and Japan. For days after, Mother was not quite herself as she wavered between sudden bursts of laughter and mortified mutterings.

*　　*　　*

Every now and then, ships from Japan steamed into Seattle
and dropped anchor in Puget Sound harbor. Sometimes it was a
battered freighter and sometimes an old warship, painted slick
and gray — a training ship for the young men of the Imperial
Navy. When a training ship arrived, the whole Japanese community burst into sudden activity, tidying up store fronts, hanging out colorful welcome banners and polishing the family cars.
It was a gay time. The Japanese consul and officers of the Seattle
Japanese Chamber of Commerce whisked away the captain and
officers of the ship and entertained them. The crew members
were dined and wined in private homes by folks of the same
"ken" or prefecture in Japan.

These visitors from Japan were all proudly driven up and down
the steep hills of Seattle in sleek, powerful, purring Cadillacs or
joint-tearing Model T Fords. The slow long drive along lovely
Lake Washington boulevard was one of the high spots for the
guests. At least that was the unshakable belief of the local Japanese. Always the sight-seeing party was escorted to Seward Park
on the southern point of the lake. Here was a bit of Oriental
heaven which the Seattle Japanese had helped to create. A magnificent vermilion torii, a replica of the famous torii at Miya-jima
in Japan, loomed gracefully on the lakeside. There was a formal
Japanese garden with pine trees, a tiny bridge, and a replica of an
ancient granite stone lantern which had been presented to the
city by the people of Yokohama in gratitude for the aid given
them during the disastrous earthquake and fire of 1923. On these
tours the local Japanese waved their arms about with the grand
air of real estate barons as if they were saying, "We, too, have a
beautiful Oriental garden, complete with torii," while the courteous Japanese guests permitted themselves to be fascinated. Although they had seen acres of lovelier landscaping in Japan the

sailors gazed and opened their mouths in astonishment. They said Seward Park was, indeed, one of the most gorgeous they had ever seen. "How charming, how picturesque!" The hosts felt prouder by the minute.

After the sailors had enjoyed the rounds of dinners, picnics, movies and the zoo at Woodland Park, they reciprocated with an "at home" tea on board ship. To entertain the entire Seattle Japanese population in a single afternoon was no small feat. Sometimes it required two days to accommodate the pressing crowd.

Of the many pleasant "at homes" I enjoyed, one of them stood out like a beacon. That particular summer afternoon at two o'clock sharp, we arrived at Smith Cove and stood in a long queue of patient, perspiring Japanese, waiting to go aboard the ship. Father suffered silently in his best black serge suit, high stiff celluloid collar, and tight-fitting straw hat. Mother looked fragile and lovely in a sheer black and white print voile dress which fluttered like butterfly wings in the sea breeze. She wore a wide-brimmed white picture hat of straw so fine and thin, I could see the blue sky and wispy clouds through the brim. In honor of the occasion, Sumiko and I proudly donned our noisy purple-flowered "happi-coats," a Western version of the coolie coat. Henry had watered and plastered down his short wiry hair, but the cowlicks sprang up defiantly like black thorns. In short-sleeved white shirt and Sunday black corduroys, he darted in and out of the line like a restless spaniel. Chubby Kenji dressed in a white sailor suit and a white gob hat, trailed after his big brother, panting and giggling.

To walk up the plank to a boat which had just come from Japan was exciting — like a state fair, an educational tour and a trip to a foreign land all rolled into one. From stem to stern, the boat had been scrubbed and polished. Brass and steel gleamed like burnished satin. Hundreds of bright flags of all nations fluttered overhead.

As usual, Father asked to meet sailors from his hometown Tochigi-ken or from neighboring Ibaragi. While the sailors were paged, we stood waiting. Everywhere the city folks and the sailors clustered in groups, bowing and chattering. Mother and Father made a game of guessing from which town the young sailors came. We walked by a knot of people whose speech sounded languid and relaxed. Father muttered, "Of course, they're from Osaka."

Mother noticed a young sailor who was conversing animatedly with his friends and she immediately labeled him as Tokyo-born. I asked Mother what a person from Ibaragi or Tochigi-ken was supposed to be like. She said, "He'll probably have a booming voice you can hear through a storm. People from that area also have a reputation for being quick tempered, frank and honest."

Just then a wiry young man with a crew-cut appeared in front of us, bowed stiffly and identified himself in a thundering voice: "I am Yamashita, from Ibaragi!"

Father and Mother returned the bow and almost whispered their acknowledgments. Yamashita-san proved to be an amiable fellow. He offered to show us around the ship, and we trotted up and down the stairs after him, inspecting the engine room, the sailors' living quarters, the steaming, humid kitchen, and the plain, bare dining room. At the canteen, he presented us with varicolored paper balls which we inflated by blowing air through a small hole. The tiny silver bells inside tinkled delicately when we tossed the balls into the air.

On one of the decks, we watched an exhibition of *sumo*, or Japanese wrestling, on an improvised stage, festooned with col-ored crepe streamers and bright red curtains. On another deck, a classic play was being put on, complete with elaborate period costumes. The dialogue in the ancient language of the samurai days sounded strange to us but Mother and Father loved it. They would have stood there all day watching if we hadn't prodded them out of the room. Just as we were about to climb a narrow stairway to the top deck, someone came tumbling and sliding down. At the bottom the man gathered himself together with great dignity. It was Mr. Sakaguchi, the old politician, his complexion as florid as the rising sun. Obviously he had been lolling among bottles of sake.

"Excuse me, please," he muttered, and hurried down the narrow hall, crashing from wall to wall. Father chuckled, but Mother sniffed indignantly at the retreating figure.

We stopped at a long table covered with white linen, laden with Japanese cookies, bean cakes and bottles of *ramunedo,* a Japanese soft drink which tasted like a supercarbonated combination of lime and lemon juice. Everytime I took a cautious sip, bubbles charged up my nose like tiny demons with needles. It tasted good.

Father and Henry and Kenji were interested in the inner workings of the ship and they disappeared with Yamashita-san. Mother, Sumiko and I roamed about aimlessly in the milling, crushing crowd. Then trouble started. A pink-faced sailor stopped Mother, looking at us bright-eyed and curious.

"*Chotto, oku-san,* just a moment. Are those your children?"

He pointed at us as if we were something Mother had dredged out of the sea. Sake had washed away his Japanese courtesy.

"Yes, they're mine. Why?" Mother snatched at our hands.

"Well, she may be your daughter," he said, rapping my head as if it were a coconut, "but this little one doesn't look like yours." He peered into Sumiko's startled face. Sumiko had an olive complexion and was deeply tanned by her daily outings to the beach. Instead of almond-shaped Oriental eyes, Sumiko had huge, flashing Latin ones. The sailor shook his head incredulously, "*Iya,* she must be a foreign child."

Mother said coldly, "She is my child." She pulled us away from him, and in our hurry to put distance between us, we ran smack into a big uniformed man. Mother apologized profusely, but the man gallantly waved it aside. His coat was decorated with fancy stripes and insignia. He straightened up, clicked his heels together and gave a slight bow as he informed Mother that he was Yoshitake and followed it with a long official title. Mother became even more apologetic. When the officer swayed slightly, the fumes of sake rolled around us like fog. He took one long, red-eyed look at Mother and then glanced at us. Mother snatched our hands again and said, "They're mine, both of them."

"So *desuka?* They're nice, very very nice like their *okah-san,*" the officer said with a loose smile, his eyes swallowing Mother in great big gulps. Mother retreated. "Oh, don't run away, young matron. I would like to invite you to my private quarters where it isn't so noisy with the crowd."

Mother mumbled her thanks and said something about finding her husband and sons. "Come, come," she scolded us, "don't dawdle." She dragged us away urgently.

The officer stumbled after us, waving his hands and commanding us to stop. We skittered around a corner, ducked through a door and ran down steep stairs, hoping to shake him. The man was determined. He kept us in sight. I found myself bounding yards ahead of Mother who was half-carrying, half-dragging Sumiko, like a sack of rice. This was more exciting than any cops and robbers game. I shrieked with frightened delight, "Here he comes, Mama."

"*Oku-sama, wakai oku-sama* . . ." the officer called plaintively.

We rushed for the stairs and scrambled up on the deck again. Just as we flitted nervously by a food booth, Father, Henry and Kenji popped out from behind the silken curtain, each holding a skewer of sweet potatoes and soybean cake squares. Henry waved his stick in my face. "Look what I have!"

Mother collapsed against Father. "*Mah*, Papa, where have you been! Please talk to that officer who is just coming up."

"What in the world are you so excited about?" Father asked, popping a sweet potato into his mouth.

Just then the officer, breathless and red-faced, rushed up to Mother who slipped quickly behind Father and pushed him forward. The two men looked at each other uncomfortably.

"Ah, pardon me. I am Yoshitake."

Father winced when the officer swayed and brought his face close. Father seemed reluctant to admit, "*Itoi toh mashi masu.*"

The officer tried to beam enthusiastically at the big happy family, "Well, well, are you enjoying yourselves here, all of you?"

"Immensely," Father said, carefully finishing the skewer. That task completed, he devoted his energy to staring fixedly at Yoshitake. The officer scuttled off, and mother was saved.

CHAPTER IV

The Japanese Touch

MOST of the time my life rolled by in pretty much the same fashion as it did for my yellow-haired, red-haired and brown-haired friends at grammar school. With them I enjoyed the national holidays — Lincoln's Birthday, Washington's Birthday, Memorial Day, the Fourth of July, Labor Day, Thanksgiving, Christmas and New Year's. But there were other times when things happened which could happen only to a Japanese.

"Tenchosetsu" was the celebration of the reigning Emperor's birthday, and the community elders surrounded the occasion with a great deal of pomp. Once a year when spring rolled around, sensei made the announcement: "Tomorrow there'll be no school because it's Tenchosetsu. We'll meet at Nippon Kan Hall at 2 P.M. I'll be taking roll call there."

I groaned. I thought it wasteful to spend a beautiful spring afternoon crowded into a dingy, crumbling hall and sit numbly through a ritual which never varied one word or gesture from year to year. But I knew there was no escape.

The next day, promptly at 2 P.M., we appeared at Nippon Kan Hall with scrubbed faces and carefully watered-down hair. The boys shuffled around self-consciously in their best suits and shoes. The girls wore fresh white middy blouses and dark skirts. We quietly took our seats with long, solemn faces as if we had come to a wake.

Up on the platform, exactly in the center, stood a square cabinet with purple velvet drapes framed around it. The drapes were held back by large, golden, sixteen-petaled chrysanthemum ornaments, the crest of the Imperial House. Four men sat stiffly at attention on the stage, two on each side of the cabinet. The men on the left side wore white gloves.

When the echo of the last cough had faded and the hall was as silent as a tomb, one white-gloved man walked gravely to the stage center in measured strides. He made a stiff quarter turn toward the cabinet, his back to the audience, and took three steps forward. Then he bent forward, sliding his hands slowly down his legs, in a deep, formal bow called the *sai-kei-rei*. He remained thus for a sacred half minute, then straightened up slowly, sliding his hands up his legs. He stepped forward again, and reverently opened the cabinet doors. There, to our humble eyes, the photograph of Emperor Hirohito himself was revealed. Only once a year was the Emperor's likeness unveiled to the public. It was a sacred moment.

The official picture-opener, not missing a cue, stepped back smoothly three paces, performed the grandiloquent *sai-kei-rei* for another half minute. Then with monumental dignity, he walked backward to his chair while the audience watched nervously. When his heels suddenly struck the chair, he froze, then sat down slowly and gravely. The audience relaxed.

The second man, who had the solemn duty of reading the scroll of "*Kyoiku Chyokugo*," the Imperial instructions to the Japanese subjects, was usually the president of the Seattle-Japanese Chamber of Commerce. I remember watching Mr. Wakamatsu perform this duty many times with grace and restraint. He was that tall, dignified man who owned the combustible café below our hotel. Although we did not understand a single word of

Nisei Daughter

the Imperial message, since it was written in a style of speech used exclusively by the Emperor, we listened with rapt attention to Mr. Wakamatsu's beautiful, clear enunciation.

But the year Mr. Sakaguchi was president of the local Chamber of Commerce, we thought the occasion lost some of its solemnity and dignity.

Mr. Sakaguchi was a hotel proprietor like Father. Short and globular with a gray-fringed, balding head, he trotted around the neighborhood distributing his charm and fat Havana cigars. Father and his friends felt a little embarrassment whenever Mr. Sakaguchi came around. It was well known that Mr. Sakuguchi's one great desire in life was to be elected president of the Japanese Chamber of Commerce. Mr. Sakaguchi poured every ounce of his oily personality into the gears and wheels of the nominating mechanism so that he might one day roll into office with ball-bearing ease. Finally his patience and diligence were rewarded. He became the president. That year he found himself on the platform at Nippon Kan Hall on Tenchosetsu, ill at ease in formal clothes. He looked as if he had encountered a morning frock for the first time in his life and he had come out second best. The coat sleeves plunged down to his knuckles. The narrow shoulders pulled his bulging, fat arms back and the split coattail dangled behind him.

When it was time for Mr. Sakaguchi to read the scroll, he stood up as if in a daze. His usual florid complexion was a waxy hue as he pattered out to the stage center. He made the quarter turn toward the picture with thoughtful precision. He took the traditional three steps forward and bent over in the elaborate *sai-kei-rei*. Then lifting the sacred scroll up high to the level of his eyes, Mr. Sakaguchi slowly unrolled it with his left gloved hand. As he began to read, he stuttered badly. He had not practiced enough. Mr. Sakaguchi stammered, he paused, he repeated himself. He raised his voice, higher and higher, to lend sincerity, at least, to this reading, but it only sounded as if he were berating us. The scroll trembled like a leaf in a storm. When it was over he performed the last *sai-kei-rei* and managed to find his seat walking backward; he sat down with his eyes closed, thoroughly shaken by this wretched travesty upon the sacred words. We had heard that in Japan, men who had committed lesser offenses than this had felt compelled to commit suicide to atone for the disgrace.

A third man then arose to speak a few thousand joyous words on this most joyous occasion, looking square and solemn. Standing erect at an angle so that his back was neither to the photograph nor to the audience, his arms clamped to his sides, he never moved a muscle. I began to feel drowsy from the closeness of the hall. The speaker's droning voice blended with the buzzing of the bluebottle flies bumping lazily against the warm windowpanes. Then a fourth man loomed up. It was Mr. Ohashi, the school principal, standing stiffly at attention. I knew that it was time to say our "banzais," for every year he led us in shouting "Banzai!" three times after him. Now he stood staring out into the audience, and, as if he had suddenly seen a terrible specter, he thrust a finger into our midst. We were shocked. It was very much out of order. Then, splitting the air with his tongue, he thundered out, "You, down there, the girls, I mean . . . take off your hats this instant. It is an insult to the Emperor that you should keep your hats on."

We rocked back in our chairs. No one said a word, but we looked around to see who was being chastised. In the rear of the room sat a group of high-school girls. As young women of impeccable taste in Western style, they had worn their best hats to an important afternoon affair. They stared defiantly back at Mr. Ohashi, but he roared at them again. "Take them off!"

Mr. Ohashi was in the finest fit of purple pique. He kept his accusing finger leveled at them and they wilted, one by one. Flushed and embarrassed, they unpinned their veils and untied their bows with trembling fingers and removed their pretty spring bonnets.

Satisfied, but still looking highly offended, Mr. Ohashi harshly commanded us to stand up. As one, we leaped to our feet. Then suddenly raising both his arms stiffly up overhead, he shouted, "*Banzai!*"

We let out a self-conscious, "Banzai!"

Mr. Ohashi lifted his arms up more violently, roaring, "BAN–ZAI!"

We shouted, "BANZAI!"

Once more it was repeated. "BANZAI!" . . . "BANZAI!"

Then a piano sounded offstage, striking the opening minor chords of "Kimi gayo," the Japanese national anthem. We sang it slowly and low as if we were reluctant to part with each note. I felt heavy-eyed and weary.

We filed out of the hall in a quiet, orderly fashion, still under Mr. Ohashi's formidable spell. Everyone milled about, excitedly talking about the girls who had been disciplined. The girls themselves stood off to one side. They sounded like an angry nest of hornets.

Then a little boy shattered the tension in the air when he shouted to his friend, "Thank God, that's over! Come on, Bozo, let's get going."

The serious pasty faces of boys and girls sprang to life again with this reminder. We scattered in all directions, as we raced home to recapture our holiday plans.

*   *   *

A happier event to which I looked forward with keen anticipation was the *undo-kai,* the Nihon Gakko picnic held every June. The whole Japanese community buzzed like a beehive in preparation at least a month ahead, and at school we practiced Japanese folk songs, folk dances and marching drills to be performed at the picnic. The boys were drilled in mass calisthenics by Naito sensei, a young student teacher from Japan. With his pale, high forehead, dark-rimmed owlish glasses and slight figure, he did not look at all athletic yet he bounded around on the boardwalk, wearing tennis shoes and a white turtle-necked sweater and counting with fierce precision, *"Ichi! Ni! San! Shi!"*

The girls chattered like magpies about the new dresses and shoes they might get. The Japanese school picnic was one occasion when every Japanese in the community turned out and all parents bought new clothes for their children. There was a terrific run on children's tennis shoes in the Japanese shoe stores, for the foot races were the most important event of our picnic. All the girls bought snowy-white canvas rubber-soled shoes with a single strap buttoning across the instep and a demure white bow at the toe. The boys wore ankle-high black and white canvas shoes with thick, black rubber soles, guaranteed to transform even a plodding turtle into a bounding hare.

On the Sunday morning of the picnic, every Japanese household was awake and stirring at an early hour. In every kitchen a woman was putting on the stove huge pots of rice to prepare a mammoth picnic meal. Mother said the rice must be exactly right that day. She washed the rice over and over again until the water in the pot was clear and fresh. She placed her hand, palm down, into the pot to measure the water, and added enough to cover her hand completely. The pot of rice was set aside for twenty minutes to soak, then placed over a high flame to boil. In a few minutes the steam was hissing and pushing the heavy lid up. White froth dribbled over the side of the pot and stiffened like tissue paper.

"Now to steam it until it sprouts." Mother turned the flame down low, put a sheet of asbestos underneath the pot and placed a heavy iron weight on the lid to keep the steam inside. After about twenty minutes, when the rice was cooked to a full-blown fluff, Mother fanned it so she could handle it to make rice balls.

"First, we'll make *maki-zushi.*"

Mother spread the cooled rice on crisp squares of toasted seaweeds. She sprinkled chopped red ginger, eel meat, cooked cold spinach and carrots down the center of the rice. With a bamboo mat she rolled the seaweed into a cylinder shape, like jelly roll, and sliced it into one-inch thickness. *Maki-zushi* not only looked colorful, it was a gourmet's favorite.

Mother assigned me to the breadboard where I chopped vegetables, fish and meat into infinitesimal particles.

"Is this small enough, Mama?"

"No, no. It's still too coarse, Ka-chan. Japanese food is supposed to be dainty as well as flavorsome. Smaller, still smaller."

Mother stirred together carrot slivers, bamboo sprouts, tiny mushrooms, taro roots and pork in soy sauce and the result was *nishime,* which she packed into her best lacquer serving box. There were ham sandwiches, fried chicken and macaroni salad. One Thermos bottle was filled with hot green tea for Mother and Father, another was filled with milk for us. Like other women, Mother cooked pounds and pounds of food. Father packed the boxes and shopping bags of food into the car trunk, muttering that there was enough to keep the family out at Jefferson Park for weeks.

We finally piled into the car, nervously adjusting new hair ribbons or neckties. When we turned into Rainier Avenue and headed south, the highway stretched bright and sunny, and far in the distance Mount Rainier loomed haughty and beautiful. It would be a fine day. We passed cars, and cars whizzed by us, filled with beaming, happy-faced Japanese and their children, all on their way to Jefferson Park.

Hundreds of Japanese swarmed over the beautiful, sprawling green lawn of the picnic ground. It was a grand feeling to be away from the city heat and traffic. Here there was nothing more confining than the graceful poplars, the cool breeze from Puget Sound and the wide expanse of blue sky. Across the road, we could see the immaculate, trim golf course.

In spite of the seeming confusion of the large crowd, the picnic was carried out in a typically neat and purposeful Japanese fashion. During the official picnic hours, we were all herded into sections according to classes, guarded by our respective teachers. We stood around a huge circular plot, roped off for the foot races; parents and spectators clustered behind us.

The class races were run off like clockwork. We chewed our nails, waiting our turn and wondering what our race would be this year. In the past, the girls in my class had run trying to balance a small bouncy rubber ball on a wooden spoon. We had tried to pick slick lima beans from the ground, one by one, with wooden chopsticks and placed the beans in china bowls. We had dashed to Japanese paper lanterns scattered on the ground, lighted the candles inside and raced with them to the finishing line, taking care not to put out the light.

The suspense grew more intense as we moved closer to the starting line. When the girls in front of us dashed off on their race, it was our turn to receive instructions. The instructor was Mr. Ohashi, sporty in white duck trousers, white shirt and green-visored cap, but still masterful and authoritative. With pounding hearts and clammy cold hands, we listened to him as if we were getting instructions for a final examination.

"This is a 'matching' race! You will find envelopes on the ground, containing cards with 'kanji.' You must match them with cards lying open-faced with ideograph symbols on them."

When Mr. Ohashi blew the "go" whistle, I leaped forward like a frightened rabbit. I sped halfway around the track and picked up an envelope. . . . My square cards had five brushed symbols (actual characters were inserted here on original manuscript), snow, spring, flower, tree and paper. I scurried around, bumping into girls, looking for the matching ideographs. By a miracle I was the second person to complete the task and I ran toward the finish line, my heart beating with joy. Then suddenly my toe caught in the grass and I fell flat on my face. The spectators groaned in sympathy. I finished an ignoble number 12 with two raw, bleeding knees.

For the boys there was the "double" foot race in which two boys ran together as partners, the right ankle of one tied to the left ankle of the other. And there was a hilarious obstacle race in which the boys dove under a huge net and crawled through on their abdomens. Heads, arms and shoulders kept bobbing out of the large net holes, trapping them.

One contest which both the boys and spectators enjoyed immensely was "cone" *wari*. The boys, about two hundred of them altogether, were divided into a red and white team. Each boy placed an ice cream cone shell, inverted, on top of his head, tying the string which pierced through the base of the cone down the side of his face and under the chin. He also tied his color band around one arm. Armed with tightly rolled bundles of newspapers, the two teams lined up at opposite ends of the field and faced each other like young gladiators.

When Mr. Ohashi blew the whistle, they charged into each other with blood-curdling yells and Indian whoops, trying to knock off their opponents' cones. The field became a tumultuous battleground of boys. Henry pranced around, as did other boys who knew the art of Japanese fencing, wielding his weapon like a young samurai. After a minute, the whistle blew again, ending the first battle. The boys repaired back to their line to be checked. Only those with whole cones participated in the second battle. Henry was "dead," as was Jiro, who, being plump and slow on his feet, had been pounced on quickly as easy prey. Dunks, the fellow who could take care of himself in any dark alley, was so fierce and aggressive few dared to touch him, and he ran wildly around the field, picking cones off with glee. When the whistle called time, Dunks's team had won.

At noon, the janitor of Nihon Gakko walked through the picnic grounds swinging the old school bell nonchalantly as if he were still on the school premises. *"Ohiru desu . . . ohiru desu.* It's lunch hour. . . . Lunch hour."

The crowd melted away into the cool green depths of the woods, hot and dusty from the races. It was a welcome relief to sit underneath the shade of a towering maple tree where Mother had already laid out the lunch on the blanket. The Katos, the Oshimas, and the Matsuis had spread their blankets under nearby trees. Dunks, Jiro and Henry arrived on the scene with armloads of the ice-cream sandwiches which were distributed free to students. Hungry from the excitement and exertion, we ate like starved bears, except for the womenfolks. They were too busy replenishing the fast-emptying dishes and exchanging food among themselves.

Mrs. Kato came up smiling, in her new navy straw hat, offering us her own concoction of pickled eggplants and yellow radishes.

Like most Japanese women, Mrs. Kato was dressed, not for a picnic, but for a formal afternoon tea. She was wearing a silk, small-patterned dark navy dress and her best shoes.

"These are tasteless *otsukemono*, but please try some," bowed polite Mrs. Kato. The pickles were very tasty, but propriety kept her from saying that they were even edible. Mother cried out with delighted surprise, "Thank you, thank you, you are so kind. I'm sure they're very delicious. I'd like to have you try some fried chicken. I did a very poor job on it, but please take pieces to your family. . . ."

Mother pressed a platter of her horrible chicken, turned to a luscious golden-brown, upon Mrs. Kato who bore it away, protesting Mother's kindness.

Mother filled another platter with *maki-zushi*, added fresh sprigs of parsley to it and took it over to Mrs. Matsui. I saw both of them bowing back and forth and soon Mother returned with Mrs. Matsui's luscious *botamochi*, a special kind of rice rolled into balls and generously covered with sweetened, crushed red beans.

"Mama, please sit down and eat. You haven't touched your plate at all!"

"Yes, yes, as soon as I take over some macaroni salad to Oshima-san."

It was a marvelous feast. I ate hot dogs, cold barbecued pork, rice balls sprinkled with sesame seeds and with bright-red pickled plums hidden in the center. The plum was so highly seasoned and salty that the thought of it still makes my mouth pucker.

I was amazed with the variety of ways in which rice appeared at the picnic. One woman served rice mixed with bits of abalone, carrots, mushroom, shreds of egg omelet and slivers of green beans. Mother had made king-sized hors d'oeuvres with her various rice balls, giving each a different flavor by combining it with vegetables, placing thin slices of vinegared smelt on top, or wrapping it in thick green kelp. Mrs. Matsui had turned rice into a dessert by making *botamochi*. My favorite rice was in the form of nutty brown crackers and paper-thin sweet wafers.

For our parents, the picnic was a rare occasion of complete relaxation and a chance to visit with friends whom they seldom saw in town. As everyone began to feel mellow and congenial, singing started here and there. Mr. Oshima was easily persuaded to sing, especially after a few bottles of sake. He crossed his legs and placed his hands dramatically on his knees. Then closing his pink, puffed eyelids and tossing his head back to get a fuller range, he started groaning a *naniya bushi*. He kept on singing, not even bothering to take a breath, until his face turned a violent blue.

Our parents loved *naniya bushi*. It was old Japan to them, a type of ballad singing in which the singer recounted favorite Japanese classic tales. It had a characteristic all its own so that once it was heard, no one could ever confuse it with any other type of singing. The singers hung on to a note for what seemed to be an eternity, turning redder and redder in the face and neck, almost to the point of asphyxiation. If I listened too sympathetically, I felt myself twisting and writhing to end this torture.

Song after song flowed from Mr. Oshima, as he gradually filled himself with such nostalgia for his homeland that an unmanly tear trickled down his wrinkled tanned cheek. Slowly he relaxed deeper and deeper into the bush behind him until he finally disappeared inside fast asleep.

After our leisurely lunch we hurried back to our places for the afternoon events. Our parents crowded around to watch us march out into the field and perform folk dances and drills. The women opened up their pretty silk Japanese parasols and fanned themselves with moon-shaped paper fans, while the men stood around in open shirt collars, sleeves rolled up, perspiration trickling down from under their straw hats.

Henry, who had always been a highly charged and gregarious person, throve in this bustling atmosphere. He was captain of the school patrol boys who directed traffic for the hundreds of cars converging upon the picnic ground. First Henry strapped himself into the patrol boy belt and waved cars in and out of the parking lot. Then he tossed his belt off and rushed into formation for the mass calisthenic demonstrations. Next he hurtled into the bandstand with his flashy saxophone. The band was loud and brassy as it swung with ease from Scottish reels to Japanese marching songs to the resounding crash and blare of "Stars and Stripes Forever."

Sprinkled here and there in the crowd were strange Occidental faces. Men and women carrying golf bags crossed the road to our side, attracted by the color and noise of the Japanese picnic. They watched with frank curiosity. Now and then some public school teachers appeared. Whenever their Japanese-American students spotted them they were instantly surrounded with cries of welcome.

When the school exhibitions were finally ended, the crowd moved en masse to the bleachers to watch the local boys play off their annual baseball tournament. The scene was gay and colorful with bobbing, twirling parasols, bright fans and handkerchiefs excitedly fluttering up breezes. Throwing aside all Japanese restraint, the issei men shed their hats and dignity and yelled themselves hoarse for their sons and favorite team in an amusing mixture of Japanese and English. Even the reticent Japanese women shrieked involuntarily as they saw a boy slide for base and disappear in a cloud of dust with the baseman diving right on top of him.

By the time the last game had been played and the spectators had cheered and applauded the champion team, it was dusk. A cleanup crew of men was already busy at work, crisscrossing over the picnic grounds, each man carrying a large paper bag and a long stick with a sharp nail protruding from its end, picking up waste paper and picnic refuse. Henry was back with the patrol boys, directing the departing traffic.

We climbed wearily into our car. Mother leaned back with a sigh, "Well, that's over with, until next year."

Kenji curled up in the corner of the back seat. Sumiko slept on Mother's lap and I sat back, tired and content. My white organdy dress was wrinkled and stained with grass, chocolate ice cream and plain black dirt. I had two square bandages on my knees and my new white sneakers were smudged and one dainty bow was missing, but I had won a shiny black notebook, two pencil tablets, a red penholder and three yellow pencils.

Father sat behind the wheel, waving at the cars which went by. Mr. Sakaguchi honked his horn at us as he drove past with his gleaming new blue car. His face was a glowing red, reflecting the color of the setting sun and the settling sake. Mr. Oshima jounced by in a jiggling Model T Ford, singing happily at the wheel. Dunks was sitting close at his elbow, directing the driving. "Pop, slow down. We ain't out on the highway yet."

After the last piece of orange peel had been picked up and the last car had rolled out to the highway, the patrol boys disbanded and Henry joined us. As Father drove slowly over the gravel road, we looked back at Jefferson Park which now looked serene and unperturbed as if it had not been assaulted with an invasion of

Japanese celebrating their biggest community event, a good old-fashioned *undo-kai.*

New Year's, as my family observed it, was a mixture of pleasure and agony. I enjoyed New Year's eve which we spent together, waiting for midnight. On New Year's eve, no one argued when Mother marched us into the bathtub, one by one. We understood that something as important as a new year required a special sacrifice on our part. Mother said the bath was a symbolic act, that we must scrub off the old year and greet the new year clean and refreshed in body and spirit.

The rest of the evening we spent crowded around the table in the living room playing *Karuta,* an ancient Japanese game. It consisted of one hundred old classic poems beautifully brushed upon one hundred cards, about the size of a deck of cards. There was one set of cards on which were written the *shimo no ku,* the second half of the poems. These were laid out on the table before the players. A reader presided over a master set of one hundred cards which contained the *kami no ku,* the first half of the poem as well as the *shimo no ku.* As the reader read from the key cards, the players were to try to pick up the card on the table before anyone else could claim it. The player or the team who picked up the greatest number of cards was the winner. An expert player knew the entire one hundred poems by heart so that when the reader had uttered the first few words, he knew instantly which card was being called out. When several experts competed the game was exciting and stimulating. But in our family only Mother and Father knew the poems, and they slowed their paces to match ours.

Mother was always the reader, chanting out the poems melodically. Sumiko, being the baby of the family, was allowed to stand on a chair at Mother's elbow and get a preview of the card being read. Sumiko would look, jump off the chair, and scurry around the table to find the card while we waited impatiently for Mother to get to the second half of the poem. I howled with indignation, "Mama, make Sumiko stop cheating! It's not fair . . . I'll never find a card as long as she peeks at the *kami no ku!*"

Mother laughed indulgently, "Now, don't get so excited. Sumi-chan's just a little girl. She has to have some fun, too."

The evening progressed noisily as we fluttered about like anxious little moths, eyes riveted on the table. Anyone who found a card would triumphantly shout *"Hai!"* and slam down on it with a force that would have flattened an opponent's fingers. Promptly at midnight we stopped. Out in the harbor, hundreds of boats sounded their foghorns to herald the New Year. Automobiles raced by under our windows their horns blowing raucously. Guns exploded, cowbells clanged, the factory whistle shrilled. Henry swept the cards off the table, leaped into the air in his billowing nightshirt and shouted "Happy New Year, everybody! Happy New Year!" We turned on the radio full blast so we could hear the rest of the city cheer and sing "Auld Lang Syne." Horrified, Father implored us, "Ohhh the guests, the guests. Lower that radio. We'll wake our guests."

Then Father and Mother slipped quietly down the hallway to the kitchen to prepare refreshments. Although the black-painted steampipe, running alongside one wall in the room, made energetic knocking noises which meant that it was piping hot, the parlor was chilly. I turned the tiny gas heater higher and Sumiko and I sat in front of it, pulling our voluminous flannel gowns over our knees and cold toes. We sat with our chins resting comfortably on our knees and huddled so close to the heater that our faces began to tighten and glow beet-red. I was floating in half sleep when I heard Mother and Father's voices murmuring gently. "*Sah*, who gets the smallest piece of pie?"

"Not me!" Sumiko jumped up defensively. Then she saw Father's eyes smiling.

Father had carried in a pot of hot coffee and fresh, honey-crusted apple pie with its golden juice bubbled through the slits. Mother brought in thick hot chocolate, with plump soft marshmallow floating on top, for us.

It was customary for the Japanese to eat buckwheat noodles on New Year's eve, but every year whenever Mother wondered aloud whether she should make some, we voted it down. Father said, "No noodles for me either, Mama. A good hot cup of coffee is what will please me most."

Father sliced the pie and as we let the flaky, butter-flavored crust melt in our mouths, we did not envy anyone eating noodles.

The next morning when we were breakfasting on fruit juice, ham and eggs, toast and milk, Mother said, "We really should be eating *ozoni* and *mochi* on New Year's morning."

We gagged, "Oh, no, not in the morning!"

"Well now, don't turn your nose up like that. It's a perfectly respectable tradition."

Ozoni was a sort of thick chicken stew with solid chunks of carrots, bamboo sprouts, giant white radishes and taro roots. Into this piping hot mixture, one dipped freshly toasted rice dumplings, puffed into white airy plumpness, in the same way one dunked doughnuts into coffee. But the rice dumpling had an annoying way of sticking to everything like glue . . . to the chopsticks, to the side of the bowl, and on the palate. It was enough to cause a panic when the thick, doughy dumpling fastened itself in the throat and refused to march on down to the stomach.

Father backed us up once more, "*Ozoni* is good, I admit, but I don't like to battle with my food so early in the morning. Let's have some more coffee, Mama."

"Well, having a whimsical family like this certainly saves me a lot of work."

Up to that moment the family was in perfect harmony about whether we would celebrate New Year's in the Japanese or the American way. But a few hours later our peace was shattered when Mother said, "*Sah,* now we must pay our respects to the Matsuis."

"Not again," Henry shuddered.

"Yes again, and I don't want to hear any arguments."

"But why must *we* go? Why can't you and Papa go by yourselves this time?"

"We are all going together for the New Year's call," Mother said firmly. "I don't want to hear another word. Put your clothes on."

We sighed loudly as we dressed ourselves. We would have to sit silently like little Buddhas and listen while our elders dredged up the past and gave it the annual overhaul. Even the prospect of Mrs. Matsui's magnificent holiday feast was dampened by the fact that we knew we would have to eat quietly like meek little ghosts and politely refuse all second helpings.

"Mama . . ." Henry shouted from his room. "What was that now, that New Year's greeting we have to say to the Matsuis? I've forgotten how it goes. '*Ake-mashite omede toh gozai masu. Konen mo, ahhh, konen mo . . .*' What comes after that? I can't remember."

Mother said, "*Soh, soh . . .* I want you all to say it properly when we arrive at the Matsui-san's home. It goes like this . . . *ake-mashite omede toh gozai masu,* which means 'This New

Year is indeed a happy occasion.' Then you say *konen mo yoro-shiku onegai itashi-masu.* 'I hope that the coming year will find us close friends as ever.'"

As we climbed up Yesler Hill to the Matsuis, we repeated the greeting over and over again. We raised our voices so we could hear ourselves better whenever a chunky bright orange cable car lurched up the hill like a lassoed bronco, inching its way furiously to the top.

The Matsui residence was a large yellow frame house which squatted grandly on an elevated corner lot. At the front door, Father and Mother and Mr. and Mrs. Matsui bowed and murmured, bowed and murmured. Standing behind our parents, we bowed vigorously, too. Then Mrs. Matsui looked at us expectantly and Mother pushed us forward. We bowed again, then started out in unison. "*Ake-mashite omede toh gozai masu.*" A long pause followed. We forgot the rest. Then Henry recalled a fragment, "*Konen mo . . . konen mo . . . ahhh,* something about *onegai shimasu.*"

The adults burst into laughter, bringing the affair to a merciful end.

In the living room, we waited patiently while Mrs. Matsui offered the best chairs to Father and Mother who politely refused them. Mrs. Matsui insisted and they declined. When at last we were all seated as Mrs. Matsui wanted — Father and Mother on the overstuffed brown mohair chairs and the four of us primly lined up on the huge davenport, our polished shoes placed neatly together and hands in our laps — she brought in tea and thin, crisp, rice cookies. As she poured the tea, she said, "Perhaps the little folks would rather have 'sodawata' instead?"

Henry and Kenji smirked at each other while Sumiko and I hung our heads, trying not to look eager, but Mother said quickly,

"Oh, no, please, Mrs. Matsui, don't trouble yourself. My children love tea." So we sipped scalding tea out of tiny, burning teacups without handles and nibbled at brittle rice wafers.

While the Matsuis and our parents reminisced about the good old days, we thumbed through the worn photograph albums and old Japanese tourist magazines. Finally Mrs. Matsui excused herself and bustled feverishly around the dining room. Then she invited us in. "*Sah*, I have nothing much to offer you, but please eat your fill."

"*Mah, mah*, such a wonderful assortment of *ogochi-soh*," Mother bubbled.

Balding Mr. Matsui snorted deprecatingly. Mrs. Matsui walked around the table with an enormous platter of *osushi*, rice cakes rolled in seaweed. We each took one and nibbled at it daintily, sipping tea. Presently she sailed out of the kitchen bearing a magnificent black and silver lacquered tray loaded with carmine lacquer bowls filled with fragrant *nishime*. In pearly iridescent china bowls, Mrs. Matsui served us hot chocolatey *oshiruko*, a sweetened bean soup dotted with tender white *mochi*, puffed up like oversized marshmallows.

Father and Mother murmured over the superb flavoring of each dish, while Mr. Matsui guffawed politely, "*Nani*, this woman isn't much of a cook at all."

I was fascinated with the *yaki-zakana*, barbecued perch, which, its head and tail raised saucily, looked as if it were about to flip out of the oval platter. Surrounding this centerpiece were lacquer boxes of desserts, neatly lined rows of red and green oblong slices of sweet bean cakes, a mound of crushed lima beans, tinted red and green, called *kinton*. There was a vegetable dish called *kimpira* which looked like a mass of brown twigs. It turned out to be burdock, hotly seasoned with red pepper.

Every now and then Mrs. Matsui urged us from the side line, "Please help yourself to more food."

And each time, we were careful to say, "*Arigato,* I have plenty, thank you," although I could have counted the grains of rice I had so far consumed. I felt that a person could starve amidst this feast if he carried politeness too far. Fortunately, Mrs. Matsui ignored our refusals. She replenished our half-empty dishes and kept our teacups filled so that without breaking the illusion that we were all dainty eaters, we finally reached a semiconscious state of satiation.

We moved heavily to the parlor to relax. Mrs. Matsui pursued us there with more green, pickled radishes and *kazunoko,* fish eggs, and a bowl of fresh fruit. She brought out fresh tea and *yokan.* To turn down Mrs. Matsui's offer so often was very rude, so we accepted with a wan smile and firmly closed our mouths over the cake and chewed.

When Father and Mother finally came to their senses and decided it was time to go home, we nearly tore the door off its hinges in our rush to get out into the hallway for our wraps.

I staggered out at last into the frosty night, feeling tight as a drum and emotionally shaken from being too polite for too long. I hoped on our next call our hostess would worry less about being hospitable and more about her guests' comfort, but that was an impudent thought for a Japanese girl.

CHAPTER V

We Meet Real Japanese

ONE evening as Father sat down to dinner he asked casually, "How would you all like to go to Japan and meet my father?"

We whooped and pounded each other in excitement.

Henry's eyes glittered. "When are we leaving?" he shouted. "I'll have to tell Miss Larson I won't be going to school for a while. And Saito sensei, too. I'm gonna get myself one of those samurai swords, a six-footer!"

"Sometime in the spring, I think. Your mother's parents are coming to America soon and they will take charge of the hotel while we visit Japan. They are on a ship right now."

I shivered with delight at the thought of the journey in a gigantic ship. But Kenji was sitting back, looking glum. Mother said, "Ken-chan, what's the matter? You're crying."

We all looked at Kenji, surprised. Crystal tears glistened tremulously in his huge, petal-shaped eyes. He suddenly burst into angry sobs, "I don't want to go, Mama."

"But, Ken-chan, Grandfather Itoi wants to see all of his *magos*. He is very old, about eighty years now, and Ken-chan, I know he will be so happy to carry you around and tell you lots of wonderful stories."

Ken-chan shook his head violently. "But I'm afraid of those earthquakes!"

I knew exactly how he felt. Kenji remembered all too clearly, as I did, the hair-raising, frightful stories about earthquakes in Japan. After the big earthquake of 1923, that was all the folks could talk about for a while. Each person told his story over and over again with loving attention to every little detail. They told of friends burnt to a crisp in raging fire. One man had seen human legs sticking out of the ground like signposts. Another told about priests who burnt incense near a pile of bones dug out of a scorched building. They sold the bones to people who were unable to find the remains of their loved ones. In the evenings I went to bed with these gruesome scenes fixed forever in my mind.

Father and Mother tried to laugh Kenji's fears away. "Most earthquakes last only a few seconds and lots of times you don't even notice them."

That night we went to bed wound up like tensed coils of spring. When we reach Japan, I thought, we will really have to start bowing. I thought of Grandfather Itoi, whose portrait hung in our living room. He was wearing a dark gray silk kimono and a *haori*, a top garment, tied in the front with a silken tassel. He looked fragile with his thin hair, high forehead and lean face. He wore the same, gentle, patient expression in his eyes as Father did.

The following days crawled maddeningly for us and for Mother. We waited impatiently for the arrival of Ojih-chan and Obah-chan. Then miraculously Obah-chan was sitting with us in the kitchen one day holding Sumiko in her lap. She had a soft, dovelike voice and the corners of her sweet, sloe eyes crinkled into fine wrinkles when she smiled. Ojih-chan was talking, talking, talking, all night about the trip while we sat around the table, listening with rapt attention. He was a small wiry man. His snapping triangular eyes peered intently over the rim of his tortoiseshell spectacles. He had a sensitive, thin, aquiline nose just like Mother's and a luxuriant, glossy mane of black hair and a walrus mustache, thicker than Father's. He was like a quiescent volcano, shifting in his seat constantly and drumming his fingers nervously on the table top as he talked.

In April, we boarded the *Arabia Maru,* really on our way. Our sleeping quarters, deep down in the hold of the ship, had a nauseating green odor, like that of metallic paint plastered on damp, sweaty walls. We were fed too much *miso shiru,* the bean paste soup, which sent shudders up and down my spine, and too much rice, but these were minor inconveniences compared to the thrill of being on a giant ship. As we went farther and farther out to sea, we saw fewer and fewer of the screeching gulls. One morning a Japanese sailor pointed down into the green, rushing waters and showed us hundreds of shiny, speckled, leaping porpoises, showing off their white bellies and swimming like mad along with our boat.

It looked as if the trip was going to be uneventful and dull, until one morning all bedlam seemed to have broken loose on ship. I was leaning over the rails, feeding my bowl of rice to the porpoises when whistles shrilled and the ship's big horn bellowed. Sailors and passengers scurried around on deck.

"It's the fire bell," someone said.

"Fire bell!" I shrieked. My hair stood on end. We were all going to burn on the ship. It was the end of everything. We would never reach Japan to see Ojih-chan, ever. I ran screaming downstairs to Mother and flung myself hysterically into her arms.

She bent down and wiped my streaming tears and nose. "This is fire practice," she said gently. "It's just a drill like the ones you have at school."

I was so relieved, I took Mother's hand and flew up the stairs so as not to miss a single second of this wonderful, exciting fire practice at sea. However, the sense that we had had a harrowing crossing haunted me until we disembarked at Yokohama.

One of Father's brothers from Tokyo met us at the port. He was taller than Father, a handsome elderly man who held himself ceremoniously erect. A summer straw hat sat squarely on his freshly barbered head, and he wore a rustling black silk *hakama* and *haori* which men put on for special formal occasions. I waited for him and Father to fall upon each other's shoulders and greet each other noisily. After all, they had not seen each other for many years. But Uncle only bowed stiffly and began a short speech of welcome. Father and Mother looked a bit startled, but they too, not to be outdone, bowed their heads and plunged into an elaborate greeting.

We goggled at the scene around us. This was a strange land of bicycles. We had thought bicycles were only for boys and girls, but here, dignified men in Western-styled business suits pedaled by industriously. A delivery boy steered his bicycle with one hand while he balanced a towering pile of wooden boxes in his other hand. Mother was astonished to see a genteel-looking elderly woman wearing a *marumage* pompadour coiffure, cycling along with haughty composure.

"Mah, mah, how time has changed," Mother chuckled.

The Japanese women wore long kimonos and stiff wide sashes as I had expected, but their kimonos were almost drab in color and pattern. The men in their kimonos topped by a Homburg or a Panama hat looked odd to us.

We whooped with joy to see hundreds of two-wheeled carriages, jinrikishas, lined up near the dock. They were just as I had pictured them to be. It turned out that we were going to ride on them to our hotel. Mother held Sumiko in her lap and I sat beside her. The jinrikisha man, small, bronzed and muscular, smiled and ducked his head a great deal. A white towel was tied around his forehead and the hem of his short blue cotton kimono was tucked up into his sash, for the sake of speed. Father and Uncle rode on ahead; Henry and Kenji followed in another carriage. Our man ran along rhythmically and effortlessly, weaving in and out of the traffic of rickshaws, pedestrians, trams and automobiles. People stared at our foreign clothes and I felt self-conscious.

At the hotel, Father and Mother removed their shoes on the concrete floor before they stepped up to the straw-matted platform. Mother unbuttoned Sumiko's black patent leather shoes.

"Take your shoes off, children. You can't walk on the *tatami* with your dirty shoes."

Henry and I stepped out of ours, resentfully. But Kenji, who had objected all along to this trip, sat down on the floor and flatly refused. "No!" he said. Mother kneeled to untie his shoestrings. Kenji kicked and screamed, filling the hotel lobby with his howls. Father said, "Never mind, Mama. We'll just have to leave the naughty boy here." Kenji sat silent and stubborn, his back turned defiantly to us, as we all filed into the dining room. We heard Kenji shouting, "I won't take my shoes off. I want to go home."

Maids in kimonos and white aprons bowed and slipped about quietly. They bowed and arranged individual trays of rice, clear soup, fish and vegetables on the floor. They bowed and departed. I wondered if we were supposed to bow in return each time. Somehow in this setting, bowing looked graceful and natural. Mother told us we were going to dine on the floor, on individual low tables. We must tuck our legs underneath us and sit on them. Henry sat tailor fashion and I did likewise, spreading my skirt modestly over my knees.

"Ka-chan and Henry!" Mother looked daggers at us. "Sit as I tell you."

"But, Mama, I can't." I had forgotten that on occasions I could wind myself up like a pretzel when I wanted to show off. Mother kept glaring at us until Henry and I had bent our knees under and were sitting properly.

I heaved a sigh. Maybe Kenji was right after all. Japan wasn't going to be much fun. Kenji was still out in the luxuriously decorated hotel lobby, shattering its quiet dignity with his screams. Finally Father's brother, unable to stand it any longer, rose from his table, "Let's not be so harsh with the little one. It's all so new and strange to Ken-chan."

He excused himself and hurried out. Soon Uncle returned, carrying in his arms a triumphant Kenji, still wearing his brown shoes, the laces tied in a mass of knots.

The next day we went to Utsunomiya where another of Father's brothers, Rokuro, and his family lived. Uncle Itoi was a physician and owned a private hospital in town. His tiny aesthetic mustache and clinical silver-rimmed glasses immediately said that he was a doctor. His wife was a small, dignified person with sharp, clear-cut features. In their home I saw the makings of a Japanese maiden by observing my Cousin Yoshiye, who was three years older than I. Bristle-headed energetic Cousin Yoshio had taken Henry and Kenji out to the yard but I stayed with Yoshiye. Yoshiye wore her hair in a long, polished mane, tied tightly at the nape of her neck with a black ribbon. Her face was sharp and aristocratic. Yoshiye was wearing a lovely, multicolored red silk kimono. She made me feel like a tomboy with her restrained, delicate movements while I rustled and hustled around as I pleased. She stared haughtily at my long white cotton stockings and short-skirted, red and white cotton dress. She sat so still, looking me over, I knew she did not approve of me.

When Aunt suggested to Yoshiye that she give one of her pretty kimonos to me, Yoshiye refused. Her face white with alarm, she said, "But I don't want to give any of them away."

Aunt Itoi looked unhappy, "I insist you give one to your cousin right now."

Yoshiye fled from the room weeping and stayed out of sight the rest of the day.

We relaxed in their quietly elegant garden which was completely surrounded with high bamboo fences. Rocks were imbedded into a grassy mound so that it looked like a miniature mountain. Stunted trees grew crookedly between these rocks. A gray stone lantern stood near a small pond, filled with velvet-black and red-gold fishes. Yoshio hacked away at a young bamboo tree showing Henry and Kenji how to carve little water buckets from the bamboo stalk.

That night I was to sleep in Yoshiye's room. Thick, padded quilts were brought out from built-in shelves and put on the floor. Yoshiye laid her head on a cylindrical padded roll. The nape of her neck rested on this pillow and her head hung back slightly over it. Lying there with her eyes closed, she looked to me as if she were waiting for an executioner's ax to fall. I pushed my pillow aside. Yoshiye and I simmered silently in the dark for a while. Then I burst out impulsively in English, "You know, I think you're awfully selfish."

"You talk so funny," she laughed.

I flung the covers back angrily. When she sat up, surprised, I slapped her face. Then I raised my arms around my head, waiting to be thoroughly pummeled. But nothing happened. Yoshiye just sank down on her quilt and cried. Aunt and Mother came into our room. Mother was mortified.

"Ka-chan! Have you forgotten you are a girl? Girls don't fight like boys."

"But, Mama, Yoshiye isn't nice. She's selfish."

"Never mind about Yoshiye. You struck her. Why can't you be more mannerly and quiet like Yoshiye?"

I was removed to another room. Although I was not sorry I had slapped my cousin, it had been an odd sensation. It was like striking a sack of flour. There had been no resistance or angry response, only a quiet crumbling away.

We immediately plunged into sight-seeing. Father trotted Henry and me out to Nikko, the famous shrine and park built by Shogun Iyemitsu. He might as well have taken a couple of puppies for all the appreciation we showed. We were curious enough, but in an undiscriminating way. After an endless trip by trains, trams, buses, and cable cars, memorable mostly for the smell of hot steel combined with boiled eggs and orange peels, we reached our destination.

We saw the *Kiri-furi No Take,* an ear-splitting, thundering waterfall. The tremendous height of the cliff and the avalanche of foaming water plummeting down into the river below gave me weak knees and a superhuman grip in my fingers as I clutched at the fence to keep from being swept down, too.

We strolled by a pretty, red-painted bridge, curved like a half-moon, and roped off on both ends. Father, in the enthusiastic tone of a newly hired guide, explained, "That's the Shinkyo Bridge, the sacred bridge of the gods. Only the Emperor of Japan may walk upon it."

I felt immediately challenged. When Father and Henry walked away to feed the young fawns, I hurried back to Shinkyo Bridge and ducked under the rope, intending to run lightly up the arch, but I found it was like trying to run up a wall. I fell on my hands and knees and tried to claw my way up, but everytime I slid back. A passer-by saw this unspeakable desecration. He froze in his tracks and sputtered, "What do you think you're doing there? Come out of there right now!"

I slid down, straightened my skirt and ran back to Father and Henry. I was careful not to brag to Father that I had laid my lowly hands and knees on the sacred bridge. But I wondered just how the Emperor managed it.

As we walked over miles and miles of pebbled pathways, winding in and out of the wooded areas, and gazed at the toriis and temples, Father whispered to us in a sepulchral tone, "Everything you see here . . . everything is nearly 400 years old."

We tried to look properly awed. To be sure, there was an atmosphere of tranquility and solemnity as if these temples and statues had been here since the days of samurais. Pigeons wheeled in and around the dark red toriis which soared majestically straight up into the sky, surrounded by massive, aged trees. The temples looked like storybook dwellings with their bright gold and crimson roofs curving heavenward. Father pointed out to us the darkened old carvings of three monkeys on the temple walls, posed in the "see no evil, hear no evil, speak no evil" postures.

As we gazed vacuously at still another temple, Father tried to whip up our flagging interest. "See there, that's 'Nemuri Neko,' the sleeping cat on that wall." Our eyes picked the mammoth figure of a reclining cat out of the tortuous carvings. "Uh huh."

Father led us to a long, low-slung shrine into which many people disappeared. At a huge gray stone urn in front of the building people stopped to sprinkle their hands with water, using long-handled dippers. Father said, "It's an old custom — people wash their hands to purify themselves before saying their prayers."

Henry and I gingerly splashed cold water on our hands, giggling nervously. The interior was dim and unlighted. The panels on the walls and ceilings crawled with ornate carvings. I caught the sickening scent of burning incense and the mysterious sound of brass gongs.

In one room, the entire ceiling was covered with the carving of a writhing, scaly, giant dragon. People were solemnly clapping their hands and looking up. Father explained, "When a person stands beneath the dragon and claps his hands together, it is said that one can hear it moan." Henry and I clapped our hands sharply. We listened, staring up at the animal. We could have sworn that it moved and groaned with a low, faint whine.

When the exhausting tour of Nikko was at last over, I felt as if I had really seen old Japan and had no need to see more.

We finally reached Takayama, the country village where Grandfather Itoi lived. It was another battling trip via jam-packed trains, hired automobiles, horse-drawn carts and jinrikishas. On country roads, farm folks seemed to know instinctively that foreigners were approaching. Wherever we went, a curious knot of people was gathered on the roadside. As we bounced by self-consciously on rickshas, they nudged each other and whispered aloud, "Look, they must be from America. They certainly wear odd clothes."

Grandfather Itoi turned out to be a much beloved old patriarch. For forty years he had served as "soncho" or the head elder of four villages, and though he was retired now, people still consulted him about farm crops and personal matters. It was relaxing to sit on the cool porch while he chatted with Mother and Father about America. Sometimes we stretched our limbs and sprawled flat on our backs and listened to Grandfather tell us "Tanuki" stories, about the crafty badger who could turn into a teapot, a drum, or a rock to escape his enemies. During these quiet afternoon hours, Grandfather invariably ordered tea and his favorite pastry, *kusamochi*, which was made of marshmallow-soft rice dough with young, crushed grass leaves mixed into it. As we sank our teeth into the freshly pounded, powdery-soft dough, the crisp fragrance of the young leaves blended perfectly with the filling of chocolatey, sweet, crushed beans.

Grandfather's home was a sprawling, one-story country house, spacious and rambling, surrounded by bamboo trees. In the daytime the entire front part of the house, sectioned wooden doors called the *amado* and the latticed paper walls called *shoji*, was pushed aside to let the sun and fresh air pour in. The interior of the building was divided into different-sized rooms by sliding walls, all papered in elegant sea-green with simple designs of pine trees painted on them.

At first we had to play by ourselves for the neighborhood children had taken an immediate dislike to us. We felt tense and unhappy as they surged around outside the fence, yelling at us, "American-jin! American-jin!" When dusk came the older boys often made a rush toward the house and pelted the *shoji* with stones, ripping holes through the taut white paper. Each evening the maids went out after them with brooms, but the children only laughed and scattered.

Henry and I knew that there would be a showdown soon, and we waited uneasily. Early one morning we slipped out of the front gate to go to the canal nearby to fish for minnows. The dust in the deserted road felt cool to our bare toes, as we strode along. Soon we heard the rustle of creeping children behind a fence a few yards ahead. I stiffened with fright. Henry whispered, "Don't let on we see them. Just keep on walking, and when we get to the bend, we'll make a dash for the canal."

We walked faster and faster, but at the end of the road, the boys sprang out in front of us, leaping and shouting.

"Yahhhh! Look at those cowards. They're afraid of us."

Henry kept on walking sturdily toward them, his fishing line held tightly in his hand.

"Oi, you, from America, you're afraid to fight, aren't you? Oi, American-jin, why don't you say something?"

Suddenly Henry charged into the group, whacking his fishing pole about him. The boys yelled with delight. The oldest was about ten, but the same size as Henry who was eight. The boys dodged around for a while and then four of them dove on Henry. There was a wild windmill of arms and legs. Henry swung his fists blindly around him, but it was a losing battle. The ten-year-old came up from behind and locked Henry's arms back so the others could pound him freely. Another small one hung on to Henry's kicking legs. Furious, I rushed at the ten-year-old and sank my teeth into his arm. I scratched viciously at his face until the boy jumped back, more out of surprise than pain, for he had not expected a girl to be so savage. It was a marvelous free-for-all. The boys gave me no quarter. They could not afford to do so. I was pulling hair and gouging at eyes as I had learned to do in alleyways back home. We were tiring fast, but we knew this was no ordinary fight. The land where we were born was being put to a test.

We made such a clamor and commotion that a maidservant at Takayama stepped out into the road. When she recognized us, she ran to our rescue, shouting and flinging her apron at the children, "What do you think you're doing, kozo tachi! Stop it!!"

She lifted the grimy-faced boys by the scruff of their kimono collars and gave them heavy blows on their heads. Henry and I panted home, spitting out grit. We were so exhausted that we didn't care who had won the fight.

Gradually the children stopped hooting at us. Henry was invited to go to the canal with the boys to net *dojos,* eel-like fishes. They never invited me nor spoke to me, but I tagged along anyway. The boys tried to ignore me as all girls deserved to be ignored, but I noticed that they sneaked many side glances, puzzled and bewildered, for in their books, girls did not behave as I did.

The season arrived when the entire household dedicated themselves to the coddling of *kaikos* or silkworms. One morning the menfolk tucked their kimono hems up, tied cotton towels around their foreheads and started pushing walls back to clear the rooms. They brought in racks of wooden frames and piled them to the ceiling. The women, their kimono sleeves tied neatly out of the way, brought in trays of mulberry leaves on which thousands of tiny white larvae fed. Every part of the house was given over to these munching worms. And how they ate! Their mass feeding sounded like the heavy patter of good Seattle rain. It drummed upon each nerve of my body until I felt as if I, too, were being fed upon. While I grew wan and exhausted from lack of sleep, the larvae thrived and fattened into lard-pale worms. Twigs were set down among them and we watched them by the hour, busily spinning their silk round and round themselves, firmly anchored to these twigs. When all the silkworms had encased themselves into cocoons, the trays were taken away and the frames moved out of the house. For the next few weeks the womenfolk gathered out in the back yard to work with these cocoons. They dipped the white peanut-shaped cocoons into pots of hot water to soften them. The odor of the cooked larvae was overpowering, but the women sat bent over their work, hour after hour, patiently unraveling the delicate threads on wooden spindles. These threads were eventually taken to the local weavers who wove them into beautiful silk fabrics on large hand- and foot-operated looms.

At Takayama I experienced my first bath, country style, in what looked like an old rain barrel. When we were in cities, we had visited public bathhouses. Sumiko and I had accompanied Mother to the women's side while Henry and Kenji had followed Father to the other side. It had been disconcerting to bathe so chummily with people I had never seen, but since they paid little attention to us, I managed to look nonchalant, too. But a rain barrel bath, I discovered, was different. Every drop of water had to be carried in from the well in the back yard. Masako, the robust country maid, went about filling the barrel stoically, bucket after bucket. I told her, smugly, that in America we have two faucets, one for cold water and one for hot, right in the kitchen sink and bathroom. She sighed, looking dreamily into the barrel as she sloshed the bucket of water inside, "I can't imagine what it would be like, to get all the water you need without working for it."

Then Masako bent down and started a fire under the tub.

"What are you doing, Masako? I'm not going to take a bath with a fire blazing under me!"

"This is the way we heat our water," she said as she threw handfuls of herbs and leaves into the water. I felt as if a delectable broth was being prepared to receive my squirming body. Masako said, "Call me when you are ready," and she left me staring into the gigantic pot.

There was no privacy for a bather here either. The tub stood just inside the open back door of the kitchen, exposed to the eyes of anyone in the yard or in the kitchen. I knew a true Japanese had a unique device of "not seeing things" if the social situation called for "not seeing things," even if the object was right in front of his eyeballs. I had seen this technique in practice time and time again. Whenever we made a call and the woman of the house did not feel properly dressed to receive callers, she would turn her face away and slip past us into the back room. Father and Mother would stare at the walls as if they had seen no one. When she later emerged, they greeted each other with ceremony and warmth as if they had just come face to face for the first time. It should have worked well for taking baths in the open, too, but I, who had been conditioned to bolting the American bathroom door securely, felt uncomfortable.

My first impulse was to drop my clothes quickly, leap into the deep barrel, and sink out of sight, but the percolating water detained me. Anyway I knew that I would be scolded for contaminating the water without a preliminary scrubbing. I cringed against the barrel, hopelessly in view. I hastily lathered myself, eyes and ears peeled, ready to duck behind the barrel should anyone approach. Then I rinsed myself hurriedly. As far as I was concerned, my bath was completed. Masako seemed to know that I was about to sneak off without the all-important soak. She popped back into the shed, tying her kimono sleeves out of the way.

"Sah, ready? This is the best part of it all . . . a nice long soak."

I cautioned Masako, in a mixture of English and Japanese, "Now be careful, that water's *atsui!*"

She lifted me up, expecting me to dive in, head first, with delight. I felt an electric shock as my toes touched the scalding water. I clung to Masako's kimono, clamped my feet firmly on the edge of the barrel and shrieked for mercy. "Let me out . . . oooout."

Masako was fast losing her temper. "What's the matter with you? Everybody loves to bathe this way."

She leaned over so that I sank into the cauldron, buttocks first. Ignoring my screams, she pried my fingers loose and let me sink to the bottom like a prime lobster. The next second I shot up to the top like a harpooned porpoise. My foot had touched the hot metal fire box.

Masako just stood, shaking her heavy mane of hair and laughing. "You look just like a frog hiding under a lily pad."

Herbs and leaves dangled limply from my dripping hair as I stood on tiptoe to keep the water from pouring into my mouth. I vowed never to take another bath in Japan. All during the rest of my stay at Takayama, I took only sponge baths and studiously avoided the simmering barrel and husky Masako.

Sometime in the heat of June, the hard-working villagers paused for a few days to observe their annual religious festival at a nearby temple called *Kuma No Jin Ja*, the Temple of Bears. At this time of year, the farmers discarded their working garments, boiled themselves in specially scented baths and donned their best clothes to relax, feast and worship at the temple. The priests, gowned in white flowing robes and wearing black, hood-like headdresses, presided at the temple ceremonies. They mumbled, bowed, chanted and burned incense at the altar. After the ritual, many dancers came out to perform ancient dances, accompanied by slender reed flutes and tiny drums.

Uncle Fujio promised to take us to the Bear Temple in the evening. After dinner, a thundershower broke through the oppressive heat, flooding the parched brown earth. Henry and I slipped into elevated rain clogs which kept our feet high and dry. Carrying huge, heavily oiled paper umbrellas over our heads, we clomped awkwardly through the dark, narrow footpaths in the woods. The wet grass flicked raindrops on our mud-spattered bare legs. Uncle Fujio lit a large round paper lantern and held it up high for us, casting a soft, swinging circular glow at our feet. Struggling along on our teetering *getas*, hooking brambles and branches into our clothes, we walked for about a mile in the soft darkness under the towering, rain-dripping trees. Suddenly we came out into an open country road. The thoroughfare was alive with lanterns swaying on the roadside stalls. The vendors were ringing their bells vigorously and calling out to the pedestrians, "This way, folks, only one cent for *kon-yaku*, right off the fire," or "Balloons, get your balloon here for one cent."

Henry and I immediately lost interest in the shrine, but Fujio-san wanted to say his prayers. People washed their hands at a well in front of a small weather-beaten temple, its unpainted timber pillars weather-scarred and pitted. Fujio-san paused at the large wooden offering box and dropped coins through the latticed top. The wooden doors of the temple were rolled back completely, revealing a somber interior eerily lighted by rows of thick, guttering white candles placed before the simple altar. Shaven, dark-eyed priests in white robes, praying on their bended knees, cast weird, giant shadows in the flickering light. I clutched at Henry's shirt sleeve to make sure that I would not be deserted in this ghostly place. Ropes, thick as a giant boa, hung down from the ceiling, and seizing one, Fujio-san pulled on it with his whole weight, again and again. Bells pealed forth, clear and musical, like silver waves breaking into the deep velvet night, undulating farther and farther into the distant country fields. Uncle Fujio took an incense stick, lighted it with the candle, and thrust it into an urn filled with sand. Then, clapping his hands sharply, he called upon the Bear God to hear his prayers.

Henry and I waited impatiently to get back to the vendors.

Smiling, Uncle Fujio let us pull him from stall to stall. We tried *konyaku* — square chunks of gelatin, dipped in sweet *miso*. We ate hot sweet potatoes, cooked over charcoal, which we tossed gingerly in our hands. We used our large kimono sleeves for pockets and stuffed them with hard brown, bullet-shaped candies, rice cookies and cakes. Henry bought a toy monkey that skittered up a stick when he pulled a string, and I picked a multi-colored celluloid pinwheel which whirled merrily in the summer breeze.

On our way back to Takayama, Uncle Fujio saw that my eyes were glued tight and I kept stumbling into the ditch. He swung me up piggy-back so I could sleep. It was comfortable to lean against Fujio-san's broad back as he jogged along, sure-footed, through the forest. Henry walked ahead with the lighted lantern and the paper umbrellas tucked under his arm. Half asleep, I watched the tall silhouettes of the black trees move sedately by in the warm blue summer night. Fireflies winked all around us. With the deep bass croaking of the bullfrogs, hidden in the damp forest carpet, and the soft, delicate chirping of the crickets growing fainter in my numbing ears, I slipped off into a contented dream.

We felt a sudden surge of warmth toward our new-formed friends, and we were reluctant to say good-by, but the time for our return to America approached. Father said, "It's nearly July. It's going to be terrifically hot from now on and we should avoid it at all cost. Children from America often get sick during these months."

As it turned out, we did not leave soon enough. Sun-browned Ken-chan, who had tumbled about so happily in the yard with his tiny playmates, came down with a high fever. He cried with aches and pains. The country doctor came. Looking wise and relaxed as he sipped tea, he said soothingly, "It is a common summer complaint. Probably the boy ate too much of that flavored ice water. Just give him an enema. He'll be all right."

But Kenji was not all right. He paled and weakened. One morning Father and Mother took Kenji away to Uncle Itoi's hospital. I overheard the maid, Masako, say to a neighbor, "They say he has '*ikiri*.' "

I didn't know then that *ikiri* meant the dreaded dysentery almost always fatal in those parts. In a few days Henry came down with the same symptoms and Grandfather sent him away to Uncle Itoi's hospital with Fujio-san.

About a week later, Mother came back to Takayama, thin and tired, to rest. But she worried and she could not stay. She hurried back, taking Sumiko with her. I remained at Takayama, dazed and horrified with the turn of events. I refused to eat. I could not sleep. I kicked the maids. Finally I was sent to Kashi where an aged, white-haired aunt lived alone with her maid, Teruko. Oba-san was a fragile, gentle creature whom I adored, for she treated me as if I were grown-up and an interesting companion. Her tiny, two-story house was filled with the delicate aroma of sweet roasted chestnuts and *kaki-mochi* crackers fried in sweet soy sauce.

At Kashi I experienced my first earthquake. I was sure that the end of the world had come. In the beginning when the dishes in the pantry began to rattle, it sounded as if mice were kicking around inside. I ran, wide-eyed and mute, to Oba-san who sat sewing in the front room.

"There is nothing to worry about, little one. Perhaps we had better step outdoors until it's over."

A low rumbling sound now accompanied the tinkling, jingling noises in the house. Teruko, who had been washing clothes in the back yard, ran into the house and swung me on her back. She and Oba-san clambered down the stone steps out into the road. Other people hurried out of their homes and shops, but there was no sign of panic. Men, women and children, all looked as if it was just routine. We went down by the riverbank, the safest place in case of fire, and stood there quietly watching houses, trees and poles quiver and jiggle. The ground trembled and heaved. Speechless with fright, I watched faces to see just how alarmed I should get, but soon it was over. When we reached our house, Teruko pointed to the stone steps in disgust, "Look what the earthquake did!" The stone steps had cracked straight down the center and the one side had turned over completely. Oba-san carefully picked her way up the stairs.

Not long after the earthquake, Uncle Fujio came to Kashi. He said I was to go back with him to Grandfather's house. Oba-san and Teruko were crying. At first I thought they were unhappy because I was leaving, but then Oba-san took me in her arms and rocked me back and forth, saying, "Poor little one, poor little one. He was such a sweet little boy." I knew one of my brothers had died.

Uncle Fujio and I climbed into the waiting jinrikisha and rode silently back to Takayama. I finally found courage to ask, "Was it Henry or Ken-chan?"

"Ken-chan yo."

I put my face down in Uncle Fujio's lap and wept long, bitter tears for Ken-chan, my little brother who had not wanted to come to Japan.

When Henry had sufficiently recovered the family came back to Grandfather's. Henry and Mother looked exhausted and pale. They sat out on the sunny porch, day after day, absorbing their strength from the warm sun and invigorating country air.

By mid-August, we were on board ship again, sailing for home with bewildered, mixed feelings. Mother was easily moved to tears whenever she thought of Ken-chan. We longed to be back home among the familiar Seattle hills, but we did not want to leave Grandfather behind us. We tried to persuade him to come with us. Henry said, breathless with hope, "There's plenty of room for you, Ojih-chan, in our big hotel. You could share my room. I wish you'd live with me, Ojih-chan!"

Ojih-chan's face, parched and browned from the sun and wind, broke into a thousand wrinkles, and he smiled tenderly. "How I would love to see your fine home in Seattle, and to watch you grow. But when a man gets as old as I, he does not feel like moving from the place where he was born and where he had lived all his life. I long to go with you, but I'm too old now. You understand, don't you?"

We didn't understand, but we nodded our heads for he looked so sad and wistful even when he smiled. Many years later I learned why he could not come with us. In 1924 my country had passed an Immigration Law which kept all Orientals from migrating to America since that year. Those who had come in before that time could stay, but there would be no more new ones. That was why Father had taken us to Japan, so Grandfather could see us and say farewell to his son who had decided to make his home across the sea. The children who had been born in America belonged there and there he and Mother would stay.

On the last lap of our return trip, we passed the narrow straits of Juan de Fuca just at eventide. Every passenger was up on deck. The Pacific glimmered in the familiar golden orange glow of sunset. Suddenly as if a heavy weight had slipped from my chest, I realized we were home again, and my visit to Japan receded into the background like a sad, enchanted dream. We had explored the exotic island of the Japanese. I had felt the charm of its people. I had been impressed by its modern cities as well as by its historic beauty, but I had felt I was an alien among them.

This was home to me, this lovely Puget Sound Harbor stretched out before us. Tomorrow we would wake to the old familiar landmarks of Seattle — Magnolia Bluff, Smith Cove, the slender pinnacle of Smith Tower, and the stretch of Alki Beach. This America, where I was born, surrounded by people of different racial extractions, was still my home.

It was going to be an exciting homecoming, too. I could almost hear Matsuko, Dunks and Jiro asking us questions about Japan as they eagerly examined Henry's toy samurai sword, my silk crepe kimono (a gift from Aunt Itoi of Utsunomiya), purple velvet Japanese stockings, Sumiko's exquisite Japanese doll, the fascinating colorful kaleidoscope tubes, miniature tea sets and fragile silken parasols in lovely pastel colors of apricot and turquoise. I felt that Japan was all this and much more, but how could I explain it to my friends? A few things I could describe, but the rest, I could only feel.

CHAPTER VI

We Are Outcasts

A GRAY gloom settled down over our family. Sumiko was ill. Always during the winter she had asthmatic attacks, but this particular winter was the worst. The little black kitten, Asthma, which Mrs. Matsui had given her because, she said, black cats could cure asthma, mewed all day long and rubbed its back against the bed. Almost every day Dr. Moon climbed the long flight of stairs and walked through the hotel without a glance at our rough-looking hotel guests who stared rudely at him. His large, clean, pink-scrubbed hands were strong and tender as he turned Sumiko over and thumped on her thin shoulder blades. Sumiko, wheezing heavily, submitted to the doctor's examination. Her eyes were black and alert as she tried not to look frightened. Dr. Moon told Father he was concerned about Sumiko's cough and the drop of blood she had spit out. He would send a specialist to see her.

Soon a short, burly man with sandy hair, growing wreathlike on his bald head bustled into the hotel. He was Dr. Stimson, director of the King County Tuberculosis Department. Father stuttered as he thanked him for taking time to come and see Sumiko, but Dr. Stimson waved Father's stumbling words aside, "No trouble, no trouble. It's my job. Well, how's the young lady feeling this morning?"

His bright blue eyes peered intently at Sumiko through thick glasses as he examined her. Dr. Stimson said Sumiko must have an X ray taken of her chest. He gave us a pamphlet describing the North Pines Sanitarium and how it took care of sick children. There were bright appealing photographs of children in sun suits and floppy white hats playing in a beautiful garden. A shuddering chill seized me. Did Sumiko have to go away? She was just six. She would be so unhappy away from all of us.

One morning Mother carefully dressed Sumiko and took her to the city clinic for an X ray. Then we waited for the fatal news with a sense of heavy foreboding. Mother moved about as if she were walking in a dream. As I sat by Sumiko's bedside, sewing dresses for our dolls, Sumiko asked me suddenly, "Do I have to go away?"

"Maybe . . ." I tried to find the right words. "It's not definite yet, Sumiko, but if you do have to, you will go to a wonderful place. It'll be just like going on a real vacation, Sumiko." I tried to be enthusiastic. "There're lots of beautiful trees and flowers and you'll go on walks and picnics with other boys and girls, all dressed in white shorts and sun hats. And you'll eat lots of ice cream, and when you come back you'll be so tanned and husky, we won't recognize you at all."

"Really?" Sumiko's enormous eyes sparkled. "How do you know?"

"I read all about it. You'll just play all day, sleep a lot and eat plenty of good food. Golly, I wouldn't mind going!"

As I talked, I thought I heard a door close but no one was in the parlor. Much later, I learned that it had been Father. He had overheard our conversation about the wonderful sanitarium and had started to laugh, but a sob came out instead. He quickly left and locked himself in the kitchen where he could cry undisturbed.

That evening Dr. Stimson came. We stood, gray-lipped, quietly waiting to hear the verdict. Dr. Stimson's eyes twinkled as he told us that Sumiko did not have tuberculosis. We cried with relief as we hugged Sumiko, swathed in a heavy flannel nightgown and smelling of camphor oil. Like a thin little sparrow burrowed deep in its nest, Sumiko cocked her Dutch-bobbed head at us and spoke carefully so as not to wheeze or cough. "I'm glad I don't have to go on that vacation!"

Dr. Stimson said Sumiko must have plenty of milk, rest and sunshine. So Father and Mother decided to rent a cottage by the sea for the summer. Father said, "Yes, we must do it this summer. We'll start looking right away for a suitable place near Alki Beach."

I leaped into the air and did ten cartwheels in a row. Sumiko, sitting hunched over in Mother's bed, rasped out a gurgling chuckle, but Henry said, "Aw, who cares about Alki. That's sissy stuff."

Henry would be going to the farm in Auburn, as he did every summer, to pick berries. It was customary for Japanese parents to send their sons to rural areas to work on farms where they could harden their muscles and their self-reliance under the vigilant eyes of a Japanese farmer. Henry was proud that he was going off to work to earn his own living, something that girls could never do.

But Sumiko and I dreamed about a little white cottage by the beach, planning in detail how we would spend our days. We would wake with the sun no matter how sleepy we might be, put on our bathing suits and dash out for an early morning dip. We would race back to our cottage, rout Mother and Father out of bed and have a wonderful big breakfast together. We would see Father off to work, help Mother with the house chores and prepare a lunch basket to spend the rest of the day on the beach. Every evening Father would join us at the beach and he would build a roaring bonfire for us. We would watch the evening sun melt the sky into a fiery mass of purple and magenta and wait until the last streak of wine had faded into the blackness behind Vashon Island. Then we would walk slowly back to the cottage, deeply tired and content. A brisk shower to rinse off the sand, the seaweed and salt water, then to bed. And all night we would listen to the muffled rhythmic beat of the ocean waves on the black sands.

Early one day, Mother and I set out to Alki to find a cottage near the beach where we always picnicked. We found a gray house with a FOR RENT sign on its window, just a block from the beach. One side of the house was quilted with wild rambler roses and the sprawling green lawn was trim behind a white-painted picket fence. When I pressed the doorbell, musical chimes rang softly through the house. A middle-aged woman wearing a stiffly starched apron opened the door. "Yes, what can I do for you?" she asked, looking us over.

Mother smiled and said in her halting English, "You have nice house. We like to rent this summer." Mother paused, but the woman said nothing. Mother went on, "How much do you want for month?"

The woman wiped her hands deliberately on her white apron before she spoke, "Well, I'm asking fifty dollars, but I'm afraid you're a little too late. I just promised this place to another party."

"Oh," Mother said, disappointed. "That's too bad. I'm sorry. We like it so much."

I swallowed hard and pointed to the sign on the window. "You still have the sign up. We thought the house was still open."

"I just rented it this morning. I forgot to remove it. Sorry, I can't do anything for you," she said sharply.

Mother smiled at her, "Thank you just the same. Good-by." As we walked away, Mother said comfortingly to me, "Maybe we'll find something even nicer, Ka-chan. We have a lot of looking to do yet."

But we scoured the neighborhood with no success. Every time it was the same story. Either the rent was too much or the house was already taken. We had even inquired at a beautiful new brick apartment facing the beach boulevard, where several VACANCY signs had been propped against empty windows, but the caretaker told us unsmilingly that these apartments were all taken.

That night I went to bed with burning feet. From my darkened bedroom, I heard Mother talking to Father in the living room. "Yes, there were some nice places, but I don't think they wanted to rent to Japanese."

I sat bolt upright. That had not occurred to me. Surely Mother was mistaken. Why would it make any difference? I knew that Father and Mother were not Americans, as we were, because they were not born here, and that there was a law which said they could not become naturalized American citizens because they were Orientals. But being Oriental had never been an urgent problem to us, living in Skidrow.

A few days later, we went to Alki again. This time I carried in my purse a list of houses and apartments for rent which I had cut out from the newspaper. My hands trembled with a nervousness which had nothing to do with the pure excitement of house-hunting. I wished that I had not overheard Mother's remark to Father.

We walked briskly up to a quaint, white Cape Cod house. The door had a shiny brass knocker in the shape of a leaping dolphin. A carefully marcelled, blue-eyed woman, wearing a pince-nez on her sharp nose, hurried out. The woman blinked nervously and tapped her finger on the wall as she listened to Mother's words. She said dryly, "I'm sorry, but we don't want Japs around here," and closed the door. My face stiffened. It was like a sharp, stinging slap. Blunt as it was, I had wanted to hear the truth to wipe out the doubt in my mind. Mother took my hand and led me quickly away, looking straight ahead of her. After a while, she said quietly, "Ka-chan, there are people like that in this world. We have to bear it, just like all the other unpleasant facts of life. This is the first time for you, and I know how deeply it hurts; but when you are older, it won't hurt quite as much. You'll be stronger."

Trying to stop the flow of tears, I swallowed hard and blurted out, "But, Mama, is it so terrible to be a Japanese?"

"Hush, child, you mustn't talk like that." Mother spoke slowly and earnestly. "I want you, Henry, and Sumi-chan to learn to respect yourselves. Not because you're white, black or yellow, but because you're a human being. Never forget that. No matter what anyone may call you, to God you are still his child. Mah, it's getting quite warm. I think we had better stop here and get some refreshment before we go on."

I wiped my eyes and blew my nose hastily before I followed Mother into a small drugstore. There I ordered a towering special de luxe banana split, and promptly felt better.

The rest of the day we plodded doggedly through the list without any luck. They all turned us down politely. On our way home, Mother sat silent, while I brooded in the corner of the seat. All day I had been torn apart between feeling defiant and then apologetic about my Japanese blood. But when I recalled the woman's stinging words, I felt raw angry fire flash through my veins, and I simmered.

We found Sumiko sitting up in bed, waiting for us with an expectant smile. Mother swung her up into the air and said gaily, "We didn't find a thing we liked today. The houses were either too big or too small or too far from the beach, but we'll find our summer home yet! It takes time." I set my teeth and wondered if I would ever learn to be as cheerful as Mother.

Later in the evening, Mr. Kato dropped in. Father told him that we were looking for a cottage out at Alki and that so far we had had no luck. Mr. Kato scratched his head, "Yahhh, it's too bad your wife went to all that trouble. That district has been restricted for years. They've never rented or sold houses to Orientals and I doubt if they ever will."

My face burned with shame. Mother and I had walked from house to house, practically asking to be rebuffed. Our foolish summer dream was over.

Somehow word got around among our friends that we were still looking for a place for the summer. One evening, a Mrs. Saito called on the phone. She lived at the Camden Apartments. She said, "My landlady, Mrs. Olsen, says there is a small apartment in our building for rent. She is a wonderful person and has been kind to us all in the apartments, and we're practically all Japanese. You'd like it here."

Mother said to me afterwards, "See, Ka-chan, I told you, there are all kinds of people. Here is a woman who doesn't object to Orientals."

The Camden Apartments was a modest, clean building in a quiet residential district uptown, quite far from Alki.

Mrs. Marta Olsen, a small, slender, blue-eyed woman took charge of the business end of the apartment while her husband and her three brothers were the maintenance men of the large building. Marta said to Mother in her soft Scandinavian accent, "I'm sorry we don't have a place large enough for the whole family."

The modest apartment on the top fourth floor was just large enough to accommodate Mother and Sumiko in the one bedroom while I occupied the sofa in the living room. Father and Henry, we decided, would stay at the hotel, but join us every evening for dinner. Marta assured us that by winter we would be all together in a larger apartment which would be vacated.

Of course, we were grateful for even this temporary arrangement, especially when we found the Olsens to be such warm, friendly folks. Marta and her husband were a middle-aged childless couple; but they apparently looked upon all the children living in the apartments as their own, for they were constantly surrounded by chattering, bright-eyed youngsters. Marta was always busy baking her wonderful butter cookies for them. It was not too long before Sumiko and I were enjoying them ourselves, and Marta and Mother were exchanging their favorite native recipes.

That summer Sumiko and I pretended we were living in the turret of a castle tower. We made daily swimming trips to Lake Washington, surrounded by cool green trees and beautiful homes. But deep in our hearts we were still attached to Alki Beach. We kept comparing the mud-bottom lake and its mosquitoes to the sparkling salt water of Puget Sound, its clean, hot sands and its fiery sunsets.

Mother was more than content with the apartment. Its windows opened up unlimited vistas of beautiful scenery. Straight across we could see a bridge rise up to meet Beacon Hill where on its crest the soft yellow building of the Marine Hospital stood magnificently alone, its soaring clean lines etched sharply against the sky. On clear days we could see the icy beauty of Mount Rainier loom up in its splendor, and in the evenings we watched the brilliant diamond lights of the Rainier Valley Highway strung across the soft blue velvet of the summer night. All this inspired Mother to stand at the bay window at odd hours of the night in a poetic trance. Once she caught a hauntingly beautiful moonlight scene and a *tanka* materialized in her mind, which she interpreted for us:

> *In the spring-filled night*
> *A delicate mauve*
> *Silken cloud*
> *Veils the moon's brilliance*
> *In its soft chiffon mist.*

The words used in *tanka* were quite different from spoken Japanese. *Tanka* was written in five, seven, five, seven, seven accents in five lines, totaling exactly thirty-one syllables, never more, never less. In reciting the poem, it was sung melodiously in a voice laden with sentiment and trembling emotion to give it proper meaning and effect. The expression *nali keli* was often employed in these poems. Whenever we wanted to tease Mother, we added this expression to every sentence we uttered. We nudged each other whenever we caught Mother standing in front of a bubbling rice pot, lost in thought. "Mama, *gohan kogeri nali keli!* The rice scorcheth."

Mother smiled at our crude humor, but we had to admit that there was something in *tanka,* the way Mother used it. With it, she gathered together all the beauty she saw and heard and felt through that window and pulled it into our little apartment for us to enjoy. Sometimes the night was blotted out with heavy fog and we could see nothing. Then Sumiko and I would sit curled on the davenport, reading and listening to the radio while Mother sat in her armchair, mending or sewing, as she listened to the sounds of a fog-bound city. At the end of the quiet evening she would recite to us the *tanka* which she had created.

> *Kiri no yo no*
> *Hodoro ni fukete*
> *Samu zamu toh*
> *Okibe no fune ka*
> *Fue nali kawasu*

> The fog-bound night
> Ever deepening in somber silence
> Tinged with chilling sadness
> Could those be ships far off at sea
> Echoing and re-echoing their deep foghorns?

On such evenings I felt suddenly old, wondering that I could like such a melancholy poem. It reminded me of the way I had come to feel about my summer experience, half sad and half at peace with the world.

Gradually I learned in many other ways the terrible curse that went with having Japanese blood. As the nations went, so went their people. Japan and the United States were no longer seeing eye to eye, and we felt the repercussions in our daily lives.

International matters took a turn for the worse when Japan's army suddenly thrust into Shanghai. City officials, prominent men and women were interviewed and they all shouted for punishment and a boycott on Japanese goods. People stopped patronizing Japanese shops. The Chinese who were employed by Japanese resigned their jobs, one after another.

I dreaded going through Chinatown. The Chinese shop-keepers, gossiping and sunning themselves in front of their stores, invariably stopped their chatter to give me pointed, icicled glares.

The editorial sections of the newspapers and magazines were plastered with cartoons of hideous-looking Japanese. The Japanese was always caricatured with enormous, moon-shaped spectacles and beady, myopic eyes. A small mustache was perched arrogantly over massive, square buck teeth, and his bow-legged posture suggested a simian character.

When stories about the Japanese Army on the other side of the Pacific appeared in the newspapers, people stared suspiciously at us on the streets. I felt their resentment in a hundred ways — the way a saleswoman in a large department store never saw me waiting at the counter. After ten minutes, I had to walk quietly away as if nothing had happened. A passenger sitting across the aisle in a streetcar would stare at me coldly.

One beautiful Sunday afternoon a carload of us drove out into the country to swim at the Antler's Lodge. But the manager with a wooden face blocked our entrance, "Sorry, we don't want any Japs around here."

We said, "We're not Japs. We're American citizens." But we piled into the car and sped away trying to ignore the bruise on our pride.

Even some of the older Japanese were confused about the Nisei. Whenever a Japanese freighter crept into the harbor to pick up its cargo of scrap metal or petroleum, a group of angry citizens turned out as pickets in protest. Quite often Nisei college students walked up and down the dock with them, wearing sandwich signs, "Halt the oil and stop the Japs!" It shocked the sensibilities of the community elders. They muttered, "Who do these Nisei think they are? Don't they realize they, too, have Japanese blood coursing through their veins?"

About this time the Matsui's son, Dick, became the talk of the folks of the Tochigi-ken prefecture. Dick had studied electrical engineering through the International Correspondence Course and had just accepted an important job with the Goto firm in Japan. The townfolk buzzed with excitement everytime someone decided to pull up stakes and go to Japan.

I remember one heated argument about Dick's decision at Mr. Wakamatsu's café, where Father had taken me for lunch. Mr. Sakaguchi, hotel manager and one-time president of the Seattle Japanese Chamber of Commerce, and Mr. Sawada, a clothing salesman, joined us.

"I say Dick's a smart lad to be going back to Japan!" Mr. Sakaguchi pounded the table so hard all the coffee cups rattled in their saucers. "Where else could Dicku get a real man's job? Certainly not here!" As he stuck out his lower lip, his round bald head made him look like an octopus.

Mr. Sawada shook his head thoughtfully. "I don't know about that, Sakaguchi-kun. It's Dicku's own decision, but if I were his parents, I would advise him to think twice about it. After all, Dicku's an American citizen; his future is here."

I liked Mr. Sawada. He was a man of gentle humor and understanding. His wife had died many years ago, leaving him with three children to rear. All his life, he worked hard as a salesman. He walked many miles every day on his route and he always walked with firm deliberate footsteps as if he were determined not to show his weariness. Mr. Sawada was one of the happiest and proudest men I knew, for one of his fondest dreams was coming true. His brilliant eldest son, George, was studying medicine.

"A future here! Bah! Words, words!" Mr. Sakaguchi exploded. "How many sons of ours with a beautiful bachelor's degree are accepted into American life? Name me one young man who is now working in an American firm on equal terms with his white colleagues. Our Nisei engineers push lawn mowers. Men with degrees in chemistry and physics do research in the fruit stands of the public market. And they all rot away inside."

Mr. Sawada insisted quietly. "That's why I think our young men should go to the Midwest or East. Jobs, all kinds of them, are open to Nisei, I hear. Take Nagai's son, for example. He took a good civil service job as an engineer in Wisconsin."

"Nagai's boy is one in a million. Most of us don't know a soul out there. You can't just go out there without contacts. I'm telling you, Dicku's the smart one. With his training and ability to use both the English and Japanese language, he'll probably be a big shot one of these days in the Orient." Mr. Sakaguchi continued to prod Mr. Sawada, "Now be frank, Sawada-kun, if you had a good job waiting for you right now in Japan, wouldn't you pick up and leave?"

Mr. Sawada replied firmly, "And leave my children? No, I wouldn't. I've lived here too long. My wife is buried here. All my friends are here. I haven't kept in touch with my relatives in Japan so I'd be a stranger, if I were to return now. Life certainly has its peculiar twists, doesn't it?"

"Indeed!" Father agreed. "After the young ones were born, our roots sank deeper here. This is our children's home, and it has become ours."

When Dick had been offered the attractive job, Mrs. Matsui came to tell us about it. She felt as proud as if the Emperor himself had bestowed a personal favor upon her family. When Mother wondered how Dick would like Japan, a country which he had never seen, Mrs. Matsui said, "Dicku feels that it's the place for him. He would work himself right up to the top without having to fight prejudice."

She said Dick had been developing an intense dislike of America over the years, and she traced it to a certain incident which Dick had never been able to forget. At work one summer at the Pike Public Market, a white man selling vegetables at a nearby stall had shouted at him peevishly, "Ah, why don't all of ya Japs go back to where ya belong, and stop cluttering up the joint."

Young and trigger-tempered, Dick had flung back, "Don't call me 'Jap.' I'm an American!"

The man had flung his head back in derisive laughter, and Dick would have torn off his apron and flung himself at him if his friends hadn't held him back.

Mrs. Matsui continued, "Dicku never forgot those words. He said that that was what every white man in this country really thought about us. He refused to go to the university because he said it was just a waste of time and money for a Nisei."

Then Dick had plunged into the correspondence course with fury, determined to be on his own so he would not have to work for a white man. When the agent from Japan approached him, Dick had snatched at the bait.

People of the same mind with Mr. Sakaguchi flatly stated, "What's so terrible about it? It's better for a man to go where he's welcome. You can't waste a man's talent and brains without wrecking his spirit."

On the other hand, young men like Jack Okada, Henry's college friend, were scornful of Dick's decision. "Dick's a fool. He thinks he's going to be kingpin out there with an American education. Those big companies can make use of fellows like him all right, but Dick's going to find himself on a social island. The Japanese hate us Nisei. They despise our crude American manners."

On the day when Dick was to sail for Japan, everyone of the Tochigi-ken prefecture turned out at Smith Cove to give him a send-off. Mother and I represented our family. Confetti and streamers laced the air as hundreds of Japanese milled around on the dock in tight circles, bowing and making their formal farewells. When the ship shuddered, sounding its deep bass horn, we fought our way through the crowd to Dick. Mrs. Matsui was smiling bravely like a samurai mother sending her son off to war. I managed to slide an arm through the crushing wall of bodies and pumped Dick's perspiring hand. He acknowledged my best wishes with an unsmiling face. In the bright sun, his face was drawn and white, making him look young and uncertain, and I wondered if Dick was having a change of heart at the last minute. Another warning horn vibrated through the air. Dick, his arms loaded with gifts and shopping bags full of fruits and packages, fought his way up as the gangplank swung off the dock. It rattled up to the lip of the ship and a sailor walked the deck, vigorously striking a brass cymbal, drowning out all conversation. It was a moment of incomparable confusion and loneliness, the clash of the cymbal mixed with the hurried last-minute farewells and the flowing tears. Another blast of the horn, then from the deck of the ship, the measured strain of "Auld Lang Syne" floated out over our heads. More confetti showered down, colored serpentines snaking swiftly through the air. Everyone was shouting, "*Sayonara* . . . good-by, good-by!"

Mrs. Matsui suddenly burst into tears. Mr. Matsui, standing

erect beside his wife, solemnly waved his straw hat at the small figure of his son on the ship, slipping away in the distance. I wanted to flee from Smith Cove. It was no longer the shining shore where the Issei had eagerly landed many years ago, but the jumping-off place for some of their young, looking to Japan as the land of opportunity. We had all felt as Dick had, one time or another. We had often felt despair and wondered if we must beat our heads against the wall of prejudice all our lives.

In the privacy of our hearts, we had raged, we had cried against the injustices, but in the end, we had swallowed our pride and learned to endure.

Even with all the mental anguish and struggle, an elemental instinct bound us to this soil. Here we were born; here we wanted to live. We had tasted of its freedom and learned of its brave hopes for a democracy. It was too late, much too late for us to turn back.

Paradise Sighted

ON my last day at Central Grammar School, romance burst into my life. During the hubbub of graduation, Haruo, the handsomest boy in the class and the top athlete, jammed a white envelope into my hands with a hurried farewell.

"Here, this is for you, Kazuko. Good luck, and I'll write you from Franklin High."

The envelope contained a snapshot of himself. Although I was so thrilled I could have floated right off into space, I stood staring helplessly at the picture, not knowing what to do with it. I wanted to put it in a beautiful frame and display it on top of the piano at home, but I knew that would bring an avalanche of disapproval upon my head from my parents. I also knew I could not hide it, for no matter where I put it, under the linoleum under my bed, or in Volume XII of the *Encyclopaedia Britannica* in the bookcase, Sumiko, the family explorer, would find it, and triumphantly show it to Mother and Father, who would deal with me from then on. No, I simply could not risk taking the snapshot home.

I took one last adoring look at it. Haruo looked wonderful in his white school sweater. A lock of black hair fell carelessly over his high forehead and he was grinning from ear to ear. Slowly I tore the glossy picture into tiny pieces and let them flutter into the wastebasket.

It was tragic. Father and Mother didn't understand. They said that anyone who thought about boy and girl friends was in danger of softening of the brain and weakening of the character. I remembered the day Mother found a dime-store ring in Henry's shirt which she was about to wash. Bashful and red-eared, Henry, then thirteen, stammered that it was from a girl named Sachiko. Mother looked grave, and she and Father closeted themselves in the parlor with Henry to talk things over. For nearly a week our home was quiet and still, as if a scandal was being muffled to death. Father and Mother were valiantly trying to recover from the shock of Henry's girl friend.

I told my best friend Matsuko about Haruo's picture. She dimpled, and smiled wisely, and opened to a page in her autograph book to let me read what was written on it. "Best wishes to the sweetest girl with the sweetest smile. I'll be seeing you at Broadway High." It was signed George Fujii. Matsuko and I parted at her doorstep with a stronger bond of friendship, hugging each other's secret happily to our hearts.

That evening I sat on the davenport, mooning out of the window. At my elbow, Henry was admiring some pictures which his friend, Kazuo, had drawn. Kazuo, who was older and different from our other friends, came to see Henry often, bringing with him drawings of the latest Japanese war planes and battleship models which he had copied from magazines. They were beautifully executed in water color, for Kazuo had talent. He also had a true, clear tenor voice, which he liked to show off, and he was nice-looking, in a dark-eyed Latin manner. He brushed his heavily oiled black hair to a patent-leather smoothness, and he moved about with the panther grace of a swordsman.

When he was very young, he had been sent to Japan to live with his grandparents. When he returned to the States, he was quite the confident, brusque, Japanese gentleman. He was called Kibei instead of Nisei because, although he was American by birth, he was more Japanese through education. Going on sixteen now, Kazuo could rattle off eloquent platitudes in beautifully correct Japanese to Father and Mother. Somehow he rubbed me the wrong way. He made me seem so sloppy and awkward.

Now Kazuo was saying, "See this airplane carrier. Japan is building some of the biggest in her naval history, because when the next war comes, it's going to be a battle of the air!"

War was all he could talk about, the great wars of the past and the great wars of the future. He talked about war is if it were an exciting chess game. Kazuo's father had been a veteran of the Russo-Japanese war and Kazuo loved to tell us about it. He described in detail how prisoners' legs were strapped to two horses and their bodies split in half when the animals were driven galloping off into opposite directions.

Kazuo talked about the inevitability of war between Japan and America. "Ha ha ha ha haaa! Listen, Kazuko-san, your brother Henry thinks that America will win a war with Japan because she's so big. Did you ever hear of such a naïve thing?"

I looked at him coldly, refusing to speak.

"Japan is so far advanced with her powerful naval fleet and fighter planes, nobody could beat her. Do you know about her one-man suicide torpedo submarines? What American warrior would consider it an honor and privilege to man one of these and go to a blazing death with a *Banzai!*" Kazuo's head trembled knowingly. "Besides, all of Nippon's men are trained to be warriors from the cradle and the proud spirit of *Bushido* is ingrained into them. Do you see anything like that here? Ha ha ha ha haaaa!"

All of a sudden I could stand it no longer. "You sound like a hyena!" I shouted. "I hate your drawings and everything you talk about. I hope we never see you again!"

I ran out of the living room, frightened at my outburst. Kazuo fled, too, and never came back. Henry was shocked and angry.

"That was pretty rotten. You hurt Kazuo's feelings badly, sis. He liked you, too. He confessed to me that he had been coming around more often because of you. I guess he was trying to show off his masculinity."

This surprising revelation only made me feel glad that Kazuo had departed. I knew that a real man was someone like Haruo, who was popular and superb in baseball and football.

Several years later, when we were all grown, we ran into Kazuo again. There were changes in him. He no longer talked about airplane carriers and war. He was too shattered by the fact that no girl wanted to go out with him.

I asked, "What makes you think so, Kazuo? I know lots of girls who would love to have dates."

"Yes, but not with a Kibei."

Kazuo looked sad and vulnerable. I knew Nisei girls turned up their noses at dating a Kibei. A Nisei girl felt insulted if a man sailed grandly through the door in front of her. She was mortified when he slouched in a chair and leaned back grandly to acknowledge introductions. Kazuo did these things, but he meant no harm. In Japan he had been waited on by females.

I noticed, too, that Kazuo's English was heavily accented and sprinkled generously with Japanese words. "Say, you want to hear my pletty new songu? *Totemo suteki yo* . . . and velly romantikku."

I had not noticed this jargon before, probably because in my early years I had thought nothing of churning the two languages together myself.

Kazuo still wore his abundant black hair slicked back. Instead of Kendo leaps, he now diligently practiced the fox trot and the tango. He had also taken to wearing long, pearl-gray trousers (snugly tucked under his armpits), with creases sharp as cleavers. Kazuo threw his head back and vocalized dramatically like an opera singer, "Miii . . . mi mi miiiiii! How you like that . . . nice, loud fool tone, eh?" He still had his head tremor. "One of these days I'm going to New Yoku for real singing lessons. This town is too smollu for me. I'll live like the true ahtist in the big city."

One day Kazuo really left for New York. Whatever I may have thought of him in my younger days, I now felt an unfamiliar stir of compassion for Kazuo. He had been shipped off to Japan in his tender years and then just as suddenly had been switched back to his homeland, which no longer fitted into his pattern of thinking. He had tried to find his bearings, however awkward and blundering. I hoped that in New York there would be people who would not care if Kazuo combed his hair horizontally or vertically, but would find his background colorful and stimulating.

My great romance with Haruo came to an abrupt end. For months I was the silent-suffering heroine, separated from Haruo by the cruel dictates of the public school system which forced him to attend Franklin High, while I went to Broadway High. His letters were delivered to me by a furtive-eyed boy. Then one day he wrote that he was returning to Nihon Gakko in the fall, and was going to be in my class. Matsuko shrieked with delight when I showed her the letter.

The momentous and greatly anticipated day arrived when Matsuko and I seated ourselves in our new classroom at Nihon Gakko. In the two years that we had been going to high school, I had seen Haruo only twice, both times at the annual Japanese school picnic, but we had kept at a discreet distance.

Familiar sun-browned faces straggled through the doorway. At long last, Haruo bounded into the room. He looked handsome as ever, his lively deep-tanned face in striking contrast to his dazzling white shirt. In my enchanted eyes, he seemed to have absorbed the vigor of the summer sun and the freshness of the invigorating wind. He walked boldly up my aisle and slid into the desk next to mine, wearing that same infectious smile I remembered so well.

"Hi, Kazuko. Had a nice summer?"

Supremely happy, I heard myself answering him calmly, "Just fine, and you?"

"Soso. I sweated it out in the country again, but it was fun."

Just then Kishida sensei punched the silver bell several times to bring order to the class and our heavenly conversation came to an end. Sensei punched the bell again for the formal bow. We bowed stiffly, arms held firmly at our sides. Before sitting down, I turned to smile at Haruo, but the smile froze on my face. I felt as if I were on the pinnacle of a mountain, looking down into Haruo's perplexed eyes. I was a good head taller than he. Haruo had not changed his appearance nor his height, but I had grown like Jack's beanstalk. I resumed my seat in a daze, my little world crashing down all around me.

The tragedy gave Matsuko good reason to worry. To her consternation, she, too, was beginning to shoot up like a bamboo tree while her secret heart, George, was expanding sideways.

Haruo and George became lost causes in our lives. While most of our girl friends remained at a dainty five feet with tiny rosebud figures, Matsuko and I watched ourselves grow with helpless dread. It was a catastrophe.

When I became elongated to five feet two, I slept with my feet planted firmly against the footboard to block the growth. At five feet four, I towered over many of the Nisei boys. At five feet five, I was enraged. Someone was responsible for this wild, cancerous growth. God and my parents shared the brunt of my anger.

At five feet six, I capitulated to fate with Oriental stoicism. I decided calmly that if I were going to be an old maid, I might as well be one without quite so much fanfare and commotion.

High school was a startling experience. For eight years at Nihon Gakko, Bailey Gatzert and Central Grammar, I had done only what I was told by my teachers. I opened my mouth only in reply to a question. I became a polished piece of inarticulateness. At high school, the teachers expected us to have opinions of our own and to express them. In classes like civics, history, current events and literature, the entire class hour was devoted to discussion and criticisms. Although I had opinions, I was so overcome with self-consciousness I could not bring myself to speak.

Some people would have explained this as an acute case of adolescence, but I knew it was also because I was Japanese. Almost all the students of Japanese blood sat like rocks during discussion period. Something compellingly Japanese made us feel it was better to seem stupid in a quiet way rather than to make boners out loud. I began to think of the Japanese as the Silent People, and I envied my fellow students who clamored to be heard. What they said was not always profound or even relevant, but they didn't seem worried about it. Only after a long, agonizing struggle was I able to deliver the simplest statement in class without flaming like a red tomato.

When I graduated from high school my future looked bright. Father and Mother had promised to let me go on to the university. Henry had started long ago and he seemed to radiate an impressive aura as a premedical student. Matsuko had won her parents over, too, about going to college, and all summer we talked of nothing else. We poured over the catalogue, planned and made our own wardrobes, and anticipated going to football games and dances with real dates.

Then one evening, Father called me into the living room. "Kazu," he said gravely, "I know how you've set your heart on going to the university this fall. When we talked it over a few months ago I thought it was an excellent idea. I still do, but Mama and I have been thinking things over, and we feel you should attend business school first."

"But why?" I cried in anguish. Business school would mean two years of steady typing, writing things down in hen scratchings so I could convert them back into plain English, and tracking down two cents in an imaginary account book. I would die of boredom. I would be left behind by Matsuko and my classmates, aging and forgotten among office machines.

Father groped for words. "There's something in the air I don't like. Some hotheads have been talking about war between America and Japan for some time now."

A chill went down my spine. I asked in a half whisper, "You don't think there'll be a war?"

"No, I don't think so, but no one can say for sure. The future seems to be clouding up with tension between the two countries. Don't misunderstand me, Kazu. It's not just this which made me change my mind. From a purely practical point of view, I want to see you acquire an office skill of some sort so you can step into a job and be independent, just in case. You may not have to use your training right away, but it will come in handy one of these days. I'm asking you to think it over, for your own sake."

Father quietly closed the discussion, leaving the matter entirely in my hands. I knew what I had to do, but I was sick and tired of making the wise decision against my will. I longed for a rip-roaring fight which would lift the roof right off the house and make the neighbors hang out of their windows.

But the next week I dutifully presented myself at the Washington State Vocational School to apply for secretarial training. Miss Thompson, a tall, efficient counselor with steel-gray bobbed hair, interviewed me with breath-taking frankness. "Now, Miss Itoi, we are accepting six of you Japanese-American girls this year. I don't want you to think that we are discriminating against people of your ancestry, but from our past experiences, we have found it next to impossible to find jobs for you in the business offices downtown. We must ask the Nisei to find their own jobs among their own people. Since your Japanese community is not large, it can absorb just so many stenographers, bookkeepers, and so on. It wouldn't be sensible for us to train too many Nisei girls who are difficult to place, would it? Our school has to maintain its high percentage in job placements for our graduates. I hope you understand our policy."

I did, and I was grateful to Miss Thompson for her straightforward approach. She left no trail of embarrassed excuses, nothing but clean-cut wounds. I knew that the Nisei girls competed fiercely among themselves for white-collar jobs in the Mitsui and Mitsubishi branch firms downtown, local newspaper establishments, Japanese banks, shipping offices and small export and import firms. Opportunities were limited. If a girl did not go to business school, the only other occupation open to her was as a domestic in a home. More fortunate girls went on to college, and so postponed their job hunting for four years.

"When the time comes, I'm sure I can find my own job," I assured Miss Thompson.

"I'm sorry it has to be this way, Miss Itoi, but we must be

realistic. Before we can accept a Nisei into the school, we must ask that you furnish us with a promise of a job after you are graduated. In the meantime, we will check your high-school record. If it's satisfactory and you are able to fulfill the rest of our requirements, we will enroll you."

I thanked her and left hurriedly, for I felt like bursting into tears. At home I sobbed on Mother's shoulder. What employer in his right mind would promise me a job when he did not know whether I could even finish business school successfully. While I sat in my pool of tears, Mother squared her tiny shoulders and went to the phone. Her social ties were numerous. For the next few hours Mother monopolized the phone so completely the telephone operator tried to put a stop to it and said, "Please limit your calls, you are on a party line."

Mother, not understanding that it was the operator, tried to get rid of the rude woman on the line by saying, "Wrong number, you have wrong number. This is Mrs. Itoi . . . Main 8504."

The next morning I found myself sitting primly in the spacious gleaming office of Mitsui and Company. I talked earnestly to Mr. Iguchi, the man who was married to a young woman whose mother was an old, old friend of the family. Mr. Iguchi looked very much the alert young executive, with trim, polished hair, trim mustache and trim dark suit. I felt that I should be talking to him about the purchase of cultured Oriental pearls, instead of trying to wheedle a promise of a job from him.

"Well, my dear young lady, I can promise you only one thing. If there is an opening when you are through with your training, and if your qualifications meet our needs, you will be considered for the job, along with the rest of the applicants."

That was good enough for me and I hoped it would be good enough for Washington State Vocational School. "Would you

. . . could you please put that in writing for me, Mr. Iguchi?"

"Why, certainly, if it will help you. As a matter of fact, I've written dozens of such letters."

Mr. Iguchi composed the letter, signed it with a flourish, and bowed me suavely out of his office. I mailed the precious letter to Miss Thompson. The next few weeks I lived near the mailbox waiting for a reply, one moment praying that I would be accepted, and in the second, hoping that I would be rejected so I wouldn't have to go to business school. The letter finally arrived.

"We are happy to inform you that your application has been approved. . . ."

Father was happy, too. So was Mother, who had been quietly worrying about me. Many of my high-school classmates had been married off soon after graduation. They had learned long ago to cook and sew, knit and crochet pineapple tablecloths and popcorn bedspreads, and they had been swamped with marriage offers by the *baishakunins,* go-between negotiators of marriages. Mother had utterly failed in her efforts to domesticate me, and I hadn't attracted a single nibble.

Once Mrs. Matsui, feeling sorry for Mother, offered to find a nice young man for me. She came calling one afternoon with a picture of a young Japanese sailor who wanted to marry a Nisei girl. Mother did not believe in picture marriages ever since her older sister, Yasuko's marriage had ended in tragedy many years ago. Yasuko had married the man Grandfather had chosen for her, but it had been an unhappy match, and since divorces were unheard of among respectable people, Yasuko had finally drowned herself. So when Mrs. Matsui came forward with her proposal, Mother wanted to refuse her services, but she could not do so very well without offending her old friend deeply. Mother decided to let the matter take its course and called me into the parlor. I had no idea what was being planned, and I thought it odd when Mother handed me a picture of a solemn, round-cheeked boy of about nineteen years. He was in a sailor's uniform, standing on the deck of a Japanese ship. I looked at the young man, then carefully examined the ship, wondering what it was all about. I returned the picture without a word, and waited for Mother to say something, but her face told me nothing. It was Mrs. Matsui's bright, eager eyes which gave it away, and suddenly to my mother's consternation and to mine, a big foolish smile spread over my face and I started to laugh. I could not stop and I was forced to retire upstairs while Mother apologized profusely to Mrs. Matsui. Mother knew I would let Mrs. Matsui know that I was not interested, but she didn't think I'd do it quite so brutally. It was well that I was going to be able to support myself.

The prospect of spending two whole years in business school while Matsuko and my other friends went to college on schedule appalled me. I decided to complete the two-year training in one year. I became an inspired business student. I typed like a demon, and attacked shorthand, the files, the calculating machine, the billing machine, the mimeograph, the account book with ferocious zeal. My one-year plan was successful. I was graduated the following June; but I had made a slip somewhere, for the next fall I found myself enrolled at North Pines Sanitarium instead of the University of Washington.

I was in a state of speechless shock when Father and Mother bundled me into Mr. Kato's car to be driven to North Pines. Our family car had internal trouble of its own and Mr. Kato had kindly offered to deliver this bundle of germs to the proper disposal station. I noticed that he had carefully draped the seats with white bed sheets, and he, who was always nattily dressed, was now sitting behind the wheel in an old faded blue workshirt, stained overalls, and a ragged, moth-eaten sweater. I knew that when he returned home, he would burn these clothes in the furnace and step into a tub of Lysol. He was making a great sacrifice and I appreciated it.

At North Pines I was put into a wheelchair and quickly wheeled away to a building for bed patients. Because I was Japanese, I turned around and solemnly waved "Good-by" to Father and Mother. I knew I should smile to assure them I was going to be brave, but I could not manage it. I waited until 9 o'clock that evening when the lights were turned off on the floor. Then I pulled the blanket over my face and quietly sobbed my heart out.

The next day I was prepared to start dying, but I found it wasn't such a simple matter to fade away into oblivion. Nurses and doctors kept breaking into my trance. From early dawn until lights out, I was confronted with a succession of pans of hot wash water, breakfast, bedpan, thermometer, sponge bath, lunch, bedpan, nap, bedpan, supper, bedpan — which I could not very well ignore.

My three roommates did not share my ideas about dying. There was Hope Loomis, about forty years old, with a genteel delicate face, chiseled fine and sharp. She looked as if she had been preserved intact from Victorian days when femininity was expressed in violet waters, lace handkerchiefs and poor health. Her dark hair was clipped short, parted on the side and smoothed so closely to the head each hair seemed to have been glued down to her scalp. She always wore a wide pink ribbon around this hair cap, tied in a large saucy bow. Two patches of pink glowed wrathfully on her parchment white cheeks.

Hope loved to talk about her T.B. history. She had first opened her baby blue eyes in a sanitarium crib. "Since then my life has been one long journey, from one sanitarium to another. The doctors gave up hope for me long ago, but here I am, still going strong."

I learned from Hope that tuberculosis need not necessarily make a person feel like throwing himself into the sea. It could actually elevate the spirit, put a sparkle of interest in a person's eyes, and provide an inexhaustible topic for conversation.

Wanda was even more startling, from a Japanese point of view. A young divorcée with brilliant agate-blue eyes, full red lips and expressive language to match them, Wanda assumed a belligerent attitude. Her corner of the room was in a perpetual hubbub, with exploding temper and energetic defiance of all hospital regulations. She almost snarled when she told us about herself, "I was hogtied and shanghaied in 'ere. Just because I had a little boy they put me away. I'm healthier than any of these flat-chested old bags who give orders around here." If she could, she would have kicked her way out of the hospital. And Wanda kicked her heels up in the air and did violent hip-reducing bicycle exercises. She was afraid of nothing. I could never let Wanda find out that I had let tuberculosis crush my spirit.

Chris, in the third corner, with her fluff of copper bright hair, laughed easily and her crisp humor took the drabness out of our routine life. I tried to analyze Chris. I couldn't understand how she could be so gay!

Although at first I had shrunk from the idea of being thrown into a room full of strange women, I thanked fate I was not rooming with three Japanese girls who would have had the same sense of futility as I did. We would have died stoically together. Now I was too fascinated by Chris, Hope and Wanda to pine away quietly.

One morning Chris was moved out of the four-bed ward into a two-bed cubicle. A few minutes later the nurse wheeled a chair up to my bed.

"Miss Itoi, would you like to move in with Miss Young?" she asked.

For a moment I lay there stupefied. I had expected Hope or Wanda to be moved in with Chris. Then I told the nurse I would like it very much. Chris beamed at me when I was settled in the new room.

"I hope you don't mind my company, Kazi. The nurse was amazed when I asked for you, but I want companionship, and not the pale vision of Miss Sanitarium or Agate Eyes."

I could only say, "I'm glad," but I felt something significant had happened. Chris had reminded me of my Japanese ancestry, but with a comforting difference. Somehow she made me feel proud of it.

I was determined to be unobtrusive, not to intrude upon Chris's sense of privacy beyond routine conversation, but it was like trying to ignore a roomful of fireworks. I could not remain untouched by her brilliant humor and her irresistible zest for living. I felt as if I were being lured into bright sunlight, inch by inch, from the pit of self-pity into which I had sunk. Every morning Chris burst through my groggy sleep in Japanese with an "*Ohayo gozai masu*" and warned me that the head nurse was on the warpath again.

At the sanitarium, I noticed that I was not quite in step with my companions. These discrepancies came as tiny shocks to me, for I had been so sure of my Americanization. I had always annoyed Father and Mother with my towering pride on this point. I could speak English so much better than they could. I felt no hesitation in wearing blood red nail polish or violent purple lipstick. But here I started to lose my confidence.

One day when we were ambulatory patients, Chris, Elaine (the tall, dark-haired girl who roomed next to us) and I agreed to invite Laura Wilson, a newcomer, to sit at our table in the dining room. Chris brought Laura over and made the introductions.

"Girls, I'd like you to meet Laura. Laura, this is Elaine and Kazi."

I greeted Laura with what I considered was one of my most cordial smiles and said, "How do you do." Laura seated herself at the table and Chris and Elaine plied her with all sorts of questions and exchanged confidences while I sat contentedly by, listening. After dinner when we had returned to our room, Chris startled me by saying, "Kazi, Laura thought you didn't care for her too much. You did seem a bit cold, you know, just sitting and not saying a word to her. Didn't you like her?"

I felt as if Chris had dashed cold water over me. I did like Laura. I had given her my best smile and yet she had taken offense. I assured Chris that I would love having Laura at our table and apologized for having seemed rude. We never talked about it again, but I was too surprised to forget Chris's strange reaction.

Weeks later the explanation dawned upon me. I noticed two new ambulatory patients, Nisei girls. They sat by themselves at the far end of the room as if they were trying to remain inconspicuous. They seemed lonely so I walked up to them and introduced myself.

"Hello, I'm Kazuko Itoi. How does it feel to be walking around now?"

They stared at me a moment as if they were trying to place me. Then they smiled shyly at me.

"I'm Nami."

"And I'm Marie."

I waited. Then Nami said simply. "It's nice, all right." And Marie just smiled. They did not invite me to sit down, but looked expectantly at me as if they were waiting for me to state my business.

With a determined smile, I asked them, "How long have you been in this ice cave?"

Nami replied gravely, "Twenty weeks." Nothing more. I looked at Marie who stammered out, "Five months."

Nami asked me in a tiny voice, "And you?"

"Seven months." It was the snappiest reply I could think of.

I tried another sure-fire topic. "Are you taking pneumo or other treatments?"

"No."

"Yes."

Nami lifted her eyes up at me with great effort. "And you?"

"Nothing."

We had wrung each other dry. Feeling thoroughly foolish and unnecessary, I tried to make a graceful exit. "Well, it was nice meeting you. I'll be seeing you. Good-by."

Then Nami and Marie came to life and literally glowed when they said, " 'By."

The girls had not meant to be unkind even though they had made me feel as if I were a spy at large. Their response was typically Japanese, and that was the way I had behaved with Laura. No wonder Chris and Laura thought I had been deliberately impolite.

From a Japanese point of view, Nami, Marie and I had behaved in the utmost decorum becoming to modest maidens. At home whenever I was introduced to friends, I always bowed low and said, "I meet you for the first time." I did not lunge at the visitor and start cross-examining him. Instead I sat down and never uttered a word unless the guest spoke to me. Then I would answer politely and briefly "yes" or "no." The important thing was to sit quietly and let the other folks talk about what they wanted to talk about, smile agreeably at all times, and keep the guest's teacup brimming full.

Then I noticed that I was too polite. I always tried to let others precede me in entering or leaving a room, and invariably I stood at the tail end of queues. But nobody cared. At first I was baffled with the perpetual rudeness of other people. Chris, Laura, Elaine and the others were so casual about such things. The person who happened to be nearest the doorway went through first. Back home it was a regular battle of will among ourselves to see who could force the other to pass through the door first or to take the most comfortable chair in the room. All this maneuvering came under *reigi* or deportment which everyone was supposed to observe rigidly, if he wanted to be respected. I remembered with a shudder how Mrs. Kato used to incite the streetcar conductor into purple apoplexy by creating a congestion, trying to outbow an equally polite companion to step into the car first. I decided to give up trying to be the most polite person at the sanitarium. When I did change my habits, nobody noticed it, but I felt more comfortable.

During my nine months' stay at the sanitarium, I became so absorbed in people and finding out about myself, that the tragedy of having tuberculosis receded into the background. But the day that Chris and I received the wonderful unexpected news that we were well enough to go home, the old fears rushed back. Chris glowed steadily in one intense light of happiness, but I tossed from one wave of joy to another wave of despair. I was afraid to go home, for I was quite sure that I could never, never be happy in my community. In the first place, I was gigantic. I had gained twenty-five pounds. And my dark past history of tuberculosis was simply unacceptable. Nobody would want me. I wept as I talked to the girls, carried away by the pathos of it all. I expected to be engulfed with the gentle sympathetic murmurs which I used to receive from my friends back home. Instead they shrieked with laughter and jollied me about my girth.

For a second I didn't know whether to cry or be angry, but when I saw them looking at me with warm affection, I suddenly felt comforted. Chris, Laura, Anne, Elaine and my other companions had accepted me into their circle as I was. They did not care that I looked different, said or did a few odd things, because basically we liked each other. For the first time in my life I felt sheer happiness in being myself.

On the day of my discharge, I found another surprise awaiting me. As we drove home, Father did not stop the car at our home in Camden Apartments, but swept by it and sped over the Beacon Hill Bridge past the impressive Marine Hospital and halted in front of a large brown and yellow two-story frame house. This was our new home. Father had moved the family when he had heard about my impending discharge. Henry, Sumiko and Asthma, our now aged black cat, rushed out at me from the front door. I had never known such delirious joy. The family could hardly wait to show me around and they rushed me up to the second floor where my bedroom awaited me, sunny and beautiful with fresh organdy curtains and deep blue rugs to match the bedspread. The house was plain but wonderfully huge with four bedrooms on the top floor, and on the ground floor a comfortable living room and a dining room large enough to hold a banquet.

Still another surprise awaited me. After the initial hubbub had died down, Henry and Minnie finally burst with the wonderful news that they were officially engaged. I congratulated Henry and hugged Minnie. We had been nodding acquaintances with the Yokoyamas for years. They were members of the same Methodist Episcopal Church, but Henry had discovered Minnie for himself at the university where Minnie was studying to be a nurse. She had bloomed into a lovely young woman, radiating buoyancy from the pert tilt of her jet, short-cropped head to her light staccato walk. Henry and Minnie had wanted to be married immediately, but each time they had approached their families with the subject, the parents had leaped to their feet in alarm. The Yokoyamas and the Itois dropped everything, rushed to call each other on the phone, and drove frantically to each other's homes for a full tribal meeting. After much imbibing of tea, shouting on the young people's part, and grave looks from the elders, it was ruled that Henry must wait until he had finished medical school and Minnie, her nurse's training. However, they had worn down enough parental resistance to become formally engaged, and this they considered a partial victory. Henry said to me in mock fierceness, "Half the battle's won. Now that you're home, you can help us talk the folks into the last half." And I nodded eagerly, delighted to take part in such a happy conspiracy.

I felt as if nothing could mar my world now. The family was together at last, healthy and happy. Father had found this marvelous big barn of a house on lovely Beacon Hill from where we could see the early morning mist rising from Lake Washington in the east, a panoramic view of Puget Sound and the city in the west. In such a setting, my future rolled out in front of me, blazing with happiness. Nothing could possibly go wrong now.

CHAPTER VIII

Pearl Harbor Echoes in Seattle

ON a peaceful Sunday morning, December 7, 1941, Henry, Sumi and I were at choir rehearsal singing ourselves hoarse in preparation for the annual Christmas recital of Handel's "Messiah." Suddenly Chuck Mizuno, a young University of Washington student, burst into the chapel, gasping as if he had sprinted all the way up the stairs.

"Listen, everybody!" he shouted. "Japan just bombed Pearl Harbor . . . in Hawaii! It's war!"

The terrible words hit like a blockbuster, paralyzing us. Then we smiled feebly at each other, hoping this was one of Chuck's practical jokes. Miss Hara, our music director, rapped her baton impatiently on the music stand and chided him, "Now Chuck, fun's fun, but we have work to do. Please take your place. You're already half an hour late."

But Chuck strode vehemently back to the door, "I mean it, folks, honest! I just heard the news over my car radio. Reporters are talking a blue streak. Come on down and hear it for yourselves."

With that, Chuck swept out of the room, a swirl of young men following in his wake. Henry was one of them. The rest of us stayed, rooted to our places like a row of marionettes. I felt as if a fist had smashed my pleasant little existence, breaking it into jigsaw puzzle pieces. An old wound opened up again, and I found myself shrinking inwardly from my Japanese blood, the blood of an enemy. I knew instinctively that the fact that I was an American by birthright was not going to help me escape the consequences of this unhappy war.

One girl mumbled over and over again, "It can't be, God, it can't be!" Someone else was saying, "What a spot to be in! Do you think we'll be considered Japanese or Americans?"

A boy replied quietly, "We'll be Japs, same as always. But our parents are enemy aliens now, you know."

A shocked silence followed. Henry came for Sumi and me. "Come on, let's go home," he said.

We ran trembling to our car. Usually Henry was a careful driver, but that morning he bore down savagely on the accelerator. Boiling angry, he shot us up Twelfth Avenue, rammed through the busy Jackson Street intersection, and rocketed up the Beacon Hill bridge. We swung violently around to the left of the Marine Hospital and swooped to the top of the hill. Then Henry slammed on the brakes and we rushed helter-skelter up to the house to get to the radio. Asthma skidded away from under our trampling feet.

Mother was sitting limp in the huge armchair as if she had collapsed there, listening dazedly to the turbulent radio. Her face was frozen still, and the only words she could utter were, "*Komatta neh, komatta neh.* How dreadful, how dreadful."

Henry put his arms around her. She told him she first heard about the attack on Pearl Harbor when one of her friends phoned her and told her to turn on the radio.

We pressed close against the radio, listening stiffly to the staccato outbursts of an excited reporter: "The early morning sky of Honolulu was filled with the furious buzzing of Jap Zero planes for nearly three hours, raining death and destruction on the airfields below. . . . A warship anchored beyond the Harbor was sunk. . . ."

We were switched to the White House. The fierce clack of teletype machines and the babble of voices surging in and out from the background almost drowned out the speaker's terse announcements.

With every fiber of my being I resented this war. I felt as if I were on fire. "Mama, they should never have done it," I cried. "Why did they do it? Why? Why?"

Mother's face turned paper white. "What do you know about it? Right or wrong, the Japanese have been chafing with resentment for years. It was bound to happen, one time or another. You're young, Ka-chan, you know very little about the ways of nations. It's not as simple as you think, but this is hardly the time to be quarreling about it, is it?"

"No, it's too late, too late!" and I let the tears pour down my face.

Father rushed home from the hotel. He was deceptively calm as he joined us in the living room. Father was a born skeptic, and he believed nothing unless he could see, feel and smell it. He regarded all newspapers and radio news with deep suspicion. He shook his head doubtfully, "It must be propaganda. With the way things are going now between America and Japan, we should expect the most fantastic rumors, and this is one of the wildest I've heard yet." But we noticed that he was firmly glued to the radio. It seemed as if the regular Sunday programs, sounding off relentlessly hour after hour on schedule, were trying to blunt the catastrophe of the morning.

The telephone pealed nervously all day as people searched for comfort from each other. Chris called, and I told her how miserable and confused I felt about the war. Understanding as always, Chris said, "You know how I feel about you and your family, Kaz. Don't, for heaven's sake, feel the war is going to make any difference in our relationship. It's not your fault, nor mine! I wish to God it could have been prevented." Minnie called off her Sunday date with Henry. Her family was upset and they thought she should stay close to home instead of wandering downtown.

Late that night Father got a shortwave broadcast from Japan. Static sputtered, then we caught a faint voice, speaking rapidly in Japanese. Father sat unmoving as a rock, his head cocked. The man was talking about the war between Japan and America. Father bit his lips and Mother whispered to him anxiously, "It's true then, isn't it, Papa? It's true?"

Father was muttering to himself, "So they really did it!" Now having heard the news in their native tongue, the war had become a reality to Father and Mother.

"I suppose from now on, we'll hear about nothing but the humiliating defeats of Japan in the papers here," Mother said, resignedly.

Henry and I glared indignantly at Mother, then Henry shrugged his shoulders and decided to say nothing. Discussion of politics, especially Japan versus America, had become taboo in our family for it sent tempers skyrocketing. Henry and I used to criticize Japan's aggressions in China and Manchuria while Father and Mother condemned Great Britain and America's superior attitude toward Asiatics and their interference with Japan's economic growth. During these arguments, we had eyed each other like strangers, parents against children. They left us with a hollow feeling at the pit of the stomach.

Just then the shrill peel of the telephone cut off the possibility of a family argument. When I answered, a young girl's voice fluttered through breathily, "Hello, this is Taeko Tanabe. Is my mother there?"

"No, she isn't, Taeko."

"Thank you," and Taeko hung up before I could say another word. Her voice sounded strange. Mrs. Tanabe was one of Mother's poet friends. Taeko called three more times, and each time before I could ask her if anything was wrong, she quickly hung up. The next day we learned that Taeko was trying desperately to locate her mother because FBI agents had swept into their home and arrested Mr. Tanabe, a newspaper editor. The FBI had permitted Taeko to try to locate her mother before they took Mr. Tanabe away while they searched the house for contraband and subversive material, but she was not to let anyone else know what was happening.

Next morning the newspapers fairly exploded in our faces with stories about the Japanese raids on the chain of Pacific islands. We were shocked to read Attorney General Biddle's announcement that 736 Japanese had been picked up in the United States and Hawaii. Then Mrs. Tanabe called Mother about her husband's arrest, and she said at least a hundred others had been taken from our community. Messrs. Okayama, Higashi, Sughira, Mori, Okada — we knew them all.

"But why were they arrested, Papa? They weren't spies, were they?"

Father replied almost curtly, "Of course not! They were probably taken for questioning."

The pressure of war moved in on our little community. The Chinese consul announced that all the Chinese would carry identification cards and wear "China" badges to distinguish them from the Japanese. Then I really felt left standing out in the cold. The government ordered the bank funds of all Japanese nationals frozen. Father could no longer handle financial transactions through his bank accounts, but Henry, fortunately, was of legal age so that business could be negotiated in his name.

In the afternoon President Roosevelt's formal declaration of war against Japan was broadcast throughout the nation. In grave, measured words, he described the attack on Pearl Harbor as shameful, infamous. I writhed involuntarily. I could no more have escaped the stab of self-consciousness than I could have changed my Oriental features.

Monday night a complete blackout was ordered against a possible Japanese air raid on the Puget Sound area. Mother assembled black cloths to cover the windows and set up candles in every room. All radio stations were silenced from seven in the evening till morning, but we gathered around the dead radio anyway, out of sheer habit. We whiled away the evening reading instructions in the newspapers on how to put out incendiary bombs and learning about the best hiding places during bombardments. When the city pulled its switches at blackout hour and plunged us into an ominous dark silence, we went to bed shivering and wondering what tomorrow would bring. All of a sudden there was a wild screech of brakes, followed by the resounding crash of metal slamming into metal. We rushed out on the balcony. In the street below we saw dim shapes of cars piled grotesquely on top of each other, their soft blue headlights staring helplessly up into the sky. Angry men's voices floated up to the house. The men were wearing uniforms and their metal buttons gleamed in the blue lights. Apparently two police cars had collided in the blackout.

Clutching at our bathrobes we lingered there. The damp winter night hung heavy and inert like a wet black veil, and at the bottom of Beacon Hill, we could barely make out the undulating length of Rainier Valley, lying quietly in the somber, brooding silence like a hunted python. A few pinpoints of light pricked the darkness here and there like winking bits of diamonds, betraying the uneasy vigil of a tense city.

It made me positively hivey the way the FBI agents continued their raids into Japanese homes and business places and marched the Issei men away into the old red brick immigration building, systematically and efficiently, as if they were stocking a cellarful of choice bottles of wine. At first we noted that the men arrested were those who had been prominent in community affairs, like Mr. Kato, many times president of the Seattle Japanese Chamber of Commerce, and Mr. Ohashi, the principal of our Japanese language school, or individuals whose business was directly connected with firms in Japan; but as time went on, it became less and less apparent why the others were included in these raids.

We wondered when Father's time would come. We expected momentarily to hear strange footsteps on the porch and the sudden demanding ring of the front doorbell. Our ears became attuned like the sensitive antennas of moths, translating every soft swish of passing cars into the arrival of the FBI squad.

Once when our doorbell rang after curfew hour, I completely lost my Oriental stoicism which I had believed would serve me well under the most trying circumstances. No friend of ours paid visits at night anymore, and I was sure that Father's hour had come. As if hypnotized, I walked woodenly to the door. A mass of black figures stood before me, filling the doorway. I let out a magnificent shriek. Then pandemonium broke loose. The solid rank fell apart into a dozen separate figures which stumbled and leaped pell-mell away from the porch. Watching the mad scramble, I thought I had routed the FBI agents with my cry of distress. Father, Mother, Henry and Sumi rushed out to support my wilting body. When Henry snapped on the porch light, one lone figure crept out from behind the front hedge. It was a newsboy who, standing at a safe distance, called in a quavering voice, "I . . . I came to collect for . . . for the *Times*."

Shaking with laughter, Henry paid him and gave him an extra large tip for the terrible fright he and his bodyguards had suffered at the hands of the Japanese. As he hurried down the walk, boys of all shapes and sizes crawled out from behind trees and bushes and scurried after him.

We heard all kinds of stories about the FBI, most of them from Mr. Yorita, the grocer, who now took twice as long to make his deliveries. The war seemed to have brought out his personality. At least he talked more, and he glowed, in a sinister way. Before the war Mr. Yorita had been uncommunicative. He used to stagger silently through the back door with a huge sack of rice over his shoulders, dump it on the kitchen floor and silently flow out of the door as if he were bored and disgusted with food and the people who ate it. But now Mr. Yorita swaggered in, sent a gallon jug of soy sauce spinning into a corner, and launched into a comprehensive report of the latest rumors he had picked up on his route, all in chronological order. Mr. Yorita looked like an Oriental Dracula, with his triangular eyes and yelllow-fanged teeth. He had a mournfully long sallow face and in his excitement his gold-rimmed glasses constantly slipped to the tip of his long nose. He would describe in detail how some man had been awakened in the dead of night, swiftly handcuffed, and dragged from out of his bed by a squad of brutal, tight-lipped men. Mr. Yorita bared his teeth menacingly in his most dramatic moments and we shrank from him instinctively. As he backed out of the kitchen door, he would shake his bony finger at us with a warning of dire things to come. When Mother said, "Yorita-san, you must worry about getting a call from the FBI, too," Mr. Yorita laughed modestly, pushing his glasses back up into place. "They wouldn't be interested in anyone as insignificant as myself!" he assured her.

But he was wrong. The following week a new delivery boy appeared at the back door with an airy explanation, "Yep, they got the old man, too, and don't ask me why! The way I see it, it's subversive to sell soy sauce now."

The Matsuis were visited, too. Shortly after Dick had gone to Japan, Mr. Matsui had died and Mrs. Matsui had sold her house. Now she and her daughter and youngest son lived in the back of their little dry goods store on Jackson Street. One day when Mrs. Matsui was busy with the family laundry, three men entered the shop, nearly ripping off the tiny bell hanging over the door. She hurried out, wiping sudsy, reddened hands on her apron. At best Mrs. Matsui's English was rudimentary, and when she became excited, it deteriorated into Japanese. She hovered on her toes, delighted to see new customers in her humble shop. "Yes, yes, something you want?"

"Where's Mr. Matsui?" a steely-eyed man snapped at her.

Startled, Mrs. Matsui jerked her thumb toward the rear of the store and said, "He not home."

"What? Oh, in there, eh? Come on!" The men tore the faded print curtain aside and rushed into the back room. "Don't see him. Must be hiding."

They jerked open bedroom doors, leaped into the tiny bathroom, flung windows open and peered down into the alley. Tiny birdlike Mrs. Matsui rushed around after them. "No, no! Whatsamalla, whatsamalla!"

"Where's your husband! Where is he?" one man demanded angrily, flinging clothes out of the closet.

"Why you mix 'em all up? He not home, not home." She clawed at the back of the burly men like an angry little sparrow, trying to stop the holocaust in her little home. One man brought his face down close to hers, shouting slowly and clearly, "WHERE IS YOUR HUSBAND? YOU SAID HE WAS IN HERE A MINUTE AGO!"

"Yes, yes, not here. *Mah, wakara nai hito da neh*. Such stupid men."

Mrs. Matsui dove under a table, dragged out a huge album and pointed at a large photograph. She jabbed her gnarled finger up toward the ceiling, saying, "Heben! Heben!"

The men gathered around and looked at a picture of Mr. Matsui's funeral. Mrs. Matsui and her two children were standing by a coffin, their eyes cast down, surrounded by all their friends, all of whom were looking down. The three men's lips formed an "Oh." One of them said, "We're sorry to have disturbed you. Thank you, Mrs. Matsui, and good-by." They departed quickly and quietly.

Having passed through this baptism, Mrs. Matsui became an expert on the FBI, and she stood by us, rallying and coaching us on how to deal with them. She said to Mother, "You must destroy everything and anything Japanese which may incriminate your husband. It doesn't matter what it is, if it's printed or made in Japan, destroy it because the FBI always carries off those items for evidence."

In fact all the women whose husbands had been spirited away said the same thing. Gradually we became uncomfortable with our Japanese books, magazines, wall scrolls and knickknacks. When Father's hotel friends, Messrs. Sakaguchi, Horiuchi, Nishibue and a few others vanished, and their wives called Mother weeping and warning her again about having too many

Japanese objects around the house, we finally decided to get rid of some of ours. We knew it was impossible to destroy everything. The FBI would certainly think it strange if they found us sitting in a bare house, totally purged of things Japanese. But it was as if we could no longer stand the tension of waiting, and we just had to do something against the black day. We worked all night, feverishly combing through bookshelves, closets, drawers, and furtively creeping down to the basement furnace for the burning. I gathered together my well-worn Japanese language schoolbooks which I had been saving over a period of ten years with the thought that they might come in handy when I wanted to teach Japanese to my own children. I threw them into the fire and watched them flame and shrivel into black ashes. But when I came face to face with my Japanese doll which Grandmother Nagashima had sent me from Japan, I rebelled. It was a gorgeously costumed Miyazukai figure, typical of the lady in waiting who lived in the royal palace during the feudal era. The doll was gowned in an elegant purple silk kimono with the long, sweeping hemline of its period and sashed with rich-embroidered gold and silver brocade. With its black, shining coiffed head bent a little to one side, its delicate pink-tipped ivory hand holding a red lacquer message box, the doll had an appealing, almost human charm. I decided to ask Chris if she would keep it for me. Chris loved and appreciated beauty in every form and shape, and I knew that in her hands, the doll would be safe and enjoyed.

Henry pulled down from his bedroom wall the toy samurai sword he had brought from Japan and tossed it into the flames. Sumi's contributions to the furnace were books of fairy tales and magazines sent to her by her young cousins in Japan. We sorted out Japanese classic and popular music from a stack of records, shattered them over our knees and fed the pieces to the furnace.

Father piled up his translated Japanese volumes of philosophy and religion and carted them reluctantly to the basement. Mother had the most to eliminate, with her scrapbooks of poems cut out from newspapers and magazines, and her private collection of old Japanese classic literature.

It was past midnight when we finally climbed upstairs to bed. Wearily we closed our eyes, filled with an indescribable sense of guilt for having destroyed the things we loved. This night of ravage was to haunt us for years. As I lay struggling to fall asleep, I realized that we hadn't freed ourselves at all from fear. We still lay stiff in our beds, waiting.

Mrs. Matsui kept assuring us that the FBI would get around to us yet. It was just a matter of time and the least Mother could do for Father was to pack a suitcase for him. She said that the men captured who hadn't been prepared had grown long beards, lived and slept in the same clothes for days before they were permitted visits from their families. So Mother dutifully packed a suitcase for Father with toilet articles, warm flannel pajamas, and extra clothes, and placed it in the front hall by the door. It was a personal affront, the way it stood there so frank and unabashedly. Henry and I said that it was practically a confession that Papa was a spy, "So please help yourself to him, Mr. FBI, and God speed you."

Mother was equally loud and firm, "No, don't anyone move it! No one thought that Mr. Kato or the others would be taken, but they're gone now. Why should we think Papa's going to be an exception."

Henry threw his hands up in the air and muttered about the odd ways of the Japanese.

Every day Mrs. Matsui called Mother to check Father in; then we caught the habit and started calling him at the hotel every hour on the hour until he finally exploded, "Stop this nonsense! I don't know which is more nerve-wracking, being watched by the FBI or by my family!"

When Father returned home from work, a solicitous family eased him into his favorite armchair, arranged pillows behind his back, and brought the evening paper and slippers to him. Mother cooked Father's favorite dishes frenziedly, night after night. It all made Father very uneasy.

We had a family conference to discuss the possibility of Father and Mother's internment. Henry was in graduate school and I was beginning my second year at the university. We agreed to drop out should they be taken and we would manage the hotel during our parents' absence. Every week end Henry and I accompanied Father to the hotel and learned how to keep the hotel books, how to open the office safe, and what kind of linen, paper towels, and soap to order.

Then a new menace appeared on the scene. Cries began to sound up and down the coast that everyone of Japanese ancestry should be taken into custody. For years the professional guardians of the Golden West had wanted to rid their land of the Yellow Peril, and the war provided an opportunity for them to push their program through. As the chain of Pacific islands fell to the Japanese, patriots shrieked for protection from us. A Californian sounded the alarm: "The Japanese are dangerous and they must leave. Remember the destruction and the sabotage perpetrated at Pearl Harbor. Notice how they have infiltrated into the harbor towns and taken our best land."

He and his kind refused to be comforted by Edgar Hoover's special report to the War Department stating that there had not been a single case of sabotage committed by a Japanese living in Hawaii or on the Mainland during the Pearl Harbor attack or after. I began to feel acutely uncomfortable for living on Beacon Hill. The Marine Hospital rose tall and handsome on our hill, and if I stood on the west shoulder of the Hill, I could not help but get an easily photographed view of the Puget Sound Harbor with its ships snuggled against the docks. And Boeing airfield, a few miles south of us, which had never bothered me before, suddenly seemed to have moved right up into my back yard, daring me to take just one spying glance at it.

In February, Executive Order No. 9066 came out, authorizing the War Department to remove the Japanese from such military areas as it saw fit, aliens and citizens alike. Even if a person had a fraction of Japanese blood in him, he must leave on demand.

A pall of gloom settled upon our home. We couldn't believe that the government meant that the Japanese-Americans must go, too. We had heard the clamoring of superpatriots who insisted loudly, "Throw the whole kaboodle out. A Jap's a Jap, no matter how you slice him. You can't make an American out of little Jap Junior just by handing him an American birth certificate." But we had dismissed these remarks as just hot blasts of air from an overheated patriot. We were quite sure that our rights as American citizens would not be violated, and we would not be marched out of our homes on the same basis as enemy aliens.

In anger, Henry and I read and reread the Executive Order. Henry crumpled the newspaper in his hand and threw it against the wall. "Doesn't my citizenship mean a single blessed thing to anyone? Why doesn't somebody make up my mind for me. First they want me in the army. Now they're going to slap an alien 4–C on me because of my ancestry. What the hell!"

Once more I felt like a despised, pathetic two-headed freak, a Japanese and an American, neither of which seemed to be doing me any good. The Nisei leaders in the community rose above their personal feelings and stated that they would co-operate and comply with the decision of the government as their sacrifice in keeping with the country's war effort, thus proving themselves loyal American citizens. I was too jealous of my recently acquired voting privilege to be gracious about giving in, and I felt most unco-operative. I noticed wryly that the feelings about the Japanese on the Hawaiian Islands were quite different from those on the West Coast. In Hawaii, a strategic military outpost, the Japanese were regarded as essential to the economy of the island and powerful economic forces fought against their removal. General Delos Emmons, in command of Hawaii at the time, lent his authoritative voice to calm the fears of the people on the island and to prevent chaos and upheaval. General Emmons established martial law, but he did not consider evacuation essential for the security of the island.

On the West Coast, General J. L. DeWitt of the Western Defense Command did not think martial law necessary, but he favored mass evacuation of the Japanese and Nisei. We suspected that pressures from economic and political interests who would profit from such a wholesale evacuation influenced this decision.

Events moved rapidly. General DeWitt marked off Western Washington, Oregon, and all of California, and the southern half of Arizona as Military Area No. 1, hallowed ground from which we must remove ourselves as rapidly as possible. Unfortunately we could not simply vanish into thin air, and we had no place to go. We had no relatives in the east we could move in on. All our relatives were sitting with us in the forbidden area, themselves wondering where to go. The neighboring states in the line of exit for the Japanese protested violently at the prospect of any mass invasion. They said, very sensibly, that if the Coast didn't want the Japanese hanging around, they didn't either.

A few hardy families in the community liquidated their property, tied suitcases all around their cars, and sallied eastward. They were greeted by signs in front of store windows, "Open season for Japs!" and "We kill rats and Japs here." On state lines, highway troopers swarmed around the objectionable migrants and turned them back under governor's orders.

General DeWitt must have finally realized that if he insisted on voluntary mass evacuation, hundreds and thousands of us would have wandered back and forth, clogging the highways and pitching tents along the roadside, eating and sleeping in colossal disorder. He suddenly called a halt to voluntary movement, although most of the Japanese were not budging an inch. He issued a new order, stating that no Japanese could leave the city, under penalty of arrest. The command had hatched another plan, a better one. The army would move us out as only the army could do it, and march us in neat, orderly fashion into assembly centers. We would stay in these centers only until permanent camps were set up inland to isolate us.

The orders were simple:

Dispose of your homes and property. Wind up your business. Register the family. One seabag of bedding, two suitcases of clothing allowed per person. People in District #1 must report at 8th and Lane Street, 8 p.m. on April 28.

I wanted no part of this new order. I had read in the papers that the Japanese from the state of Washington would be taken to a camp in Puyallup, on the state fairgrounds. The article apologetically assured the public that the camp would be temporary and that the Japanese would be removed from the fairgrounds and parking lots in time for the opening of the annual State Fair. It neglected to say where we might be at the time when those fine breeds of Holstein cattle and Yorkshire hogs would be proudly wearing their blue satin ribbons.

We were advised to pack warm, durable clothes. In my mind, I saw our permanent camp sprawled out somewhere deep in a snow-bound forest, an American Siberia. I saw myself plunging chest deep in the snow, hunting for small game to keep us alive. I decided that one of my suitcases was going to hold nothing but vitamins from A to Z. I thought of sewing fur-lined hoods and parkas for the family. I was certain this was going to be a case of sheer animal survival.

One evening Father told us that he would lose the management of the hotel unless he could find someone to operate it for the duration, someone intelligent and efficient enough to impress Bentley Agent and Company. Father said, "Sam, Poe, Peter, they all promised to stay on their jobs, but none of them can read or write well enough to manage the business. I've got to find a responsible party with experience in hotel management, but where?"

Sumi asked, "What happens if we can't find anyone?"

"I lose my business and my livelihood. I'll be saying good-by to a lifetime of labor and all the hopes and plans I had for the family."

We sagged. Father looked at us thoughtfully, "I've never talked much about the hotel business to you children, mainly because so much of it has been an uphill climb of work and waiting for better times. Only recently I was able to clear up the loans I took out years ago to expand the business. I was sure that in the next five or ten years I would be getting returns on my long-range investments, and I would have been able to do a lot of things eventually. . . . Send you through medical school," Father nodded to Henry, "and let Kazu and Sumi study anything they liked." Father laughed a bit self-consciously as he looked at Mother, "And when all the children had gone off on their own, I had planned to take Mama on her first real vacation, to Europe as well as Japan."

We listened to Father wide-eyed and wistful. It had been a wonderful, wonderful dream.

Mother suddenly hit upon a brilliant idea. She said maybe the Olsens, our old friends who had once managed the Camden Apartments might be willing to run a hotel. The Olsens had sold the apartment and moved to Aberdeen. Mother thought that perhaps Marta's oldest brother, the bachelor of the family, might be available. If he refused, perhaps Marta and her husband might consider the offer. We rushed excitedly to the telephone to make a long-distance call to the Olsens. After four wrong Olsens, we finally reached Marta.

"Marta? Is this Marta?"

"Yes, this is Marta."

I nearly dove into the mouthpiece, I was so glad to hear her voice. Marta remembered us well and we exchanged news about our families. Marta and her husband had bought a small chicken farm and were doing well. Marta said, "I come from the farm ven I vas young and I like it fine. I feel more like home here. How's everybody over there?"

I told her that we and all the rest of the Japanese were leaving Seattle soon under government order on account of the war. Marta gasped, "Everybody? You mean the Saitos, the Fujinos, Watanabes, and all the rest who were living at the Camden Apartments, too?"

"Yes, they and everyone else on the West Coast."

Bewildered, Marta asked where we were going, what we were going to do, would we ever return to Seattle, and what about

Father's hotel. I told her about our business situation and that Father needed a hotel manager for the duration. Would she or any of her brothers be willing to accept such a job? There was a silence at the other end of the line and I said hastily, "This is a very sudden call, Marta. I'm sorry I had to surprise you like this, but we felt this was an emergency and . . ."

Marta was full of regrets. "Oh, I vish we could do someting to help you folks, but my husband and I can't leave the farm at all. We don't have anyone here to help. We do all the work ourselves. Magnus went to Alaska last year. He has a goot job up there, some kind of war work. My other two brothers have business in town and they have children so they can't help you much."

My heart sank like a broken elevator. When I said, "Oh . . ." I felt the family sitting behind me sink into a gloomy silence. Our last hope was gone. We finally said good-by, Marta distressed at not being able to help, and I apologizing for trying to hoist our problem on them.

The next week end Marta and Karl paid us a surprise visit. We had not seen them for nearly two years. Marta explained shyly, "It was such a nice day and we don't go novair for a long time, so I tole Karl, 'Let's take a bus into Seattle and visit the Itois.'"

We spent a delightful Sunday afternoon talking about old times. Mother served our guests her best green tea and, as we relaxed, the irritating presence of war vanished. When it was time for them to return home, Marta's sparkling blue eyes suddenly filled, "Karl and I, we feel so bad about the whole ting, the war and everyting, we joost had to come out to see you and say 'good-by.' God bless you. Maybe we vill see you again back home here. Anyvay, we pray for it."

Marta and Karl's warmth and sincerity restored a sense of peace into our home, an atmosphere which had disappeared ever since

Pearl Harbor. They served to remind us that in spite of the bitterness war had brought into our lives, we were still bound to our home town. Bit by bit, I remembered our happy past, the fun we had growing up along the colorful brash waterfront, swimming through the white-laced waves of Puget Sound, and lolling luxuriously on the tender green carpet of grass around Lake Washington from where we could see the slick, blue-frosted shoulders of Mount Rainier. There was too much beauty surrounding us. Above all, we must keep friends like Marta and Karl, Christine, Sam, Peter and Joe, all sterling products of many years of associations. We could never turn our faces away and remain aloof forever from Seattle.

CHAPTER IX
Life in Camp Harmony

GENERAL DeWitt kept reminding us that E day, evacuation day, was drawing near. "E day will be announced in the very near future. If you have not wound up your affairs by now, it will soon be too late."

Father negotiated with Bentley Agent and Company to hire someone to manage his business. Years ago Father had signed a long-term lease with the owner of the building and the agent had no other alternative than to let Father keep control of his business until his time ran out. He was one of the fortunate few who would keep their businesses intact for the duration.

And Mother collected crates and cartons. She stayed up night after night, sorting, and re-sorting a lifetime's accumulation of garments, toys and household goods. Those were pleasant evenings when we rummaged around in old trunks and suitcases, reminiscing about the good old days, and almost forgetting why we were knee-deep in them.

The general started issuing orders fast and furiously. "Everyone must be inoculated against typhoid and carry a card bearing the physician's signature as proof."

Like magic we all appeared at the old Japanese Chamber of Commerce building on Jackson Street and formed a long, silent queue inside the dark corridor, waiting to pass into the doctor's crowded office. The doctor's pretty young wife, pale and tired, helped her husband puncture the long line of bare brown arms.

On the twenty-first of April, a Tuesday, the general gave us the shattering news. "All the Seattle Japanese will be moved to Puyallup by May 1. Everyone must be registered Saturday and Sunday between 8 A.M. and 5 P.M. They will leave next week in three groups, on Tuesday, Thursday and Friday."

Up to that moment, we had hoped against hope that something or someone would intervene for us. Now there was no time for moaning. A thousand and one details must be attended to in this one week of grace. Those seven days sputtered out like matches struck in the wind, as we rushed wildly about. Mother distributed sheets, pillowcases and blankets, which we stuffed into seabags. Into the two suitcases, we packed heavy winter overcoats, plenty of sweaters, woolen slacks and skirts, flannel pajamas and scarves. Personal toilet articles, one tin plate, tin cup and silverware completed our luggage. The one seabag and two suitcases apiece were going to be the backbone of our future home, and we planned it carefully.

Henry went to the Control Station to register the family. He came home with twenty tags, all numbered "10710," tags to be attached to each piece of baggage, and one to hang from our coat lapels. From then on, we were known as Family #10710.

On our last Sunday, Father and Henry moved all our furniture and household goods down to the hotel and stored them in one room. We could have put away our belongings in the government storage place or in the basement of our church, which was going to be boarded up for the duration, but we felt that our property would be safer under the watchful eyes of Sam, Peter and Joe.

Monday evenings we received friends in our empty house where our voices echoed loudly and footsteps clattered woodenly on the bare floor. We sat on crates, drank bottles of coke and talked gayly about our future pioneer life. Henry and Minnie held hands all evening in the corner of the living room. Minnie lived on the outskirts of the Japanese community and her district was to leave in the third and last group.

That night we rolled ourselves into army blankets like jelly rolls and slept on the bare floor. The next morning Henry rudely shouted us back into consciousness. "Six-thirty! Everybody wake up, today's the day!"

I screamed, "Must you sound so cheerful about it?"

"What do you expect me to do, bawl?"

On this sour note, we got up stiffly from the floor, and exercised violently to start circulation in our paralyzed backs and limbs. We jammed our blankets into the long narrow seabag, and we carefully tied the white pasteboard tag, 10710, on our coat lapels. When I went into the bathroom and looked into the mirror, tears suddenly welled in my eyes. I was crying, not because it was the last time I would be standing in a modern bathroom, but because I looked like a cross between a Japanese and a fuzzy bear. My hideous new permanent wave had been given to me by an operator who had never worked on Oriental hair before. My hair resembled scorched mattress filling, and after I had attacked it savagely with comb and brush, I looked like a frightened mushroom. On this morning of mornings when I was depending on a respectable hairdo so I could leave town with dignity, I was faced with this horror. There was nothing to do but cover it with a scarf.

Downstairs we stood around the kitchen stove where Mother served us a quick breakfast of coffee in our tin cups, sweet rolls and boiled eggs which rolled noisily on our tin plates. Henry was delighted with the simplicity of it all. "Boy, this is going to be living, no more company manners and dainty napkins. We can eat with our bare hands. Probably taste better, too."

Mother fixed a stern eye on Henry, "Not as long as I'm around."

The front doorbell rang. It was Dunks Oshima, who had offered to take us down to Eighth and Lane in a borrowed pickup truck. Hurriedly the menfolk loaded the truck with the last few boxes of household goods which Dunks was going to take down to the hotel. He held up a gallon can of soy sauce, puzzled, "Where does this go, to the hotel, too?"

Nobody seemed to know where it had come from or where it was going, until Mother finally spoke up guiltily, "Er, it's going with me. I didn't think we'd have shoyu where we're going."

Henry looked as if he were going to explode. "But Mama, you're not supposed to have more than one seabag and two suitcases. And of all things, you want to take with you — shoyu!"

I felt mortified. "Mama, people will laugh at us. We're not going on a picnic!"

But Mother stood her ground. "Nonsense. No one will ever notice this little thing. It isn't as if I were bringing liquor!"

"Well!" I said. "If Mama's going to take her shoyu, I'm taking my radio along." I rescued my fifteen-year-old radio from the boxes which were going down to the hotel. "At least it'll keep me from talking to myself out there."

Sumi began to look thoughtful, and she rummaged among the boxes. Henry bellowed, "That's enough! Two suitcases and one seabag a person, that's final! Now let's get going before we decide to take the house along with us."

Mother personally saw to it that the can of shoyu remained with her baggage. She turned back once more to look at our brown and yellow frame house and said almost gayly, "Good-by, house."

Old Asthma came bounding out to the front yard, her tail swaying in the air. "And good-by, Asthma, take good care of our home. *Yoroshiku onegai shimasu yo.*"

A swallow swooped down from the eaves. "Oh, soh, soh, good-by to you, too, Mrs. Swallow. I hope you have a nice little family."

Mother explained that she had discovered the swallow's little nest under the eaves just outside Sumi's bedroom window, filled with four beautiful blue-speckled eggs like precious-colored stones. The swallow darted low and buzzed over Asthma like a miniature fighter plane. We watched amazed as it returned time and time again in a diving attack on Asthma. Mother said, "She's fighting to protect her family." Asthma leaped into the air, pawed at the bird halfheartedly, then rubbed herself against Mother's woolen slacks.

"Quarter to eight," Dunks gently reminded us. We took turns ruffling Asthma's fur and saying good-by to her. The new tenants had promised us that they would keep her as their pet.

We climbed into the truck, chattering about the plucky little swallow. As we coasted down Beacon Hill bridge for the last time, we fell silent, and stared out at the delicately flushed morning sky of Puget Sound. We drove through bustling Chinatown, and in a few minutes arrived on the corner of Eighth and Lane. This area was ordinarily lonely and deserted but now it was gradually filling up with silent, labeled Japanese, standing self-consciously among their seabags and suitcases.

Everyone was dressed casually, each according to his idea of where he would be going. One Issei was wearing a thick mackinaw jacket and cleated, high-topped hiking boots. I stared admiringly at one handsome couple, standing slim and poised in their ski clothes. They looked newly wed. They stood holding hands beside their streamlined luggage that matched smartly with the new Mr. and Mrs. look. With an air of resigned sacrifice, some Issei women wore dark-colored slacks with deep-hemmed cuffs. One gnarled old grandmother wore an ankle-length black crepe dress with a plastic initial "S" pinned to its high neckline. It was old-fashioned, but dignified and womanly.

Automobiles rolled up to the curb, one after another, discharging more Japanese and more baggage. Finally at ten o'clock, a vanguard of Greyhound busses purred in and parked themselves neatly along the curb. The crowd stirred and murmured. The bus doors opened and from each, a soldier with rifle in hand stepped out and stood stiffly at attention by the door. The murmuring died. It was the first time I had seen a rifle at such close range and I felt uncomfortable. This rifle was presumably to quell riots, but contrarily, I felt riotous emotion mounting in my breast.

Jim Shigeno, one of the leaders of the Japanese-American Citizens' League, stepped briskly up front and started reading off family numbers to fill the first bus. Our number came up and we pushed our way out of the crowd. Jim said, "Step right in." We bumped into each other in nervous haste. I glanced nervously at the soldier and his rifle, and I was startled to see that he was but a young man, pink-cheeked, his clear gray eyes staring impassively ahead. I felt that the occasion probably held for him a sort of tense anxiety as it did for us. Henry found a seat by a window and hung out, watching for Minnie who had promised to see him off. Sumi and I suddenly turned maternal and hovered over Mother and Father to see that they were comfortably settled. They were silent.

Newspaper photographers with flash-bulb cameras pushed

busily through the crowd. One of them rushed up to our bus, and asked a young couple and their little boy to step out and stand by the door for a shot. They were reluctant, but the photographers were persistent and at length they got out of the bus and posed, grinning widely to cover their embarrassment. We saw the picture in the newspaper shortly after and the caption underneath it read, "Japs good-natured about evacuation."

Our bus quickly filled to capacity. All eyes were fixed up front, waiting. The guard stepped inside, sat by the door, and nodded curtly to the gray-uniformed bus driver. The door closed with a low hiss. We were now the Wartime Civil Control Administration's babies.

When all the busses were filled with the first contingent of Japanese, they started creeping forward slowly. We looked out of the window, smiled and feebly waved our hands at the crowd of friends who would be following us within the next two days. From among the Japanese faces, I picked out the tall, spare figures of our young people's minister, the Reverend Everett Thompson, and the Reverend Emery Andrews of the Japanese Baptist Church. They were old friends, having been with us for many years. They wore bright smiles on their faces and waved vigorously as if to lift our morale. But Miss Mahon, the principal of our Bailey Gatzert Grammar School and a much-beloved figure in our community, stood in front of the quiet crowd of Japanese and wept openly.

Sumi suddenly spied Minnie, driving her family car. The car screeched to a halt and Minnie leaped out, looking frantically for Henry. Henry flung his window up and shouted, "Minnie! Minnie! Over here!" The bystanders, suddenly good-humored, directed her to our moving bus. Minnie ran up to the windows, puffing, "Sorry I was late, Henry! Here, flowers for you." She thrust a bouquet of fresh yellow daffodils into his outstretched hand. Henry shouted, "Thanks — I'll be seeing you, I hope."

When our bus turned a corner and we no longer had to smile and wave, we settled back gravely in our seats. Everyone was quiet except for a chattering group of university students who soon started singing college songs. A few people turned and glared at them, which only served to increase the volume of their singing. Then suddenly a baby's sharp cry rose indignantly above the hubbub. The singing stopped immediately, followed by a guilty silence. Three seats behind us, a young mother held a wailing red-faced infant in her arms, bouncing it up and down. Its angry little face emerged from multiple layers of kimonos, sweaters and blankets, and it, too, wore the white pasteboard tag pinned to its blanket. A young man stammered out an apology as the mother gave him a wrathful look. She hunted frantically for a bottle of milk in a shopping bag, and we all relaxed when she had found it.

We sped out of the city southward along beautiful stretches of farmland, with dark, newly turned soil. In the beginning we devoured every bit of scenery which flashed past our window and admired the massive-muscled work horses plodding along the edge of the highway, the rich burnished copper color of a browsing herd of cattle, the vivid spring green of the pastures, but eventually the sameness of the country landscape palled on us. We tried to sleep to escape from the restless anxiety which kept bobbing up to the surface of our minds. I awoke with a start when the bus filled with excited buzzing. A small group of straw-hatted Japanese farmers stood by the highway, waving at us. I felt a sudden warmth toward them, then a twinge of pity. They would be joining us soon.

About noon we crept into a small town. Someone said, "Looks

like Puyallup, all right." Parents of small children babbled excitedly, "Stand up quickly and look over there. See all the chick-chicks and fat little piggies?" One little city boy stared hard at the hogs and said tersely, "They're *bachi* — dirty!"

Our bus idled a moment at the traffic signal and we noticed at the left of us an entire block filled with neat rows of low shacks, resembling chicken houses. Someone commented on it with awe, "Just look at those chicken houses. They sure go in for poultry in a big way here." Slowly the bus made a left turn, drove through a wire-fenced gate, and to our dismay, we were inside the over-sized chicken farm. The bus driver opened the door, the guard stepped out and stationed himself at the door again. Jim, the young man who had shepherded us into the busses, popped his head inside and sang out, "Okay, folks, all off at Yokohama, Puyallup."

We stumbled out, stunned, dragging our bundles after us. It must have rained hard the night before in Puyallup, for we sank ankle deep into gray, gluttinous mud. The receptionist, a white man, instructed us courteously, "Now, folks, please stay together as family units and line up. You'll be assigned your apartment."

We were standing in Area A, the mammoth parking lot of the state fairgrounds. There were three other separate areas, B, C and D, all built on the fair grounds proper, near the baseball field and the race tracks. This camp of army barracks was hopefully called Camp Harmony.

We were assigned to apartment 2–1–A, right across from the bachelor quarters. The apartments resembled elongated, low stables about two blocks long. Our home was one room, about 18 by 20 feet, the size of a living room. There was one small window in the wall opposite the one door. It was bare except for a small, tinny wood-burning stove crouching in the center. The flooring consisted of two by fours laid directly on the earth, and dandelions were already pushing their way up through the cracks. Mother was delighted when she saw their shaggy yellow heads. "Don't anyone pick them. I'm going to cultivate them."

Father snorted, "Cultivate them! If we don't watch out, those things will be growing out of our hair."

Just then Henry stomped inside, bringing the rest of our baggage. "What's all the excitement about?"

Sumi replied laconically, "Dandelions."

Henry tore off a fistful. Mother scolded, "*Arra! Arra!* Stop that. They're the only beautiful things around here. We could have a garden right in here."

"Are you joking, Mama?"

I chided Henry, "Of course, she's not. After all, she has to have some inspiration to write poems, you know, with all the '*nali keli's.*' I can think of a poem myself right now:

> Oh, Dandelion, Dandelion,
> Despised and uprooted by all,
> Dance and bob your golden heads
> For you've finally found your home
> With your yellow fellows, *nali keli,* amen!"

Henry said, thrusting the dandelions in Mother's black hair, "I think you can do ten times better than that, Mama."

Sumi reclined on her seabag and fretted, "Where do we sleep? Not on the floor, I hope."

"Stop worrying," Henry replied disgustedly.

Mother and Father wandered out to see what the other folks were doing and they found people wandering in the mud, wondering what other folks were doing. Mother returned shortly, her face lit up in an ecstatic smile, "We're in luck. The latrine is right nearby. We won't have to walk blocks."

We laughed, marveling at Mother who could be so poetic and yet so practical. Father came back, bent double like a woodcutter in a fairy tale, with stacks of scrap lumber over his shoulder. His coat and trouser pockets bulged with nails. Father dumped his loot in a corner and explained, "There was a pile of wood left by the carpenters and hundreds of nails scattered loose. Everybody was picking them up, and I hustled right in with them. Now maybe we can live in style with tables and chairs."

The block leader knocked at our door and announced lunchtime. He instructed us to take our meal at the nearest mess hall. As I untied my seabag to get out my pie plate, tin cup, spoon and fork, I realized I was hungry. At the mess hall we found a long line of people. Children darted in and out of the line, skiing in the slithery mud. The young stood impatiently on one foot, then the other, and scowled, "The food had better be good after all this wait." But the Issei stood quietly, arms folded, saying very little. A light drizzle began to fall, coating bare black heads with tiny sparkling raindrops. The chow line inched forward.

Lunch consisted of two canned sausages, one lob of boiled potato, and a slab of bread. Our family had to split up, for the hall was too crowded for us to sit together. I wandered up and down the aisles, back and forth along the crowded tables and benches, looking for a few inches to squeeze into. A small Issei woman finished her meal, stood up and hoisted her legs modestly over the bench, leaving a space for one. Even as I thrust myself into the breach, the space had shrunk to two inches, but I worked myself into it. My dinner companion, hooked just inside my right elbow, was a bald headed, gruff-looking Issei man who seemed to resent nestling at mealtime. Under my left elbow was a tiny, mud-spattered girl. With busy runny nose, she was belaboring her sausages, tearing them into shreds and mixing them into the potato gruel which she had made with water. I choked my food down.

We cheered loudly when trucks rolled by, distributing canvas army cots for the young and hardy, and steel cots for the older folks. Henry directed the arrangement of the cots. Father and Mother were to occupy the corner nearest the wood stove. In the other corner, Henry arranged two cots in L shape and announced that this was the combination living room-bedroom area, to be occupied by Sumi and myself. He fixed a male den for himself in the corner nearest the door. If I had had my way, I would have arranged everyone's cots in one neat row as in Father's hotel dormitory.

We felt fortunate to be assigned to a room at the end of the barracks because we had just one neighbor to worry about. The partition wall separating the rooms was only seven feet high with an opening of four feet at the top, so at night, Mrs. Funai next door could tell when Sumi was still sitting up in bed in the dark, putting her hair up. "*Mah,* Sumi-*chan,*" Mrs. Funai would say through the plank wall, "are you curling your hair tonight again? Do you put it up every night?" Sumi would put her hands on her hips and glare defiantly at the wall.

The block monitor, an impressive Nisei who looked like a star tackle with his crouching walk, came around the first night to tell us that we must all be inside our room by nine o'clock every night. At ten o'clock, he rapped at the door again, yelling, "Lights out!" and Mother rushed to turn the light off not a second later.

Throughout the barracks, there were a medley of creaking cots, whimpering infants and explosive night coughs. Our attention was riveted on the intense little wood stove which glowed so violently I feared it would melt right down to the floor. We soon learned that this condition lasted for only a short time, after which it suddenly turned into a deep freeze. Henry and Father took turns at the stove to produce the harrowing blast which all but singed our army blankets, but did not penetrate through them. As it grew quieter in the barracks, I could hear the light patter of rain. Soon I felt the "splat! splat!" of raindrops digging holes into my face. The dampness on my pillow spread like a mortal bleeding, and I finally had to get out and haul my cot toward the center of the room. In a short while Henry was up. "I've got multiple leaks, too. Have to complain to the landlord first thing in the morning."

All through the night I heard people getting up, dragging cots around. I stared at our little window, unable to sleep. I was glad Mother had put up a makeshift curtain on the window for I noticed a powerful beam of light sweeping across it every few seconds. The lights came from high towers placed around the camp where guards with Tommy guns kept a twenty-four hour vigil. I remembered the wire fence encircling us, and a knot of anger tightened in my breast. What was I doing behind a fence like a criminal? If there were accusations to be made, why hadn't I been given a fair trial? Maybe I wasn't considered an American anymore. My citizenship wasn't real, after all. Then what was I? I was certainly not a citizen of Japan as my parents were. On second thought, even Father and Mother were more alien residents of the United States than Japanese nationals for they had little tie with their mother country. In their twenty-five years in America, they had worked and paid their taxes to their adopted government as any other citizen.

Of one thing I was sure. The wire fence was real. I no longer had the right to walk out of it. It was because I had Japanese ancestors. It was also because some people had little faith in the ideas and ideals of democracy. They said that after all these were but words and could not possibly insure loyalty. New laws and camps were surer devices. I finally buried my face in my pillow to wipe out burning thoughts and snatch what sleep I could.

Our first weeks in Puyallup were filled with quiet hysteria. We peered nervously at the guards in the high towers sitting behind Tommy guns and they silently looked down at us. We were all jittery. One rainy night the guards suddenly became aware of unusual activity in the camp. It was after "lights out" and rain was pouring down in sheets. They turned on the spotlights, but all they could see were doors flashing open and small dark figures rushing out into the shadows. It must have looked like a mass attempt to break out of camp.

We ourselves were awakened by the noise. Henry whispered hoarsely, "What's going on out there anyway?"

Then Mother almost shrieked, "*Chotto!* Listen, airplanes, right up overhead, too."

"I wonder if by accident, a few bombs are going to fall on our camp," Father said, slowly.

I felt a sickening chill race up and down my spine. The buzzing and droning continued louder and louder. We heard Mrs. Funai and her husband mumbling to each other next door. Suddenly the plane went away and the commotion gradually died down.

Early the next morning when we rushed to the mess hall to get the news, we learned that half the camp had suffered from food poisoning. The commotion had been sick people rushing to the latrines. The guards must have thought they had an uprising on hand, and had ordered a plane out to investigate.

Henry said, "It was a good thing those soldiers weren't trigger-happy or it could've been very tragic."

We all shuddered as if we had had a brush with death.

Quickly we fell into the relentless camp routine in Puyallup. Every morning at six I was awakened by our sadistic cook beating mightily on an iron pot. He would thrust a heavy iron ladle inside the pot and hit all sides in a frightful, double-timed clamor, BONG! BONG! BONG! BONG! With my eyes glued together in sleep, I fumbled around for my washcloth and soap, and groped my way in the dark toward the community washroom.

At the mess hall I gnawed my way through canned stewed figs, thick French toast, and molten black coffee. With breakfast churning its way violently down to the pit of my stomach, I hurried each morning to the Area A gate. There I stood in line with other evacuees who had jobs in Area D. Area D was just across the street from A, but we required armed chaperones to make the crossing. After the guard carefully inspected our passes and counted noses, the iron gate yawned open for us, and we marched out in orderly formation, escorted fore and aft by military police. When we halted at the curb for the traffic signal to change, we were counted. We crossed the street and marched half a block to the Area D gate where we were counted again. I had a $16 a month job as stenographer at the administration office. A mere laborer who sweated it out by his brawn eight hours a day drew $12, while doctors, dentists, attorneys, and other professionals earned the lordly sum of $19 a month. For the most part, the camp was maintained by the evacuees who cooked, doctored, laid sewer pipes, repaired shoes, and provided their own entertainment.

I worked in the Personnel Department, keeping records of work hours. First I typed on pink, green, blue and white work sheets the hours put in by the 10,000 evacuees, then sorted and alphabetized these sheets, and stacked them away in shoe boxes.

My job was excruciatingly dull, but under no circumstances did I want to leave it. The Administration Building was the only place which had modern plumbing and running hot and cold water; in the first few months and every morning, after I had typed for a decent hour, I slipped into the rest room and took a complete sponge bath with scalding hot water. During the remainder of the day, I slipped back into the rest room at inconspicuous intervals, took off my head scarf and wrestled with my scorched hair. I stood upside down over the basin of hot water, soaking my hair, combing, stretching and pulling at it. I hoped that if I was persistent, I would get results.

Thus my day was filled, hurrying to Area D for work, hurrying back to Area A for lunch, then back to D for work again, and finally back to A for the night. The few hours we had free in the evenings before lights out were spent visiting and relaxing with friends, but even our core of conversation dried out with the monotony of our lives. We fought a daily battle with the carnivorous Puyallup mud. The ground was a vast ocean of mud, and whenever it threatened to dry and cake up, the rains came and softened it into slippery ooze.

Sumi and I finally decided to buy galoshes, and we tracked down a tattered mail-order catalogue nicknamed the Camp Bible. We found a pageful of beautiful rubber galoshes, marked "not available." Then I sent out an S.O.S. to Chris . . . please find us two pairs of high-topped galoshes. Chris answered a week later, "It looks as if there's a drought on galoshes. I've visited every store in town and haven't found a single pair. One defensive salesman told me very haughtily that they were out of season. I'll keep trying though. I'm going to try the second-hand stores and those hot fire sales on First Avenue."

Sumi and I waited anxiously as our shoes grew thick with mud.

Finally Chris sent us a bundle with a note. "No luck on First Avenue, but I'm sending you two old pairs of rubbers I dug out of our basement."

They fitted our shoes perfectly, and we were the envy of all our friends — until the *geta* craze swept through the camp. Japanese *getas* are wooden platform shoes. When I first saw an old bachelor wearing a homemade pair, his brown horny feet exposed to the world, I was shocked with his daring. But soon I begged Father to ask one of his friends who knew a man who knew a carpenter to make a pair for me. My gay red *getas* were wonderful. They served as shower clogs, and their three-inch lifts kept me out of the mud. They also solved my nylon problem, for I couldn't wear stockings with them.

One Sunday afternoon Joe Subotich from the hotel visited us unexpectedly. He waited for us in a small lattice enclosure just inside the gate where evacuees entertained visitors. Joe, his round face wreathed in smiles, was a welcome, lovable sight. He and Father shook hands vigorously and smiled and smiled. Joe was wearing the same old striped suit he wore every Sunday, but he had a new gray hat which he clutched self-consciously.

Joe handed Father a large shopping bag, bulging with plump golden grapefruit. "This for you and the Mrs. I remember you like grapefruits." Then he pulled out bags of nuts and candy bars from his pockets, "And these for the children."

We cried, "Thank you Joe, how thoughtful of you." We showered him with questions, about Sam, Peter and Montana.

"Everybody's fine. Sam's still chasing drunks out. Everybody making lotsa more money, you know, and everybody drinking more. We have to t'row them down the stairs and call the cops all the time. It's joost like the time of the First World War, lotsa drinking and fighting. You remember, Mr. Itoi."

We asked about Seattle. Was it still the same?

"Oh, the buildings and everything the same, but more people in town. Everybody coming in for war jobs. Business booming in Skidrow." He glanced at the high wire fence and shook his head.

"I don't like it, to see you in here. I don't understand it. I know you all my life. You're my friend. Well, I gotta go now and catch that bus."

Father and Henry walked to the gate with Joe. He smiled a brief farewell on the other side of the fence, clapped on his new hat over his balding head and walked quickly away.

The grapefruit was the first fresh fruit we had seen in Puyallup. Every time I held a beautiful golden roundness in my hand, a great lump rose in my throat — Joe's loyalty touched me.

Before a month passed, our room was fairly comfortable, thanks to Father. With a borrowed saw and hammer, he pieced together scrap lumber and made a writing table, benches and wall shelves above each cot. He built wooden platforms for our suitcases, which we slid under our cots out of sight. He fixed up a kitchen cabinet which to all appearances contained nothing but our eating utensils, but an illegal little hot plate crouched behind its curtain. It was against the fire regulations to cook in the room, but everyone concealed a small cooking device somewhere.

Just as we had become adjusted to Area A, Henry announced he had applied for a job in the camp hospital in Area D. Minnie and her family lived in Area D and she worked as nurse's aide in the hospital. But when Henry told us happily that we had to move, Sumi and I screamed, "Oh, no, not again! But we just got settled!"

Henry smiled smugly, "Hospital orders, I'm sorry."

Father looked around the room which he had worked over so

lovingly, "Ah! *Yakai da na*, what a lot of bother, after I went to all the trouble fixing it up."

Mother was the only one pleased about the prospect. "My friends have written they can see mountain peaks from the Area D barrack doors on a clear day. And if they climb to the top of the baseball grandstand, they get a magnificent view. When are we moving?"

"I don't know, Mama. They'll notify me in a few days."

That very day after lunch hour, a truck rolled by our door. A tough-looking, young bearded Nisei, standing on the running board, bawled at us, "Get your stuff together. We're picking you up in a couple of hours."

We spat out an indignant "Well!" and then began to throw our things together. Wet laundry was hanging in the back yard and this we slapped into our seabags with the unwashed dishes and cups we had used for lunch. Father wrenched shelves and cabinets from walls and lashed tables and benches together. When the truck returned, we were ready after a fashion. Our paraphernalia had refused to go back into the original two suitcases and one seabag per person. We had to wear layers of sweaters, jackets, coats and hats. We carried in our arms pots and pans and the inevitable *shoyu* jug, the radio and the little hot plate. The energetic truck crew threw baggage and furniture into the back of the open truck, and we perched on top of it all.

Area D boasted such exclusive features as the horse race tracks, the spacious baseball grounds, grandstands, display barns, concession buildings and an amusement park. Area D people dined in a mammoth-sized mess hall, formerly a display barn for prize livestock. From one end of the barn to the other were hundreds of long tables and benches lined up in straight uncompromising rows.

The advantages of Area D stimulated strange ambitions in some people, often to the discomfort of the rest. One day an un-employed physical education instructor looked at the beautiful, huge empty lot in front of the mess hall and he was inspired. The ground was level, hard and covered with fine gravel, a perfect set-up for mass calisthenics. Too many people, he reasoned, were developing flabby muscles and heavy paunches with this seden-tary camp life. It was a deplorable situation. One morning a rash of bulletins appeared on posts and walls of buildings. "Calisthenic drills will start tomorrow at 5:30 A.M. in front of the mess hall. Everyone must turn out on time."

When I read the word "must," I dug my heels in, ready to resist anyone who came around to drag me out of bed. Early the next morning Mother was the only one in our barrack who stirred awake in the darkness to meet with the other pre-dawn people. She said, "I'm just going out of curiosity, not for my health. I'd break into a hundred pieces if I jumped around like a young girl."

Father mumbled defensively through his blankets, "The gov-ernment gave me the first vacation of my life and no one's going to interfere with it." We snuggled down deeper under our covers; down the length of the barracks I heard fifty-odd people snoring contentedly and accumulating sleep and fat.

An hour later Mother returned puffing like an exhausted steam engine, hair over her eyes, and blouse pulled out from her skirt. She crawled into bed.

"No breakfast for me today, I need the rest. I just went through the most unspeakable torture. I just wanted to stand by and watch, but that sharp-eyed leader shouted me into formation. I was so embarrassed, I went right in and leaped around with the rest of them."

"Were there a lot of people?" we asked.

"Quite a few, but mostly old folks. Some of them couldn't even straighten their knees. Ah, but that leader had such a fine resonant voice, it practically lifted me off the ground. But what atrocious Japanese! The only time I understood his directions was when he counted 'Ichi! Ni! San! Shi!' He has a crippled arm and couldn't show us what he wanted us to do. It was quite a frustrating morning."

Mother never returned to the calisthenics. She said she was too old for it, and we said we were too young. We paid no attention to the bulletins which pleaded for more bright-eyed turnouts, but only wide-eyed old men and bachelors, who thrived on four hours of sleep, showed up. They went through the drills the best they could, which was always several counts behind the laboring drillmaster. One morning the young man himself did not show up and rumor had it that he was on the verge of a nervous breakdown. Thus the "return to health" program quietly collapsed.

Sunday was the day we came to an abrupt halt, free from the busy round of activities in which we submerged our feelings. In the morning we went to church to listen to our Reverend Everett Thompson who visited us every Sunday. Our minister was a tall and lanky man whose open and friendly face quickly drew people to him. He had served as missionary in Japan at one time and he spoke fluent Japanese. He had worked with the young people in our church for many years, and it was a great comfort to see him and the many other ministers and church workers with whom we had been in contact back in Seattle. We felt that we were not entirely forgotten.

With battered spirits we met in the dimly lighted makeshift room which served as our chapel under the baseball grandstand, and after each sermon and prayer, we gained new heart. Bit by bit, our minister kept on helping us build the foundation for a new outlook. I particularly remember one Sunday service when he asked us to read parts from the Book of Psalms in unison. Somehow in our circumstances and in our environment, we had begun to read more slowly and conscientiously, as if we were finding new meaning and comfort in the passages from the Bible. " 'The Lord hear thee in the day of trouble; the name of the God of Jacob defend thee . . . Be not far from me; for trouble is near; for there is none to help . . . The Lord is my light and my salvation; whom shall I fear? The Lord is the strength of my life; of whom shall I be afraid?' "

As we finished with the lines, " 'Thou hast turned for me my mourning into dancing: thou hast put off my sackcloth, and girded me with gladness; to the end that *my* glory may sing praise to thee, and not be silent. O Lord my God, I will give thanks unto thee for ever,' " the room seemed filled with peace and awe, as if walls had been pushed back and we were free. I was convinced that this was not the end of our lives here in camp, but just the beginning; and gradually it dawned on me that we had not been physically mistreated nor would we be harmed in the future. I knew that the greatest trial ahead of us would be of a spiritual nature. I had been tense and angry all my life about prejudice, real and imaginery. The evacuation had been the biggest blow, but there was little to be gained in bitterness and cynicism because we felt that people had failed us. The time had come when it was more important to examine our own souls, to keep our faith in God and help to build that way of life which we so desired.

After dinner we hurried with our blankets to a large plot of green velvet lawn to listen to an open-air record concert. The recreation leader borrowed records from music lovers and broadcast them over a loud-speaker system so we could all enjoy them. Always a large crowd of young people was sprawled comfortably over the lawn, but when the concert started, they became so quiet and absorbed I thought I was alone, lying on my back and looking up at the dazzling blue summer sky. Something about the swift billowing clouds moving overhead and the noble music of Dvorak or Beethoven brought us a rare moment of peace.

We had been brought to Puyallup in May. We were still there in August. We knew Puyallup was temporary and we were anxious to complete our migration into a permanent camp inland. No one knew where we were going or when we were leaving. The sultry heat took its toll of temper and patience, and everyone showed signs of restlessness. One day our block leader requested us to remain in our quarters after lunch, and in the afternoon a swarm of white men, assisted by Nisei, swept through the four areas simultaneously for a checkup raid. A Nisei appeared at our door. "All right, folks, we're here to pick up any contraband you may have, dangerous instruments or weapons. Knives, scissors, hammers, saws, any of those things."

Father's face darkened, "But we need tools. I made everything you see here in this room with my own hands and a few tools! There's a limit to this whole business!"

The young man tried to control his rising temper. "Don't argue with me, Oji-san. I'm just carrying my orders out. Now, please, hand over what you have."

Father gloomily handed him the saw which Joe had mailed to him from Seattle. We knew that Father was keeping back a hammer and a small paring kitchen knife, but we said nothing. The Nisei seemed satisfied, and mopping his forehead, he headed for the next door neighbor, looking unhappy and set for another argument.

Later, we were ordered to turn in all literature printed in Japanese. Mother went to the central receiving station to plead with the young man. "I have a few things, but they're not dangerous, I assure you. Why does the government want to take away the little I have left?"

The Nisei explained patiently, "No one is taking them away from you, Oba-san. They'll be returned to you eventually. Now what have you there?"

Mother smiled. "A Bible. Pray tell me, what's so dangerous about it?"

The Nisei threw his arms up, "If it's printed in Japanese, I must have it. What else?"

"Not my *Manyoshu*, too?" The *Manyoshu* was a collection of poems, a Japanese classic.

"That too."

"But there isn't one subversive word in it!"

"Again, I repeat, I'm not responsible for these orders. Please, I have work to do."

Mother reluctantly handed him the Bible and the *Manyoshu*. She held up a tiny, pocket-sized dictionary, and said, "I'm keeping this."

"All right, all right." He let Mother go, muttering how difficult and stubborn the Issei were.

Within two weeks, we were told we were moving immediately to our relocation camp. By then we knew we were headed for Idaho. Mr. Yoshihara, one of Father's friends, had volunteered to go ahead as carpenter and laborer to help build our permanent camp. He wrote:

> Our future home is set right in the midst of a vast Idaho prairie, where the sun beats down fiercely and everything, plant and animal life, appears to be a dried-up brown, but there are

compensations. A wonderful wild river roars by like a flood. I am informed it is part of the Snake River. There is a large barracks hospital at one end of the camp and a gigantic water tank towers over the camp like a sentry. There'll be adequate laundry and toilet facilities here. The apartments are only a little larger than the ones in Puyallup, but we cannot expect too much. After all, it's still a camp.

We were excited at the thought of going to unknown territory, and we liked the Indian flavor of the name "Idaho." I remembered a series of bright, hot pictures of Idaho in the *National Geographic* magazine, the sun-baked terrain, dried-up waterholes, runty-looking sagebrush and ugly nests of rattlesnakes. I knew it wasn't going to be a comfortable experience, but it would be a change.

CHAPTER X

Henry's Wedding and a Most Curious Tea Party

EARLY one steamy morning in the middle of August, we set off for Idaho on an old relic of a train adorned with gaslights, rococo wall panelings and stiff mohair seats. When we started rolling through the Hood River region along the Columbia River, we all pressed our faces against the windows and drank in the extravagant beauty in hushed reverence. The country was bathed in the warm gold of the bright sun, turning the clouds into a pearly opalescence against the sapphire summer sky. Mountains reared proudly above us and the tumbling blue river below sparkled with the effervescence of liquid brilliants.

A porter announced dinner. Looking like grimy chimney sweeps, we sat down shyly at white tables, laden with sparkling silverware. Sprays of roses trembled in slender vases. I gazed at the chicken dinner set before me, expecting, any moment, to have my plate whisked away and to be handed the more familiar canned wieners and beans. After I swallowed my first cautious mouthful, I compelled myself to relax, and fingered the slender stem of the water goblet luxuriously as I stared at the magnificent scenery speeding by.

Our car became hot and humid, but we didn't dare open the inner window because cinders would come blowing in as from a bellows. At night the MP's ordered everyone to pull the window shades down. Somehow we felt as if we were traveling in hostile country through which we must pass in utmost secrecy. Mother, Sumi and I occupied two facing seats. All night we twisted and turned on the prickly mohair. Heavy-footed botflies kept bumbling into our sweat-stained faces. Through the endless hours our train climbed the mountains, crawling like a dying caterpillar, squeaking, creaking, jolting to sudden halts, and then sliding helplessly backwards. When dawn finally broke through in sharp white slits all around the window, I threw open the shade and gulped at the sunlight. The scenery had changed drastically overnight. The staring hot sun had parched the earth's skin into gray-brown wrinkles out of which jagged boulders erupted like warts. Wisps of moldy-looking, gray-green sagebrush dotted the land. In the midst of this bare prairie, our train clanked to a standstill for a ten minute stop. When the MP told us we could step outside, we rushed out of the cars like excited children on a field trip, curious to feel the prairie under our feet. I noticed that barbed wire fences had been hastily strung up on both sides of the railroad tracks and the MP's had stationed themselves along them. Farmers, women and children were gathered along the other side of the fences, staring silently at us. There were no farmhouses in the vicinity so I assumed they had made a special trip to see us. With our glistening faces and baggy clothes we were not looking our best, and we turned away, embarrassed.

That afternoon the train joggled into a small town where we were transferred to a fleet of busses. The two-hour ride through open country was quiet. Everyone stared woodenly out of the windows. From about a mile away we caught sight of our camp, its neat rows of mica-covered barracks flashing in the brilliant sun.

Camp Minidoka was located in the south central part of Idaho, north of Snake River. It was a semiarid region, reclaimed to some extent by an irrigation project with the Minidoka Dam. From where I was sitting, I could see nothing but flat prairies, clumps of greasewood, and the jack rabbits. And of course the hundreds and hundreds of barracks, to house ten thousand of us.

Our home was one room in a large army-type barracks, measuring about twenty by twenty-five feet. There were smaller rooms on both ends of the barracks reserved for couples, and larger rooms to accommodate a family of more than five. The only furnishings were an iron pot-belly stove and the cots.

On our first day in camp, we were given a rousing welcome by a dust storm. It caught up with us while we were still wandering about looking for our room. We felt as if we were standing in a gigantic sand-mixing machine as the sixty-mile gale lifted the loose earth up into the sky, obliterating everything. Sand filled our mouths and nostrils and stung our faces and hands like a thousand darting needles. Henry and Father pushed on ahead while Mother, Sumi and I followed, hanging onto their jackets, banging suitcases into each other. At last we staggered into our room, gasping and blinded. We sat on our suitcases to rest, peeling off our jackets and scarves. The window panes rattled madly, and the dust poured in through the cracks like smoke. Now and then when the wind subsided, I saw other evacuees, hanging on to their suitcases, heads bent against the stinging dust. The wind whipped their scarves and towels from their heads and zipped them out of sight. It seemed as if we had been sitting for hours in the stifling room before we were aroused by the familiar metallic clang of the dinner triangle.

The mess hall was a desolate sight with thick layers of dust covering the dining tables and benches, and filling teacups and bowls. The cooking in the kitchen filled the building with steaming vapor and the odor of fried fish. As we stood in the chow line, we stared out of the window, wondering when the storm would subside.

I saw a woman struggling toward the building. A miniature tornado enveloped her and she disappeared from sight. A few seconds later when it cleared, I saw that she had been pulling a child behind her, shielding it with her skirt. The little girl suddenly sat down on the ground and hid her face in her lap. The mother ripped off her jacket, threw it over her daughter's head and flung herself against the wind, carrying the child. Someone pulled the two inside the mess hall. For the next half hour we ate silently, accompanied by the child's persistent sobs.

Just as suddenly as the storm had broken out, it died. We walked out of the mess hall under a pure blue sky, startling in its serenity. It was as if there had been a quiet presence overhead, untouched and unaffected by the violence below, and the entire summer evening sky had lowered itself gently into a cradle of peace and silence.

The night sky of Idaho was beautiful and friendly. A translucent milk-glass moon hung low against its rich blue thickness, and diamond-cut stars were flung across it from horizon to horizon. This was a strange, gaunt country, fierce in the hot white light of day, but soft and gentle with a beauty all its own at night.

In the deepening blue shadows, people hurried to and fro, preparing for their first night in camp. The Issei men stomped along in their wooden *getas*, their loose suspenders swinging rhythmically with each step, while the Issei women in cool cotton print *yukatas*, Japanese house kimonos, slipped along noiselessly. They bowed to each other, murmuring, *"Oyasumi nasai.* Rest well."

These familiar words echoing in the alien darkness of the prairie were welcome sounds. I suddenly saw that these people were living their circumstances out with simple dignity and patience, and I felt ashamed of my own emotional turbulence. That night we let ourselves sink deep into the yawning silence of the prairie which was shattered only by the barking of the worried coyotes.

Idaho summer sizzled on the average of 110 degrees, and for the first few weeks I lay meekly on my cot from morning till night not daring to do more than totter to the mess hall three times a day. I could well understand why the natives who had first stumbled into this territory had called it "Idaho," meaning "sunshine" in Indian. The almighty sun was king here, its pressure overwhelming, overpowering. The sun beat down from above and caught us on the chin from below, bouncing off the hard-baked earth, and browning us to such a fine slow turn that I felt like a walking Southern fried chicken. The sun dried our laundered sheets into stiff billboards, and our dresses hung like paper-doll cutouts on the line.

When September came we slowly emerged from our stupor. The sun no longer stabbed the back of our necks and we walked upright again. Now when I awoke in the mornings, the air felt cool and crisp.

The momentum of the invigorating change carried me along into a job at the camp hospital as ward secretary. Henry had already been working at the hospital for weeks and Minnie was there also, as a nurse's aide. Sumi and her young friends, who spent their days roaming through the camp looking for excitement, soon tired of their vacuous lives, and in desperation signed up as nurse's aides, too. They livened the hospital wards with their bright-eyed, teen-age enthusiasm. Even Father began to study the job situation with his usual thoroughness. He was, of course, looking for work which would not require too much heavy labor. Ditch-digging was out of the question. So was cooking. He had had enough of it, cooking back and forth between Seattle and Alaska. Father finally settled on becoming a member of the Internal Security staff — a policeman, no less, complete with uniforms of olive-drab army shirt, olive-drab trousers and leggings, looking for all the world as if he were about to revive World War I. Mother, who was not well, stayed home to mop the floor, handwash the family laundry, iron and mend our clothes, attend the English language class, choir practice, prayer meetings, and a Japanese doll-making class.

By fall, Camp Minidoka had bloomed into a full-grown town. Children went to school in the barracks, taught by professional teachers among the evacuees and people hired from the outside. Except for the members of the administration staff at the main building and the head of the hospital staff, the evacuees themselves supplied the entire labor pool in the camp, in the mess halls, in the hospital, on the farm, on roadwork, and in internal policing. A small library was started with the donation of books from Seattle and the neighboring towns. All church activities, Protestant, Catholic and Buddhist, were in full session. The ministers, who had served among the Japanese people back home, moved to Twin Falls, a small town nearby, and continued their good work among us. Our own Mr. Thompson and his family were with us again.

During our spare hours, we confiscated scrap lumber, piece by piece, from the lumber pile which was supposedly guarded night and day by the Internal Security staff. Since the staff was made up of evacuees themselves, the enormous pile diminished little by little. A coffee table, a writing table, a glamorous dressing table, low chairs and tall chairs gradually made their appearance in our tiny apartment. Rows of shelves lined the bare walls. New suitcase platforms lay hidden under our cots. We bought gallons of shellac, and white paint, yards of white organdy for curtains, and blue damask for the cots and the clothes closet. We had a living room, powder room, three bedrooms, a study, storage room, and a kitchen all in one, a Rube Goldberg dream come true. It had everything except the kitchen sink and privacy. People kept walking in when we were in rumpled pajamas, trimming toenails, or creaming our faces.

Winter in Minidoka was as intense an experience as summer had been. In preparation for the paralyzing cold, a crew of men raced from room to room, pounding slabs of white fiberboard to the walls. The fresh white coverings gave us a finished decorator's touch, for until then our four walls had looked like skeletons with their ribs of two by fours bare and exposed. We gave a lusty cheer for the government when we were told that they would provide winter clothing for those who needed it. Mother was the first to go after her clothing allotment. When she came home with the bundle, we all gathered around her excitedly to see what she had. She held up a dangling pair of longjohns, olive-drab army trousers of World War I, and a navy pea coat.

"They're good quality woolens," she said calmly, "and they'll certainly keep me warm. Only thing, it's too bad we aren't all males."

Sumi and I protested hysterically that we were all going to look like members of the Internal Security staff since these clothes were exactly what Father and his friends wore on patrol duty.

Henry snorted disgustedly at us, "Oh, women! Why should you care what you look like in camp?"

We haughtily announced we would rather freeze than lose our femininity. Even when winter swept in with wild shrieking winds and tons of snow, we remained steadfast. The dull gray-brown of the prairie disappeared, and we moved as if in a dream through a muffled white world. There was nothing but whiteness all around us, the white-mantled barracks, the white dunes and the blank white sky. Father, Mother and Henry bundled into their stiff pea coats and army breeches, but Sumi and I clung stubbornly to our slacks and coats, which flapped in the blizzard like cheesecloth. The zero cold drew tears from our eyes and crystallized them on our cheeks. Ice formed on our umbrellas. We stopped smiling to keep our faces from cracking. And our skin slowly changed to an ominous purple, the color of eggplants.

It was only after a man living in our block became lost one night in a snowstorm and died from exposure, that we finally gave in. We ran to the clothing office, and on bended knees, begged for "Longjohns, pea coat, waistcoat, anything!" The man in charge pointed to the almost empty shelves, and said laconically, "Out of luck, I'm afraid. Nothing in your size."

We stared at him, dumbfounded by his callous attitude. "We don't care about size or looks! We just want something to keep us warm. What about army blankets? We'll make our own."

The man gave us what was left, size forty longjohns, sleeveless, collarless waistcoats which hung down to our knees, and wonderful thick, bear-sized pea coats. We were especially fond of those pea coats with their stiff, enormous berthas which we could flip up at the first warning whistle of a snowstorm. We agreed that it was much better to look like headless mariners than to become a block of ice and chip slowly away into nothing. That night we remembered the government in our prayers for our warm clothing. It had also taught us a lesson that man, or at any rate woman, cannot live on pride alone.

We had lived in camps through four seasons, and each season

had served as a challenge to us. In the meantime we had drifted farther and farther away from the American scene. We had been set aside, and we had become adjusted to our peripheral existence. The great struggle in which the world was engaged seemed far away, remote from our insulated way of life.

Then one day a group of army personnel marched into our dreaming camp on a special mission and our idyllic life of nothingness came to a violent end. They made a shocking announcement. "The United States War Department has decided to form a special combat unit for the Nisei. We have come to recruit volunteers."

We gasped and we spluttered. Dunks Oshima who had brought the news to us was on fire. Dunks had grown into a strapping young man with a brilliant record for high-school sports. He eyed us fiercely as he cried, "What do they take us for? Saps? First, they change my army status to 4–C because of my ancestry, run me out of town, and now they want me to volunteer for a suicide squad so I could get killed for this damn democracy. That's going some, for sheer brass!"

That was exactly the way most of us felt, but the recruiting officers were well prepared to cope with our emotional explosion. They called meetings and we flocked to them with an injured air.

An officer, a big, tall, dark-haired man with formidable poise spoke to us. "You're probably wondering why we are here, recruiting for volunteers from your group. I think that my explanation is best expressed in the statement recently issued by our President, regarding a citizen's right and privilege to serve his country. I want to read it to you:

> No loyal citizen of the United States should be denied the democratic right to exercise the responsibilities of his citizenship, regardless of his ancestry. The principle on which this

country was founded and by which it has always been governed is that Americanism is a matter of the mind and the heart. Americanism is not, and never was, a matter of race or ancestry. Every loyal American citizen should be given the opportunity to serve this country wherever his skills will make the greatest contribution . . . whether it be in the ranks of our armed forces, war production, agriculture, Government service, or other work essential to the war effort.

It all sounded very well. It was the sort of declaration which rang true and clear in our hearts, but there were questions in our minds which needed answering. The speaker threw the meeting open for discussion. We said we didn't want a separate Nisei combat unit because it looked too much like segregation. We wanted to serve in the same way as other citizens, in a mixed group with the other Americans. The man replied, "But if the Nisei men were to be scattered throughout the army, you'd lose your significance as Nisei. Maybe you want it that way, because in the past you suffered with your Japanese faces. Well, why not accept your Japanese face? Why be ashamed of it? Why not capitalize on it for a change? This is no time for retiring into anonymity. There are powerful organizations who are now campaigning on the Coast to deport you all to Japan, citizens and residents alike. But there're also men and women who believe in you, who feel you should be given the chance to stand up and express yourselves. They thought that a Nisei combat unit would be just the thing so that whatever you accomplish, whatever you achieve, will be yours and yours alone."

We saw that the speaker was sincere and believed earnestly in this cause. Then we asked him another burning question. "Why had the government ever put us here in the first place? Why? Why? Why?"

The man looked at our wounded faces and said, "I can't answer that question. I can only repeat what you already know, that the government thought evacuation was necessary. The evacuation occurred, and right or wrong, it's past. Now we're interested in your future. The War Department is offering you a chance to volunteer and to distinguish yourselves as Japanese-American citizens in the service of your country. Believe me, this combat unit is not segregation in the sense you think it is."

The tension in the mess hall eased, and questions and answers flowed more naturally. After the meeting we returned to our barracks to continue the debate. Dunks came with us.

"What's a fellow to do?" Dunks said wryly. "They've got us over the barrel. If we don't do our bit, you can bet your boots there won't be much of a future for us here. Those racists on the Coast will see to that."

I put in, "I'll wager, though, that some of those characters will be dead set against a Nisei combat team."

Henry snorted, "Those scrooges will be agin anything which might make us look good."

Dunks said, "It's the general public I'm thinking about. They're the ones who count. They want proof of our loyalty. Okay, I'm giving it to them, and maybe I'll die for it if I'm unlucky. But if after the war's over and our two cents don't cut any ice with the American public, well, to blazes with them!"

The next day Henry announced, "Tomorrow I'm going down to volunteer." No one said a word. Father stared down at his veined hands. Mother's face turned into a white mask.

"Please don't feel so bad, Mama."

Mother smiled thinly, "I don't feel bad, Henry. In fact, I don't feel anything just now."

Father spoke to her tenderly, "Mama, if Henry had been born

in Japan, he would have been taken into the army and gone off to war long ago."

"That's right. And I guess it's about time we all stopped thinking about the past. I think we should go along with our sons from now. It's the least we can do."

Father said, gratefully, "That's what I wanted to hear. At least we're together on this matter. Imagine what Dunks must be going through."

Mrs. Oshima had refused to speak to her son ever since he had decided to volunteer. "Is this what we deserve from our children," she said, "after years and years of work and hardship for their sake? Ah, we've bred nothing but fools! They can be insulted, their parents insulted, and still they volunteer. The Nisei never had backbones!"

Early the next morning, Dunks, and George and Paul, sons of Mr. Sawada, the clothing salesman, swarmed into our apartment on their way to the camp hospital for their physical.

"Let's go, Hank, before the crowd gets there."

They left with a great clatter and boisterous shouting. Father, Mother, Sumi and I sank to our cots feeling as if we had emerged from a turbulent storm which had been raging steadily in our minds since Pearl Harbor. The birth of the Nisei combat team was the climax to our evacuee life, and the turning point. It was the road back to our rightful places.

A few days later Henry made another announcement. He and Minnie were going to be married, and soon. We were speechless. Father stopped sandpapering his greasewood cane. Mother stopped writing at her desk. Sumi and I stared at our parents, wondering how they would react. Henry and Minnie had been rebuffed so often on this matter in Seattle, we were prepared for fireworks.

Now they stood before us, both looking as if a storm were about to burst over their heads. We were all pleasantly surprised, however.

Mother was the first to recover. "If Minnie's folks approve, it's all right with us, isn't it, Papa?"

Father agreed. "But how do your parents feel? After all, Henry will be leaving."

Minnie almost sighed, "They said it's all right with them, if it's all right with you."

"Then in that case, we must get together and talk it over."

Henry opened his mouth to protest, but thought better of it. The old folks must have their conference, for such things were as inevitable as the Japanese bow. They conferred that night and it ended, as we all knew it would, with unanimous approval of the marriage. Henry said that after he was stationed in camp he planned to find an apartment nearby and Minnie would join him.

The events that followed in order to get Henry and Minnie properly married are forever pasted into our family memory album, in all its glorious confusion, as one of the most strenuous, tumultuous and happy experiences of our entire camp career. Minnie made up her mind to have a full-blown civilized wedding, camp or no camp. To Minnie, the fact that we were planted way out in the wilderness was no deterrent at all. If she had had the slightest inclination, I was sure she could have willed even the most scraggly clumps of sagebrush to bloom calla lilies and orchids to adorn the wedding altar.

Early the next morning, Henry and Minnie invaded the Administration Building to get a one-day pass to Twin Falls for themselves, Mrs. Yokoyama, Mother, Sumi and me. On that one precious day in town, we were to apply for the marriage license, shop for the wedding gown and veil, make appointments with the minister, the photographer, and the restaurant for the wedding dinner. Normally a town pass took about a week to be officially processed, but Henry and Minnie pounded private doors and desk tops until they had the permit safely in their hands by evening.

Early the next morning we rode to Twin Falls, crowded into the back of an army truck. Although a raw, slicing wind whipped through between the canvas cover and slowly turned us into ice figures, the thought of our first day of freedom in town brightened our eyes. Sumi chattered excitedly, "First thing I'm going to do, I'm buying a chocolate ice-cream soda."

We shivered and concentrated our thoughts on hot coffee and hot roast beef sandwiches.

Minnie breathed deeply, "I hope I find my wedding dress."

When our truck rolled to a stop at a corner in front of a drugstore, we fell silent. We wondered how the townspeople would react to us. Would their glances be just curious or would they be filled with suspicion and hostility? A well-dressed matron looked at us with startled eyes and open mouth as we jumped out of the back of the army truck one by one. Under her frank appraisal we felt at a distinct disadvantage, but we pretended indifference. Eager to go on our errands, we scattered happily off in all directions, like marbles from a little boy's bag. Henry and Minnie dashed off to get their marriage license, while Mrs. Yokoyama, Mother, Sumi and I invaded the five-and-ten cent store. Mrs. Yokoyama and Mother went berserk in the household goods section and bought teacups, needles and thread, cotton goods, laundry soap, alarm clocks and light bulbs, all scarce commodities in camp. Sumi and I stormed our way to the cosmetic counter and found our favorite purple lipstick and purple nail polish. At noon we all stood in front of a restaurant, trying to decide whether we should walk in together or split into two parties and go to different eating places. Somehow we felt we ought not to travel in droves or congregate in public in large groups. One Japanese face was conspicuous enough, and a party of them might be downright obnoxious. We finally decided to stay together, since Mrs. Yokoyama and Mother preferred each other's company, and Sumi and I were reluctant to see them go off by themselves. We walked timidly inside, hoping that we would not attract too much attention. Only one raw-boned, weather-beaten farmer stared at us. We made for the corner where we huddled close against the wall, trying to blend into the wallpaper design. Like children out on a spree not to be seen or heard, we quietly swooned over our roast chicken, crisp French fried potatoes, tender golden carrots, fluffy coconut cream pie and aromatic hot coffee. At the end of the meal, we fought down an impulse to scrape our dishes and take them back to the dishwasher, a ritual we had learned at the mess hall. And we remembered just in time to stop at the cashier's window to pay for the dinners.

The rest of the afternoon we accompanied Minnie on the hunt for the all-important wedding gown. In one department store, a cheerful, buxom saleslady melted in ecstasy when she learned that Minnie was to be a bride. "My dear, how absolutely luscious! I have the latest assortment of gowns for you."

She lovingly draped a voluminous satin creation against her full-blown Brünnhilde bosom and hips. Minnie suggested delicately, "It's lovely, but I wear a size nine."

"My dear, everything we have here is size sixteen," she stated flatly, implying that all women wore size sixteen, except for the subnormal and scrawny. She added warmly, "But that's all right, honey, we can fix that easy enough. Come on, let's put this on."

The saleslady cast the billowing satin over Minnie's head like a fisherman with his net, drowning Minnie's feeble protest. In an instant she was swarming over Minnie with a pincushion, and soon the gown was a perfect fit. The woman had deftly tucked the dress with straight pins up and down Minnie's back so that it resembled a dinosaur's spine. The sleeves were folded back six inches and the waistline, which had dangled at Minnie's knees, was doubled and hoisted over the abdomen so that it resembled the silken pouch of a kangaroo.

"It's delicious, delectable!" the saleswoman said, fluttering about. "I just love that neckline," she added, trying to lift our gaze above this wanton surgery. "Don't you think she looks scrumptious in it?"

Sumi and I were too fascinated by the glittering row of straight pins down Minnie's back to say anything. Mrs. Yokoyama and Mother, ever polite and noncommittal, smiled and nodded at no one in particular.

The only other department store in town also had the latest assortment of gowns, all size sixteens, complete with fingerprints, footprints and lipstick smears. We trudged into an exclusive women's shop. A svelte, streamlined woman, wearing a plain, simple, tight-fitting dress which looked as if it had been woven right onto her epidermis, told Minnie haughtily, "We have no wedding gowns," as if she considered weddings unfashionable.

When the fourth dress shop proved just as barren, Minnie's lips started to tremble, "What am I going to do?"

The saleswoman who had waited on her suggested that we try Sarah Ann's down two blocks. Minnie blurted out happily, "Is there another store?"

Minnie flew out of the door and preceded us down the street by a full block as we loped after her wearily. Inside Sarah Ann's we found Minnie in a delirium, swishing back and forth in front of a mirror, dressed in a beautiful gown of delicate white lace, with a floating skirt of white net. Minnie told us with a hysterical catch in her voice, "This was the only one they had left, and it was size nine!"

We collapsed. The wedding was saved.

There was not a single bridal headdress to be found in town, but nothing could discourage Minnie now. She bought a dozen baby pearl necklaces, wire, and yards of netting. Out of these she patiently fashioned a handsome coronet, worked into it an intricate orange-blossom design with the tiny seed pearls, and set it off with the white cloud of veiling. It was an exquisite work of art.

Minnie wanted wedding music for the ceremony, but the Thompsons, in whose apartment in Twin Falls the wedding was to take place, had no piano. Minnie was undaunted. "Don't worry, I'll find something!" I knew she would, even if she had to go out and fashion one herself out of greasewood, and run a pack of coyotes down for the ivory in their mouths. A few days later Henry and Minnie crashed into our room, hauling behind them a battered black oversized suitcase. Minnie patted it affectionately, "There it is, Kaz. We borrowed it from a voice teacher here in camp. She thought her portable organ was more important to bring than a suitcase of clothes. It's going to play the wedding march for us."

Minnie snapped open the top, revealing crumbling organ keys which reminded me of yellowed, decaying teeth. And it bellowed and belched like a vulgar old man enjoying himself after dinner. My only function was to pump the air and press the keys, and it took over completely in an uninhibited double forte roar. The wedding march swelled out from our apartment as I practiced, so that everyone in our block was pacing his walk to Lohengrin.

Henry stood over me, bitterly wringing his hands, "Can't you tone that thing down, Sis? Everybody looks up at our window and smirks! And everybody under the sun knows I'm getting married now."

I told him blandly that the only way to quiet this organ down was to take a hatchet to it. Besides now Minnie wouldn't have to send announcements.

Tuesday night, the night before the wedding, there was another calamity. Henry fell headlong into a deep ditch and sprained his ankle. He was half dragged, half carried, moaning and cursing to the hospital by the indomitable Minnie. There Henry sheepishly offered himself up to the tender mercies and ribbings of the hospital staff.

We arose early on the wedding day and the entire Yokoyama and Itoi clan formed a beaming parade up to the Administration Building where the army truck awaited us. Mr. Yokoyama and Father reeked of mothballs in their dark suits and heavy winter overcoats. The womenfolks were delighted to have the opportunity to wear their best clothes and best hats swathed in veiling. The air was crystal cold and the road was iced and slick as a mirror. We found the two-mile hike to the Administration Building fraught with danger as we slid about on high heels. Our frantic breathing steamed our hat veils until they sagged moist and limp like damp cobwebs in front of our struggling red faces.

In Twin Falls, we stopped off first at The Album for the wedding and family pictures. On such short notice, the photographer could give us only a morning appointment before the wedding. It was unconventional, but for once Minnie did not mind. So six women crowded into the small dark dressing room to help dress the bride and help arrange her coiffure. Dunks, who had come with the party to act as one of the witnesses, rushed out to the florist for the bridal bouquet, corsages and boutonnieres while Henry sat forlornly in the corner, contemplating his purple gout. The hysteria of the wedding preparations was plainly reflected in all our faces in the finished picture. The photographer valiantly tried to make the eleven of us relax and look natural at the precise second. He darted all around us, unclenching Mr. Yokoyama's fists, adjusting a sausage curl here and pulling out a creeping cuff, until his brown thin wisp of hair stood up and floated like sea anemone. He pleaded, "Please, the bridegroom, loosen your cheek muscles. Don't look so grim, even though it is your wedding day!"

"The gentleman with the glasses, keep your chin down. Lower. Lower." He was talking to Father. Father finally photographed with a double chin and four eyes shining out from behind his bifocals.

From there the wedding party moved on to the Reverend Mr. Thompson's apartment where the ceremony took place. I wish I could have seen the wedding myself, but my only recollection of it is confined to the bathroom. I remember distinctly that Mrs. Thompson had the loveliest shade of jonquil yellow linen towels hanging on the rods, and the bathtub faucet dripped steadily in dignified accompaniment to the Lohengrin wedding march.

Before the ceremony began, Dunks had thoughtfully hidden the crouching uncouth-looking black organ and me behind the davenport at the far end of the small living room. When I started playing "Clair de Lune" to create a soft, shimmering effect, the organ howled like a drunken village idiot. Everyone turned and gave me delicately shocked glances. Henry shot out from the kitchen where he and the bride had been waiting for the march to the altar. He hissed fiercely at us, "God bless it, I knew this would happen. Get that thing out of here."

"Where?" Dunks lifted the organ up off the floor and looked wildly around the little room.

"In there, behind that door!" Henry pointed at a white-curtained French door.

The organ and I were whisked out of the living room, and we blundered into a bedroom where the Reverend Thompson was meditating, waiting for the proper mood and moment to step out into the living room. He helped us squeeze the chuckling, gloating organ between the bed and the wall. I sat primly on the host's bed, barely pumped the air, and started the opening number again, but the organ thundered out like a full-bodied pipe organ at a skating rink. Sumi dashed in, "Henry says it's still too loud."

The organ and I were pushed out of the bedroom, and we sat out in the hallway. They closed the living-room door and the bedroom door for good measure. I played, but bugle-eared Henry was still not satisfied. There was only one other retreat. The organ and I were exiled to the bathroom. Dunks said, wiping his brow, "Henry'd better be satisfied now or you'll both have to leave by the window."

There was not enough room for an extra chair so I made myself comfortable on the toilet seat and waited for Sumi's signals, two raps on the door, to start the music. I played only a few bars of the wedding march when Sumi rapped on the door four times to halt. Evidently the trip that Henry and Minnie made from the kitchen to the living room required only three steps. While Mr. Thompson was solemnizing the ceremony, I meditated earnestly into the bathtub. After it was all over Sumi flung open the bathroom door and cried, starry-eyed, "It was wonderful! The music sounded as if it were floating right down from heaven!"

After a merry wedding feast at the Blue Ox, the army truck hurtled us back to Camp Minidoka before they locked the gates.

The happy bridal couple remained behind to spend their three days' honeymoon in Twin Falls.

Since Henry and Minnie had not been able to invite their many good friends to the wedding because of rigid rules concerning town passes, they decided to have a bang-up wedding reception in camp for their friends and their parents' friends. While Henry and Minnie feverishly penned invitations, we all rallied around to help them with their party. We wangled special permission to use the huge recreation barracks for the occasion. It was completely bare except for a thick blanket of sand on the floor and window sills. We swabbed the floors, washed the windows, and collected chairs of all shapes and sizes. We made a gigantic tea table with long boards placed on dozens of wooden horses. After it was covered with snowy white sheets and graced with borrowed silver candelabra, the table took on the massive dignity of a royal banquet table. Mrs. Yokoyama and Mother arranged a beautiful floral centerpiece of blush-pink gladiolas in a wide silver bowl.

Minnie said she wanted music for her reception, and I recoiled in horror, "Oh no, not again!"

Minnie laughed, "Relax, Kaz. I ran into an honest-to-goodness piano this time, recently donated to the camp by one of the churches in Buhl. Besides you don't have to play. I want you to help as tea hostess."

The piano was trucked in and tenderly lifted into the barracks. It was old and decrepit, like a dried-out hag. Its front panel was torn out, exposing an emaciated set of stringy ribs. Henry went into an apoplectic fit. "Take it back, wherever you found it! I won't have my guests entertained with that thing!"

Minnie stood her ground. "I'm going to have music — chamber music. I've already asked three girls to make up a string trio."

Tears poised perilously in Minnie's eyes until Henry was forced to retreat. "You may have your chamber music, honey, but we'll have to put a curtain in front of that thing."

Sunday afternoon, the stage was finally set for a formal hat-and-gloves reception. The silver tea set, the coffee urn, china cups and saucers, gleaming silverware, silver trays of nuts and mints, all borrowed, were set in their proper places. Confronted with this polished glamour, the ugly bare rafters and the two by four planks crisscrossing the walls receded hastily into the background. Behind the curtain the rebuffed piano stood among the gallon cans of ice cream. Outdoors, the pale yellow sun was doing its best to soften the sting of the sharp March wind. It was a perfect day for a brisk walk for our guests, some of whom would be walking several miles to our end of the camp. I anticipated a delightful afternoon with people drifting in and out for the next two hours to chat with the bride and groom and the in-laws, to meet new people and to renew old acquaintances. It would be a brief return to an urban affair, a blend of laughter, the polite tinkle of silver against teacups, and soft, bouncy music.

But we had overlooked one important thing. In our runaway enthusiasm for a genuine tea party with all the trimmings, we had forgotten that the Issei were accustomed only to Japanese tea parties. We had planned an American one.

I first sensed that something was wrong when two o'clock came and no one appeared. During the first hour, only a handful of Nisei sat around, rattling their teacups nervously. Their voices echoed painfully clear up and down the large hall and the conversation threatened to die from sheer embarrassment. There was only one explanation. The old folks were observing the Japanese time-honored custom of being substantially late. To an Oriental, arriving on the appointed hour implied a childlike eagerness, while to be late to a tempting dinner party or entertainment indicated self-restraint and modesty. We were Orientals, too, and we waited patiently. Finally at three o'clock, they came, all at once. They paused politely at the doorway, slipped modestly into the hall, bowing graciously to the right and to the left. They all gravitated to the far end of the hall where there was nothing and nobody. There they seated themselves and waited for things to happen. Soon there were not enough chairs, and a number of Issei stood pressed against the walls, trying to look as inconspicuous as possible. We sent young men out on a frenzied search for more chairs, crates, anything sittable, for it was all too evident that Issei guests must never be left standing. Minnie discovered something else that was wrong. "They don't even have refreshments to occupy them!"

Tami and Kazie, Minnie's sisters, Sumi and I rushed to our guests. We bowed to them. We waved our hands toward the beautifully set table and said in our most charming hostess voices, "*Dozo*, please, won't you step up to the table and help yourself to some refreshments?"

The first Issei woman to whom I spoke, bowed deeply and thanked me, murmuring, "*Dozo,* please don't trouble yourself over me!"

She remained firmly seated. I went down the line, bowing and pleading with each man and woman. Each Issei smiled graciously and remained glued to the chairs and walls. After the twentieth woman had tried to bow me away, "Thank you so much, it's very kind of you, but please don't bother," I nearly sobbed in frustration. We went into a huddle. Maybe we should give a demonstration of what goes on at an American tea party. Henry, Minnie and the hostesses walked to the table, asked for tea and coffee, and helped themselves to refreshment. Our guests watched our every move, vastly interested and relieved to have the monotony broken by human activity. I felt so completely unnerved I fumbled at the cake plate, pushed the cake off on the table, and dropped cashew nuts into my coffee cup. We drifted casually among people, bantering here and there. I swallowed scalding hot coffee so vigorously tears came into my eyes. A sweet-faced woman who had been watching me for some time with a quizzical expression on her face, looked away politely. I finally pulled Mother behind the curtain.

"Mama, we invited your friends to refreshments, but they're not co-operating. They make me feel as if I were trying to shove food down their throats."

Mother reflected a moment. "I'm afraid you'll have to serve them, Ka-chan. They're uncomfortable with the arrangements here. It's just like telling your guests at home to find their way into the kitchen, when they get hungry, and help themselves."

"But, Mother, there're nearly a hundred guests, and to serve them. . . ."

But there was no other way out. I inquired of each person, "I would like to bring you some refreshment. Which do you prefer, tea or coffee?"

They were very evasive. They said, "*Arigato,* thank you, thank you. Either will be just fine."

In the end, I served tea and coffee alternately and things ran smoothly for a while.

As I roamed among the guests, looking for empty teacups to fill, I felt vaguely uncomfortable as if something else was off-key. It was some time before I discovered that it was the stony silence which fell upon the crowd every now and then. It always occurred when the chamber music started playing. Only the sound of the string trio, sawing on and on, filled the hall until the music began to sound lonely and self-conscious. I mentioned it to Sumi. Her eyes gleamed as she tried to penetrate our guests' minds. "You know what? They think it's not polite to talk or eat when the music is being played."

We immediately started circulating through the crowd to divert attention from the music and start a move back to general conversation, but our voices sounded loud and forced in the polite silence. Waves of chilled disapproval snapped our voices off one by one, until we were all listening helplessly to the hard-working musicians. After the girls had finished a medley of Victor Herbert tunes, Tami went up to them with refreshments which they accepted eagerly. A wave of applause broke through the crowd. The girls, holding a dish of ice cream and cake in one hand and a teacup in the other, looked at their audience with baffled smiles, and then with a great show of nonchalance, started eating.

At another moment, Sumi hissed at me, "The candles aren't lit!" We had been so occupied trying to keep the reception from grinding to a complete standstill, we had forgotten to light them. I found matches behind the curtain, whipped it aside and marched out to the table. Then the familiar, appalling silence filled the barracks. I glanced up to see what had gone wrong and I met one hundred pair of eyes turned upon me, giving me their full and undivided attention. I swallowed. There was only the sound of my high heels clicking sharply on the bare floor as I walked around the long table, lighting what seemed to me then at least one hundred candles. I saw Sumi watching me from behind the curtain, tears of laughter streaming down her face. When I glared at her, she only rolled her eyes to the ceiling and shrugged her shoulders in a hopeless gesture. When I finished my little chore, I felt the mood of expectancy mount to an excited tension. I wished with all my heart then that I could have rendered a beautiful solo of "The Indian Love Call," but I had nothing more to offer my public. As I slowly moved back behind the curtain, I was a little disappointed to find that I hadn't rated even a slight burst of applause after my splendid performance.

The bulk of our guests who had arrived on Japan Time dutifully remained until four o'clock because the invitation had said from "Two to four, Sunday afternoon." By then we were feeling sorry we had not planned a solid round of entertainment to fill the terrible vacuum. Promptly at four, everyone prepared to leave. They rushed at Henry and Minnie and the in-laws to offer their congratulations, all at once, and the babble and laughter rose to a hilarious pitch. Freed of teacups and cake plates, freed from the concert and the strange candle-lighting ceremony, the Issei milled about happily. It was nearly six o'clock when the last guest departed. We stumbled into our chairs, more hysterical than relieved. To try to force East to meet West had been a terrible mistake. Our American tea party with Japanese guests had nearly been a complete failure.

Eastward, Nisei

BY 1943, scarcely a year after Evacuation Day, the War Relocation Authority was opening channels through which the Nisei
could return to the main stream of life. It granted permanent
leave to anyone cleared by the FBI who had proof of a job and
a place to live. Students were also released if they had been accepted into colleges and universities.

The West Coast was still off-limits, but we had access to the
rest of the continent where we could start all over again. The
Midwest and East suddenly loomed before us, an exciting challenge. Up till then America for me had meant the lovely city
of Seattle, a small Japanese community and a desperate struggle
to be just myself. Now that I had shed my past, I hoped that I
might come to know another aspect of America which would in-
ject strength into my hyphenated Americanism instead of pulling
it apart.

Matsuko, my childhood friend, was one of the first to leave
camp. Through a church program, the Reverend Mr. and Mrs.
W. Trumble of Chicago had become interested in helping individual evacuees. They had written Matsuko, telling her about a
job as a stenographer in a large department store and inviting her
to live with them. From Chicago, Matsuko deluged me with enthusiastic letters, telling me what wonderful folks the Trumbles
were and how happy she was with her job. She said she no longer

felt self-conscious about her Oriental face and that she was breathing free and easy for the first time in her life. Matsuko urged me to leave Minidoka and spoke to the Trumbles about me. One day I received a cordial letter from a Dr. and Mrs. John Richardson. Dr. Richardson was a pastor at a Presbyterian Church in a suburb of Chicago. He told me of a dentist, desperately in need of an assistant, who was willing to hire a Nisei. I was to live with the Richardsons.

I accepted Dr. Richardson's invitation posthaste, feeling as if it were a dream too good to be true. Father and Mother, although reluctant to see me go, accepted my decision to leave as part of the sadness which goes with bearing children who grow up and must be independent.

So when it was early in spring and the snow had thawed, I boarded a train in Shoshone, numbed with excitement and anxiety. For two days and two nights I remained wide-eyed and glued to my seat as we rushed headlong across the great continent. We finally hit Chicago, and I felt helpless in the giant, roaring metropolis, with its thundering vitality, perpetual wind and clouds of smoke. Hundreds of people and cars seemed to be rushing at each other at suicide speed. I was relieved to see that they were much too busy to notice the evacuees who had crept into town. I plunged and swam through this heaving mass of humanity until I found a taxi.

The Richardson residence was a large, two-story brown frame house in the suburbs. I pressed the doorbell with a nervous cold finger. A small woman with a beautiful halo of white hair and gentle gray eyes greeted me warmly. "Come in, Monica, I'm Mrs. Richardson. My husband and I've been expecting you. Here, let me help you with your suitcase." Her quiet, gracious manner disarmed me completely.

Dr. Richardson came out of his study, beaming. He was a great oak of a man, tall and solidly built. The rugged cut of his features, his deep vibrant voice, everything about him revealed a personality of strong purpose and will. He shook my hand so vigorously I felt like a tiny wren swaying on the end of a swinging branch.

"We're so glad to see you, Monica, so very glad," he said. "I hope you'll like it here."

I learned that the Richardsons had been China missionaries for many years. Mrs. Richardson brought out pictures of her sons, all three in the armed services: Gordon, the physician, in the army; Paul, in the navy; and John, the youngest, also in the army, somewhere in the Pacific. It was a curious sensation to be talking to these folks who knew and loved so much about China, a nation at war so long with Japan. I felt even stranger when I learned that Paul, the second son, was learning Japanese in naval intelligence. Eventually he would go out to meet his Japanese enemy, and John had probably already encountered them. Our entire relationship was interwoven in the grim business of war, and yet the Richardsons made me feel from the start that we were friends, that we had something in common, something which had nothing to do with politics, war and hate.

After we had chatted a while, Dr. Richardson remembered he had a call to make, and clapping on his hat and overcoat, he rushed out, telling me to make myself at home now that I *was* home.

Mrs. Richardson led me upstairs into an attractive, modestly furnished room. "This is yours, Monica. It was John, Jr.'s before he left for the army. I've emptied the closet and drawers so you may use them as you wish."

Mrs. Richardson walked to the window overlooking the spacious back yard and opened it slightly. A spring breeze wafted through the freshly starched curtain, bringing into the room the cool freshness of the trees, the lawn and the flower garden below. There was serenity and peace in this house which I knew was the reflection of this gentle woman's character.

"I'll go away now and let you rest," she said. "When you're ready, come downstairs for supper."

I stood alone in the room, very close to tears. It seemed as if I had at last come to the end of a long journey, and walked into a resting place for tired souls. I lay on the bed, weary, with the comfortable weariness which comes after release from tension. It was wonderful to have a room of my own again. I even had an elm tree of my own, towering right outside the south window, which broke the sunlight pouring into my room into a cool, shadowy pattern of dark-green leaves. There was a yellow bowl filled with fresh-cut flowers placed on the dresser. And I noticed that the night table standing beside my bed was covered with a Chinese scarf, a beautiful piece of rich blue satin, the intricate flowered design hand-embroidered with gold, carmine, jade green and purple threads. Mrs. Richardson must have placed it there for my enjoyment. I settled into my pillow with a warm feeling. I knew that I would become terribly lonely for my family now and then, but its sharpness would be dulled in this home, for here there was kindness and love, deep and unshakable. Tomorrow I would be able to write a gay letter to Father and Mother, telling them about my new friends.

In the beginning I worried a great deal about people's reactions to me. Before I left Camp Minidoka, I had been warned over and over again that once I was outside, I must behave as inconspicuously as possible so as not to offend the sensitive public eye. I made up my mind to make myself scarce and invisible, but I discovered that an Oriental face, being somewhat of a rarity in the Midwest, made people stop in their tracks, stare, follow and question me. At first I was dismayed with such attention, but I learned that it was out of curiosity and not hostility that they stared.

Much of the time people mistook me for Chinese, and they told me how well they thought of the Chinese, who were our allies, and what a dynamic personality Madame Chiang Kai-shek was. Once in a department store, a young wide-eyed sales-girl fluttered up to me, "May I have your autograph, Miss Wong?" I regretfully told her I was not Miss Wong, but for a fleeting second I felt the vicarious thrill of a celebrity. The young clerk had been thinking of Miss Anna May Wong who was in the same department store that day demonstrating cosmetics.

On another occasion, I was mistaken for Ming Toy, a Chinese fan dancer. As I stood waiting for a bus on a corner, a strange man dashed across the street, grinning widely and waving his hand at me. He came up, all graciousness.

"Good afternoon, Miss Toy! Er, ah, you are Miss Toy?"

I was confused for a moment. My name was "Itoi" and many times people dropped the first letter and simply called me "Miss Toy." I said, "Yes," hesitantly, wondering what this was leading up to. The man brightened. "Well, Miss Toy, I thought your number pretty snappy. How about lunch so we can talk about booking you at our cabaret. We can use a fan dancer now."

My jaws dropped, and I was unable to find words to express my shock. I flagged down an empty taxicab and dashed away, followed by the bewildered man who shouted after me, "Just a moment, Miss Toy! You are the fan dancer, aren't you?" People stopped to watch Ming Toy, the fan dancer, dive into a taxi.

Sometimes there were decided advantages to having an Oriental face, especially when shopping. When I stepped into a department store or a market, a clerk would spot me instantly and rush up to wait on me, burning with curiosity. The clerks were invariably pleasant and sociable and they complimented me on my English.

Matsuko had blossomed into an attractive young lady about town with a wide circle of friends, and she took me in hand. I was overwhelmed to find that we were made welcome everywhere, especially in the church groups. We enjoyed dinner parties, concerts and dances with our new friends, and no one looked askance at us.

I wrote letters to Henry, Minnie and Sumi, telling them about this refreshing attitude and the naturalness I felt in the Midwest, urging them to leave camp at once. Henry had been rejected by the army on account of his poor eyesight and he was chafing in camp, watching all of his friends go off to war. Soon I received word from home that Henry and Minnie had found jobs in a tuberculosis sanitarium in St. Louis, and Sumi had been accepted into the Cadet Nurse's Corps. She was going to study at a Long Island hospital. We had a wonderful, brief reunion when the three of them stopped off at Chicago before they resumed the trips to their respective destinations. They met the Richardsons, fell in love with them, and said that they felt like new people. Henry and Minnie were happy about their new jobs because they would be working together. Sumi was enthusiastic about her nurse's training, and at the thought of seeing New York. We felt a twinge of regret when we had to say good-by again. We promised each other that eventually we would try to move to a central point and call Mother and Father out. It would be like old times again, but much better.

The first morning I reported for work as dental assistant to

Dr. J. J. Moller, I was on my toes, glowing with eagerness and what I hoped was bright-eyed intelligence. When I stepped into Dr. Moller's office, I thought I had blundered into an exclusive beauty salon. The walls and ceilings were painted a soft dove blue, lighted up by handsome floor lamps. Huge barrel armchairs and a modernistic low davenport lounged about smugly on thick blue rugs.

Dr. Moller, in a starched white coat, glided out of the inner office. He was tall and lithe, and somewhere in his middle forties. Penetrating steel-gray eyes, set deep in their sockets, glittered like ball-bearings. The thin lips were a straight slit above a jutting, granite jaw. His words were sparsely efficient.

"Come in. I'll show you around."

Beyond the reception room there was an office furnished with a handsome desk, an electric typewriter, an expensive-looking file cabinet. The operating room was fitted with an electrically operated dental chair — a luxurious white master unit studded with mysterious accessories. There was also a powder room for women patients. But the tiny laboratory was dingy and disorderly. It looked like a junkyard with a profusion of cans and glass jars piled on top of each other. It seemed to be the center of frenzied activity.

As if it were an afterthought, Dr. Moller discussed salary. "Now, I've been paying my help fourteen dollars a week. To tell the truth, no girl is worth that much in the beginning. In your case, however, I'm making an exception and I'll pay you fifteen dollars."

I thought about the scarcity of jobs and accepted his offer.

From the beginning, Dr. Moller trained and groomed me with relentless zeal. His motto was efficiency. There must never be a wasted movement. He said, "Always utilize both hands.

Never let one dangle idly. If you can do a job with just one hand, then find another task for the other."

No one could approach the dedication that Dr. Moller showed for his work. Every evening he hurried out for a quick supper and rushed back to work until way past midnight. One morning I found him vigorously vacuuming the rug in the reception room. He was muttering, "Don't know what the cleaning woman does around here, but the floor's never clean, the furniture's never dusted properly. That's the way inferior people operate."

With a vehement flourish, he swept out into the next office mumbling, "From tomorrow, you get down here an hour earlier and clean the rooms, but don't think you're going to get paid more. I'm actually paying you more than I ordinarily do."

I told Matsuko about my employer. She was shocked.

"He sounds like a slave driver. If I were you, I'd leave him."

"That'd really make him angry. Maybe he'll go around telling everybody Nisei aren't any good."

I was thinking what Mr. Beck, the director of the War Relocation Authority Employment Office, had said: "Whatever you do, don't quit at the drop of a hat. If you switch jobs too often, the Nisei are going to get a reputation as poor risks."

Matsuko replied, "Bosh and nonsense. It's one thing to work hard, and another to be trampled on. I guess I'm lucky to have a boss like Mr. Pritchard. He's the most considerate and kind person I've ever met."

I decided to hang on a little longer.

Within two weeks, I had been promoted to cleaning woman, receptionist, secretary, bookkeeper and laboratory worker. This was too much for me, and my efficiency began to deteriorate. Soon I was crashing into closed doors, dropping cans of white plaster powder, and stabbing innocent patients with dental instruments in my zeal to pass them to the doctor quickly, and never waste a motion.

One day I made the terrible mistake of fainting at work. The summer afternoon was sultry, and for two hours I had assisted on a gold-filling job. It looked as if it would take another hour before it was completed. The work required close attention and timing, firing the gold foils to the right temperature and pinpointing them down into the exact spot indicated by Dr. Moller's instrument. I had to stand motionless at attention on the other side of the patient with perspiration streaming down the back of my neck. I felt gradually mesmerized by the monotony of the work, and the thick humidity, and the dead silence in the room, broken only by the soft metallic tick-tick-tick-tick of the electric gold plugger. The blood slowly settled to my feet and I knew I was going to faint. I told Dr. Moller that I was not feeling well. I wanted to crawl to the reception room where I could sit down in one of the deep comfortable chairs for a while, but I didn't quite make it. I blacked out at the door. The next thing I knew, I was looking up at a ceiling, and desk and chairs were hanging upside down above. The sight made me dizzy and I had to close my eyes again. Then I remembered where I was lolling. I struggled to my feet and saw Dr. Moller calmly working away. I went into the laboratory, poured water down my throat, rearranged my hair and uniform and went back to work.

After the patient left the office, Dr. Moller thundered out in a white rage. "What was the dumb idea of fainting in the presence of a patient? What if someone had walked in and found you lying on the floor, what an impression you would have made."

It was the last straw. I was through. I told him with intense satisfaction, as if I were dropping great chunks of ice on his head. "I am quitting, Dr. Moller, right now. I'm leaving for good."

Dr. Moller's temper came to a screeching halt. He roared like a wounded lion. "But you can't leave me just like that! I'll report you to the War Relocation Office. Besides you owe me two weeks' notice before you can quit. Mr. Beck will see to that for me."

"Very well, I'll stay on the two weeks, but not a day longer."

That evening at dinner time, I told the Richardsons I had quit, and all that had happened.

Mrs. Richardson shook her head. "I'm terribly sorry. I can't understand such a man. But I'm glad you gave your notice, because we have good news for you. We have arranged for you to return to college. Our friends, the Scotts, were China Missionaries. Now Dr. Scott is the president of Wendell College in Indiana, and today we received a letter from him, saying he would be glad to have you enroll, if you wish."

"If I wish? I've never wanted anything more in my life, Mrs. Richardson. But . . ."

She interrupted me, smiling, "And that isn't all. The college is offering you a work scholarship which will take care of your tuition fees. Then there is a minister's widow who lives on the campus grounds, a Mrs. Ashford, who wants you to come and live with her. She is all alone and you would be a companion to her."

Dr. Richardson said, "Well, Monica, you've had your share of downs, but you're going to have your ups from now on."

This good news was almost too much to bear after the hectic day with Dr. Moller. I tried in vain to tell the Richardsons how happy I was, and was immensely relieved when Dr. Richardson reached for his Bible and began the usual after-dinner worship so I could sob quietly while we bowed our heads for the prayer.

CHAPTER XII

Deeper into the Land

I ENROLLED at Wendell College in southern Indiana. The cluster of ivy-covered red brick buildings stood gathered on the edge of a thick-wooded bluff which rose almost three hundred feet, overlooking the stately Ohio River. Wendell College was a Presbyterian-affiliated liberal arts school, and the atmosphere of its campus reflected a leisurely pace of life, simplicity and friendly charm. Young people from all walks of life were there . . . studying for the ministry, the teaching profession, the medical profession and other varied fields. There was also a distinct international air with foreign students from all parts of the world: South America, China, Java, India.

Mrs. Ashford, the widow with whom I lived on the edge of the campus, was an example of the college town's friendliness. She was a comfortable, motherly woman with silky, honey-colored hair done up in a bun, and merry blue eyes. Her husband had been a minister and college official. He had died several years before, and Mrs. Ashford had been living alone ever since. In the tall, two-storied gray frame house, my new friend had prepared a cozy room for me upstairs, where I could study quietly. Despite a stiff knee, Mrs. Ashford was up at dawn to fire up the furnace and prepare breakfast. I awakened to her cheerful call and the fragrant aroma of coffee wafting up to my room. In the evenings when I returned home from school, we sat in the two wooden rocking chairs in the sitting room, chatted about the days' events, listened to a favorite radio program or two, then I went upstairs to study. And always before bedtime, Mrs. Ashford called me down to the kitchen for a light snack because she firmly believed that mental work was just as exhausting as physical labor. Thus she provided me with the companionship I needed and a wealth of enchanting memories which I could conjure up at the thought of Wendell . . . the warm fragrance of freshly baked nutbread and homemade cookies filling the house on a cold winter night, the creaking porch swing where I could relax on warm spring evenings to watch the fireflies pinpoint the dark blue night, as I breathed in the thick sweet scent of lilacs surrounding the house.

There were three other Nisei girls enrolled at Wendell. Two were from southern California, and the third from my own home town. Faculty and students alike went out of their way to make us feel a real part of the campus life. We were swept into a round of teas and dinner parties, and invited to join the independent women's organization. The sororities included us in their rush parties, too, although because of a national ruling we could not be asked to join. I knew about this policy, and although I had ceased to feel personally hurt about it, one sorority apparently felt troubled by the restriction imposed on it. One day its officers, Alice Week, Lorraine Brown and the faculty advisor, Miss Knight, paid me a special visit. I remember how Alice looked at Miss Knight as if she were taking a deep breath before the plunge, and then spoke gently to me. "Monica, we've enjoyed meeting you, and we hope we'll get to know a lot more of each other from now on. But there are national restrictions placed on our membership. Although many of us sincerely want to invite you into our group, we can't. I hope you understand."

After a moment of embarrassed silence, I managed to say, "Yes, Alice, I do know about this from back home. I understand."

Lorraine said, "We felt we should tell you about it, Monica, rather than say nothing. We didn't want you to think we were ignoring you for personal reasons."

"Thank you. I really appreciate your visit." I knew this call had cost them something in pride, and it took moral honesty to have come in the spirit in which they did.

In the following years I came to know and like Alice, a charming and earnest young woman, who took valedictory honors in my graduation class, and Lorraine, a talented music major. My constant companion was Marta Sanchez, a vivacious dark-eyed girl from Bogotá, Colombia, who spoke with her expressive hands whenever her English failed her. We both liked music and played the piano about the same way, loud and stormy. We were frustrated "classical" students who yearned to play jazz with the abandon of George Gershwin. Marta was studying to be a doctor because, as she said, there was a great need for them in her country. Then there was Anna Jong from Bangkok. She had been a student in China until the time Japan had pushed into its interior. Anna had fled to safety by walking long, cruel miles southward. She had come to Wendell through the auspices of the Presbyterian Mission Board. Anna wanted to be a geologist. I also became good friends with Sylvia Arnold and her brother John from Dayton, Ohio, both of whom were studying to go into the Christian service.

The professors were at once friendly and casual. Although during class hours they were distant and insistent that we study, we grew to know them, their wives and their children, well at school and church functions and from day-to-day encounters at the post office and stores. There was one distinguished-looking language professor whom I always called whenever I wanted to get a ride into town on a Saturday. Dr. Konig and his wife always went into town on week ends, taking a carload of students with them. There was another, tall, gruff-mannered economics professor whom we could sometimes persuade to move classes out to the cool green lawn under the trees on warm spring days. And whenever I was faced with a vexing personal problem, I immediately hied myself to Dr. or Mrs. Scott who diffused affection and understanding like a glowing hearth fire. It was a far cry from the dignified and austere University of Washington where I hurried alone from class to class along the sprawling pathways.

I had been intimidated by the racial barriers in the business and professional world and I wasn't brave enough to explore or develop my other interests. It seemed useless to do so in the face of closed doors. So when I entered the University of Washington, I clung to literature, my first love, saying to my friends that I wanted to teach. We all knew this was a fancy, too, destined to wither.

Now my interests exploded in a number of directions — music, history and current events, religion and philosophy, sociology. But above all, I discovered that I liked people, as individuals and unique personalities. Whatever career I chose, it would have something to do with people. And since I had to come to the Midwest and was embarked on a life more normal and happier than I had dared hope for, I gradually uncoiled and relaxed enough to take more honest stock of my real inclinations. I was attracted to psychology courses and did well in them. After talking it over with my advisor, I decided to go into Clinical Psychology.

The first two school years at Wendell I worked for my tuition and board, waiting on tables in the women's dormitory. Being physically inept, I never learned to hoist the huge tray over my head with one hand as most students did within the first week. Instead I staggered and groaned under the weight of the tray until at last I was offered a job as secretary to Dr. Scott, and not a day too soon, I thought, for I had worn deep dents into my sides from carrying trays on my hips. During summer vacations, I went home to the Richardsons in Chicago where I worked as a stenographer in a law firm. Father's foresight in persuading me to go to business school was paying off at last.

My second year at Wendell, just before Christmas, I had a letter from Father and Mother, who were still in camp, urging me to spend the holiday with them. "It would be so nice to have at least one of you back." They enclosed a check for the railroad fare. So I packed a suitcase, kissed Mrs. Ashford "Good-by and Merry Christmas," and set off for Camp Minidoka.

At Shoshone, my last stop, I went into a crumbling old hotel and sat in its overheated lobby to wait for the bus to take me into camp. Bewhiskered, wrinkled old men lounged silently, reading every word in the newspaper, reaching around now and then to spit tobacco juice into the battered brass spittoon. I wondered if Father's hotel in Seattle was now filled with dried-up, dusty remnants of humanity like these.

At Camp Minidoka, I was startled to see an MP again, standing at the gate. I had forgotten about such things as MP's and barbed-wire fences. Mother rushed out of the gate shelter, her face beaming. "Ka-chan! It was so good of you to come. Have you been well and happy?" She looked closely into my face. I was relieved to see Mother looking well and still full of smiles, although I noticed a few gray streaks in her smooth jet-black head of hair as I hugged her.

"Where's Papa?" I asked.

"He had a bad cold, and he's resting at the hospital now. He'll be home in a day or two."

Although Mother tried to hide it, I learned that Father had had a close brush with pneumonia.

The camp was quiet and ghostly, drained of its young blood. All of the able-bodied Nisei men had been drafted into the army. The rest of the young people had relocated to the Midwest and East to jobs and schools. Some of the parents had followed them out. But the Issei who still wanted to go back West and had a home or a business to return to, remained in camp, hoping that the military restriction on the Coast would be lifted at the end of the war.

When I stepped into our old barracks room, I felt as if I had returned to a shell of a prison. The room had been stripped down to two cots, and it yawned silent and bare. The white walls were now filmed over with a dingy gray from the coal smoke. The wall where Sumi's cot had stood, formerly plastered with movie actors' pictures, was empty and dotted with black pinholes. The dressing table, once cluttered with rows of nail polishes, lipsticks and bottles of cologne, stood stark and empty. Only Mother and Father's brush and comb sets lay there, neatly, side by side.

That evening Mother and I went to see Father at the hospital. From a distance down the hall I could see him sitting up in bed. What had been a firm-fleshed, nut-brown face, was now thin-chiseled and pinched. His high forehead gleamed pale. I did not have the heart to ask whether this was only the result of his illness.

I had written to Father and Mother about everything which had happened to me since I left camp, but they wanted to hear about it all over again. For two hours I talked, telling them in detail about the Richardson family, how I had been able to return to school, and about my new friends at Wendell. Mother had been studying me as I talked. She said, "You've become a happy person, Ka-chan. I remember those days back in Seattle when the war started, I wondered when any of us would ever feel secure and happy again. We worried a great deal about our children."

Father told me that things were not going too well with his business in Seattle. From the looks of the monthly reports, Father suspected that somebody was siphoning huge sums of money into his own pockets, and juggling books to make it appear that vast improvements were being made, which Father had no way of checking. Father said that Henry was going to Seattle soon to look into the matter. Henry had given up thoughts of pursuing his medical career for the present, and he and Minnie decided to leave St. Louis and go back to Seattle to help Father with his business comeback. Minnie's folks planned to return to their former home, too.

"At least I still have the business," Father said philosophically. "I'm a lot luckier than many of my friends who lost everything."

Mr. Kato had lost his hotel lease and his entire personal property had been carted away from the hotel by men, posing as government storage men, who said they were going to move everything into the storehouse. Mr. Kato and his wife said they would probably work together as houseman and cook in a home, for a while, when they returned to Seattle until they had a better plan. For the present, they were waiting their days out, looking for mail from their son Jiro who was somewhere in Europe.

Mr. Oshima had been released from the internment camp in

Missoula. He and his wife intended to return to the barber business provided they could find a suitable shop. They were living in suspended anxiety for their son Dunks had been taken prisoner of war by the Germans.

Mrs. Matsui had joined her daughter, now married, in New York. Mother said Mrs. Matsui was toying with the idea of returning to Japan where her son Dick was, but Dick had written, saying that he wanted to return to the States. She was in a dilemma. Mrs. Matsui also mentioned that she had run into Kazuo, our former Seattle childhood friend. Kazuo was now a happily married man with three children, and he was star soloist in his church choir.

I also learned that Genji, the model boy whom we had disliked so much at Nihon Gakko was now studying for the ministry in the East. And Mr. Ohashi, the old schoolmaster, was operating a bookstore in Colorado. There was also a rumor that the Nihon Gakko building might be converted into apartment houses for the returning evacuees.

Father asked me to call on his best friend, Mr. Sawada, the former clothes salesman. "He's all alone here now since his daughter has left for Chicago. As you know, George was killed in Italy, and now his other son, Paul, is reported missing in action. Mr. Sawada often asks about you." I remembered long ago how hard Mr. Sawada had worked to send George to medical school, and how he straightened up whenever he talked about his children.

I found Mr. Sawada in an untidy room. Half-filled teacups stood on windowsills and a saucer overflowed with cigarette butts. An odd wired cage stood on a stool near the stove, a ragged gray sweater flung over it. Mr. Sawada grinned as he caught me staring at it. "This is where Shozo lives," he said. He pulled the sweater off to show me a disgruntled black crow. "For hours I sat out there on the prairie before I could persuade him to light on my shoulder. Since then we've become good friends. Sometimes I let him fly around in here, but he gets it so messy. I think one messy old man in the room is enough, don't you?"

I laughed. Mr. Sawada was still his cheerful, casual self. He told me he was eager to return to Seattle. When I said that I didn't want to go back there for a long, long time, he said, "You young ones feel everything so keenly. It's good, but sometimes you must suffer more for it. When you get old like me, Kazuko-san, things are not so sharply differentiated into black and white. Don't worry, I'll be happy in Seattle. The common people there won't hold grudges for long, and neither will I. All the fire and emotion will have died down. All I want is to live out my days there peacefully."

We sat silently together for a moment. Then I stood up to leave. "It was nice seeing you again, Mr. Sawada. Please take good care of yourself, and I hope you will hear good news about Paul soon."

"Hah, *arigato*. I'm praying."

"And I was terribly sorry to hear about George."

Mr. Sawada said quietly, "He walked into it, that boy of mine. Maybe you heard . . . he volunteered to go on a special mission."

"Yes, Father told me about it."

I lapsed into an unhappy silence, thinking how painful it must be for him to talk about it. He spoke to me gently, as if he were trying to put me at ease. "Kazuko-san, I want to show you a letter which he wrote me when he was on the train, on his way to Camp Shelby. After you read it, you will understand why I do not feel as lonely as you think I do." He walked to a bookshelf on which stood a photograph of George in uniform. A Japanese Bible lay in front of it. From between its pages, Mr. Sawada withdrew the letter and handed it to me.

In the quiet of the little room where I heard only the loud ticking of the alarm clock and Shozo strutting up and down on his horny little feet, I read George's letter, written only a few hours after he had told his father good-by at the camp gate.

He wrote: "I feel I owe it to myself and to you to tell you some of the things I should have said and didn't when the time came for us to part. I don't know why I didn't. Perhaps, because I was overly reticent; perhaps, it was because we were Japanese, but mainly, because I think I was a little bit self-conscious."

George went on to say that as the train carried him away, he was thinking back over their happy family life. He recalled family picnics, the sorrow when his mother died, the family struggles and triumphs. "When Evacuation Day came," George wrote, "I was stricken with bitterness, and I remember how you comforted me. I could not then understand why you tried to restore my faith in this country which was now rejecting us, making us penniless. You said wisely: 'It is for the best. For the good of many, a few must suffer. This is your sacrifice. Accept it as such and you will no longer be bitter.' I listened, and my bitterness left me. You, who had never been allowed citizenship, showed me its value. That I retained my faith and emerged a loyal American citizen, I owe to your understanding. When the time came for enlistment, I was ready."

There were tears in my eyes. I heard Mr. Sawada say, "With this letter, George will comfort me always. I know that George understood and loved me well."

I thanked him for letting me read the letter. He took Shozo out of the cage and walked to the door with me. "Well, Kazuko-san, study hard. But don't forget to keep one eye out for your future husband!"

I laughed, in spite of my brimming eyes, and walked quickly away.

The days passed by too quickly and it was time to leave Camp Minidoka. Father and Mother accompanied me to the camp gate. It was one of those crisp winter mornings when the pale sky and the snow were bathed in a taut cold pink.

"Ah, well, this parting is not a sad one for us, is it, Mama?" Father said. "It isn't as if she were a young son going off to war."

"This is what happens to all parents. Children grow, and they must fly away. But it is well . . . you all seem so happy in your letters, Henry and Minnie in St. Louis, and Sumi way out there in the East. When the war came and we were all evacuated, Papa and I were heartsick. We felt terribly bad about being your Japanese parents."

"No, don't say those things, Mama, please. If only you knew how much I have changed about being a Nisei. It wasn't such a tragedy. I don't resent my Japanese blood anymore. I'm proud of it, in fact, because of you and the Issei who've struggled so much for us. It's really nice to be born into two cultures, like getting a real bargain in life, two for the price of one. The hardest part, I guess, is the growing up, but after that, it can be interesting and stimulating. I used to feel like a two-headed monstrosity, but now I find that two heads are better than one."

Father beamed, "It makes us very happy to hear that."

"In spite of the war and the mental tortures we went through, I think the Nisei have attained a clearer understanding of America and its way of life, and we have learned to value her more. Her ideas and ideals of democracy are based essentially on religious principles and her very existence depends on the faith and moral responsibilities of each individual. I used to think of the government as a paternal organization. When it failed me, I felt bitter and sullen. Now I know I'm just as responsible as the men in Washington for its actions. Somehow it all makes me feel much more at home in America. All in all, I think the Issei's losses during this war are greater."

"If we consider material losses, maybe so, but our children's gain is our gain, too. Our deepest happiness we receive from our children," Father said.

"What are you and Mama going to do, the first thing after you return to Seattle?"

Father had a ready reply.

"Oh, first, we'll go and say 'Hello and thank you' to Joe, Sam and Peter for looking after the hotel. After that, we will take a walk along the waterfront and maybe dine on a crab or two. Then we will buy a little house and wait for visits from you all with your little children."

Mother smiled in assent. I gave a quick hug to Father and Mother and stepped inside the bus. As I looked out of the window, I saw them standing patiently, wrapped in heavy dark winter clothes, Father in his old navy pea jacket, Mother in black wool slacks and black coat. They looked like wistful immigrants. I wondered when they would be able to leave their no-man's land, pass through the legal barrier and become naturalized citizens. Then I thought, in America, many things are possible. When I caught Father and Mother's eyes, they smiled instantly.

I was returning to Wendell College with confidence and hope.

I had discovered a deeper, stronger pulse in the American scene. I was going back into its main stream, still with my Oriental eyes, but with an entirely different outlook, for now I felt more like a whole person instead of a sadly split personality. The Japanese and the American parts of me were now blended into one.